D1475204

CREATE YOUR FUTURE

A Memoir by John G. (Jack) Healey

Create Your Future
A Memoir by John G. (Jack) Healey

Published by Snail Press
Los Angeles, CA

Printed in the United States of America

First Printing, 2015

ISBN 978-0-692-50438-3

Illustration by Shepard Fairey / obeygiant.com
Photographic reference by Simon Cole
Cover Design by Christie Little

Proceeds from this publication will go to Human Rights Action Center.

Thank you for your continued support.
www.humanrightsactioncenter.org

Dedication

In loving memory of my mother, Mary Olivia Gaughan Healey, who taught me to hear the cry of those without a voice.

And

To Feryal Gharahi, trusted colleague and friend, who pushes me to think bigger, push harder, and fight uncompromisingly for the cause of human rights around the world.

And

To those whose voices have been silenced by oppression and tyranny. May our voices thunder for you.

Contents

Acknowledgments 7

Prologue: They Dance Alone 11

Chapter 1   Foundations:1938–1951. 13

Chapter 2   The Seminary years: 1953–1962 33

Chapter 3   I Begin To March: 1962–1966 41

Chapter 4   Priesthood: 1965-1968 46

Chapter 5   Awakening 54

Chapter 6   Baby Steps to Out of Control Skiing 61

Chapter 7   American Freedom from Hunger Foundation: 1968–1973. 66

Chapter 8   Next Steps: 1974–1976 81

Chapter 9   The Peace Corps Years: 1977–1981 89

Chapter 10   Too Small to Win: 1981–1994 108

Chapter 11   The Conspiracy of Hope: 1985–1986 121

Chapter 12   Amnesty after a Conspiracy of Hope 134

Chapter 13   Human Rights Now! Tour: 1987-1988 140

Chapter 14   Amnesty after Human Rights Now!. 163

Chapter 15   The National Stadium of Death: 1990 169

Chapter 16   The Work Continues at Amnesty 178

Chapter 17   Human Rights Action Center: 1994–Present 187

Chapter 18   Groundwork: October 14–22, 2001 199

Chapter 19   Aung San Suu Kyi Campaign 203

Chapter 20   Symbols of Hope. 211

Chapter 21   Haiti: February 2, 2010. 214

Chapter 22   Defend Our Native People 217

Chapter 23   Chen Shui-bian Vengeance in Taiwan 220

Chapter 24   Words have Power and One Document Can Lift the Whole World . . . 223

Chapter 25   One Person Can Lift the Whole Damn Thing 226

Credits 228

References 230

Bibliography 231

Acknowledgments

THE STORIES I SHARE IN THIS BOOK ARE MEANT TO INSPIRE readers to act and to raise their voices and make them thunder. My life is proof that you don't need money, fame or a prestigious background to make a difference in this world. You need passion. And, I have learned, you need friends and allies. Friends and supporters share equal credit for the work we've been able to accomplish.

Feryal Gharahi challenges me to go further and push harder. And she tells it like it is with irony and humor. I could not have accomplished the work of the past 33 years without her voice in my head and her brain and her heart. Aram Jafarey has taught me logic mixed with warmth.

Dick Gregory has kept me laughing and focused on the goal since 1971. No matter his fame or position, his friendship is firm. Jimmy Miller, fellow Pittsburgh native, has been a loyal friend and ardent supporter of the work with his wife Cheryl. Their dedication to freeing Aung San Suu Kyi culminated in a dinner they hosted for a now-free Aung San Suu Kyi in 2012. Matt Burrows has been my faithful pro bono counsel for 25 years, ensuring I can focus on the work without worry. Henry and Carol Goldberg make sure I continue in my human rights work and maintain balance. Beckie Healey deserves special thanks for her vital support of AFFHF and Peace Corps. She was a big sister to many of the young volunteers and a steady and kind partner to me.

Heartfelt thanks go to the following for your support and passion: Will Ferrell and Viveca Paulin, Judd Apatow and Leslie Mann, Lyle and Lisi Poncher, Phil Kent, Dan Adler and family, Fannie Lou Hamer, James Groppi, John Lewis, Reg Petty, Elsa and Norm Rush, the Freston brothers, Barry Dane, Shepard and Amanda Fairey, Simon Cole, Dr. David Brown, Don Foster, John and Maria Taglioli, David Milch, Muhammed Ali, Jason Rothberg, Amy Poncher, Jonathan Kadin, Father James Hannon, the Capuchin Order, Bob Pittman, John Sykes, Cardinal Sean O'Malley, Bishop John Corriveau, Peter Benenson, Sean MacBride, Mike Johns, Noam Chomsky, Anjelica Huston, Anca Albu, Tony Mac, Lili Haydn, Tom Morello, Maggie Q, Jae Choi, Jay Tu, Douglas Busby, David Kornhauser, Sydney Scribner, Cassa Van Kundra, Stan and Liz Salett, June Guterman, Joanne Barker, Kris Hahn, Rick Garson, Jack Magee, Michael Johns, David Slemmons,

Emily Trautman, Stanley Friedman, Sheron Leonard, Charlie Hernandez, all the roadies of the four musical tours, and my seminary classmates.

Big projects build close friendships. Many of the teenagers who organized Walks for Development (hunger hikes) in the '70s continued into lifelong activism and remain dear friends. There are too many to name here, but your continued dedication to making the world a better place is a daily inspiration to me. The first regional coordinator I hired at Young World Development in Los Angeles was named Moira Sher. That began a friendship that has endured to this day. Moira introduced me to a variety of people in the entertainment industry. When I met her, she was married to filmmaker Jack Sher, and both became good friends. She introduced me to Joe Strummer, former lead singer of The Clash, who worked with me on a punk rock album for human rights. To the hundreds of thousands who trekked thirty miles every year to end hunger, thank you. May your effort continue to your children and grandchildren.

The employees at the Freedom from Hunger Foundation, Peace Corps, and Amnesty International did the work from top to bottom, and I'm truly grateful for all their hard work and for the many friendships formed over the years. Jeremy Woodrum, Dan Beeton, and hundreds of dedicated Burmese contributed tirelessly to the work of bringing democracy to Burma.

Once known to me only through their music, these artists became lifelong allies in the fight for human rights and the type of friends who show up when asked. We pick up right where we left off no matter the time between visits. I respect each and every one and cherish my friendship with them: Sting, The Police, Peter Gabriel, U2, Wynton Marsalis, Tracy Chapman, Jackson Browne, Bruce Springsteen, Youssou N'Dour, Bryan Adams, Joan Baez, Neville Brothers, Lou Reed, Paul Simon, Joe Strummer, Pearl Jam, Susan Silver, REM, and the 130 artists that played for human rights.

My late friend Bill Graham guided this absolute neophyte through the intricacies of producing two major national and international tours with big performers. The planning and hard work for the Conspiracy of Hope and Human Rights Now! tours was nothing compared to the challenge of dealing with multiple personalities, handlers, logistics, the Amnesty board, and especially me. I love him and miss him. I thank the Board of Directors of Amnesty, USA and International Secretariat in London.

Finally, telling my stories was important to me because I am in awe that I was allowed to participate in these events. Putting them on paper was mind boggling. This publication was made possible only with the help of several skilled writers and editors over the past ten years.

Cynthia Okayama Dopke interviewed and recorded me for hours, meticulously transcribing stories. She captured my voice and the details so important to me. Mike Haack captured the historical significance of the times to put context to my story. Under his careful hand the Molly Maguires are remembered, and the dictatorships and corrupt governments (sometimes our own) are exposed. Grace Powell edited the early versions of this work, skillfully correcting grammar and adding salient details to reveal the heart of the message.

Eve Mykytyn used both chisel and scalpel to combine the two previous versions into one cohesive, readable work. Where the story bogs down for the reader, it is because I am not easy to silence and wanted every story included. Michelle (Burke) Foster not only wrote portions of the final product, but took on project management and editing. Michelle kept us all on track while ensuring my voice remained and excess chatter was silenced. I also want to thank my intern James Mason Cohen, who wrote a piece with me about the Chile concert for his blog. It is repeated here as the prologue.

Finally, I send loving thanks and gratitude to my family. I thank my father and mother as well as my brothers and sisters: Martin, Mary Olivia, Virginia, Elaine, Evelyn (Naomi), Eugene, Joseph, Agnes, Carole, and Mike for their love. My mother was well cared for by my sisters and for that I say special thanks. My brother Mike watched out for me as a young boy in our cold attic and has continued the task all through my life. Naomi was not only a faithful sister but was a second mother to me. She protected me as fiercely as I tried to protect my mother. We're an Irish clan with fire and love and passion. Here's hoping our collective offspring can share a bit of our family history through the stories told here.

To those with nowhere to turn, I say rise up. Believe in your own talent when you feel weak. Believe in your dreams and make them a reality. I know you will produce plays and poems and art and music and be able to step into the breach when needed. Take your place. Demand your rights and protect others that need help.

Prologue: They Dance Alone

OCTOBER 1990, SANTIAGO, CHILE. THERE WAS NOT A DRY eye in Santiago's National Stadium as the first notes of Sting's "They Dance Alone" faded into the night. With handkerchief-covered heads and photos around their necks, the Mothers of the Disappeared danced onto the stage in memory of the men they lost—the fathers, husbands, and sons who were "disappeared" by the Chilean government. My breath was taken away by the pain and suffering that filled those words and that stadium. I think even the mountains cried that day for the atrocities that had happened there. But the concert, *A Hug to a Hope,* was about renewal. Held two years after the last show of Amnesty's Human Rights Now! tour, it was a time to heal from the violence of the Pinochet dictatorship.

My good friend Pino Sagliocco took me to the top of the stadium where the majestic Andes Mountains swathed the 68,000 young people who were grasping for the first time the suffering their parents and grandparents had endured. We stood together, taking in the cleansing that was taking place. "This is what you've done," he said.

I knew that together we had done what we could to avenge the pain, suffering, and death that took place in that stadium. I said a silent thank you to my own widowed mother, remembering her words from long ago, telling me how I would know when I'd become a man:

"When you learn to walk the highways and byways of life," she said, "and learn to listen to the weeping and the wailing of the poor, then and only then will you be a man."

CHAPTER 1

Foundations:1938–1951

I WAS LUCKY, AND I KNEW IT AT AN EARLY AGE. OUTSIDERS wouldn't know it by looking—I was the youngest of eleven kids, scrawny and nearly blind in one eye. My father died in a horrific streetcar accident when I was two, and our sole income for years was the small monthly check that arrived in our mailbox courtesy of FDR's recently created social security fund. But I knew I was lucky. I was raised by a mother who gave me a voice.

Mary Olivia Gaughan was a quiet, beautiful woman with a magnificent face. She was gentle and easy. Peace and calm were her nature. Nothing rocked her in the essentials: her God, her faith, her belief in our people, her belief in our need to survive and thrive. She was always good, always simple, and an always-present focus was the center of her life and loves. That simplicity rattles a less than-perfect me even now. I secretly envied those virtues. None of us could misbehave around her. We do not know how this happened, but we all behaved, at least until we got away from her.

I was born March 24, 1938, midway through my mother's forty-sixth year. She and I had a natural bond. I charmed her, and she was quiet strength for me to lean on and trust...love on call, always. Many people enjoyed spending time with that quiet woman, like the "trash" collectors and the insurance man. Workers would often stop by for a

Martin Healey attended Carnegie University night school, where he studied metal alloys.

cup of coffee or two. She gave off a kind of solace, which no one discussed, yet everyone felt.

My father, Martin Healey, began working in the Pennsylvania coal mines at age twelve. He managed to get out of the mines and into the steel mill in 1922 and became a self-made metallurgist by the mid-1930s. He started out as a security guard, put himself through night school, and became well-respected in his field. He worked on alloys and heat treatments of iron, steel, and glass at Superior Steel in Carnegie, PA—not a bad job with World War II looming. His skill and determination carried our big family through the Depression with little damage.

Because he died when I was two, I don't have the memories of my father that my ten siblings have, but his loss devastated my mother and our family. The streetcar driver who took his life took much more than that. He took away my sisters' handsome hero and my brothers' big daddy, who could do anything. His death would cripple most of my family for years.

But my father's passing didn't make much difference to me at the time—one powerful person was enough, and she was a force, that mother of mine. At that time, my self-assigned task was to keep my mother happy and feeling good. I made a decision early on that my job was to take care of her and lift her spirits.

Battle of Stalingrad. Family history says that Martin Healey was part of the team at Superior Steel that patented a bullet before World War II called SuVaneer, which was used at the Battle of Stalingrad. Superior Steel 1942 Ad.

We all vied for mother's attention, but I was the curious one. I asked her questions that nobody else thought to ask. She told me about her time as a teacher, and what it was like for her to teach in the school for the miners' children. I learned about life for Irish Catholics in the mining towns throughout Pennsylvania. She told me tales of the Molly Maguires, the coal miners who banded together to fight the unsafe conditions of the mines, and how twenty Mollies were hanged after the deaths of some of the mine supervisors. She taught me that the death penalty was a weapon of the rich and powerful against the poor, and never the other way around. I learned that her grandfather had known John L. Lewis, head of the United Mine Workers Union. While Lewis may not be in the history books, my mother made sure I remembered who he was and what he meant to the Irish and to the nation.

She told me what happened when a miner died on the job, and I began to understand oppression. My Uncle Tony McHugh, a short guy who used to take me on walks, died in a mine cave-in. When the cart came from the mine and stopped in front of your home, it was over and there was no

Mary Healey while on a picnic. My mother loved being surrounded by her children. L– R. Agnes, Mike, Jack, Elaine, Carole, mother.

more to say. The miner's family descended from impoverished to shambles. Life was different from then on, and it was hard, very hard, for a very long time.

I learned about the five thousand Ku Klux Klan members who marched through Irishtown against the Irish Catholics in Carnegie, Pennsylvania, in 1923. The Irish, including my dad, staged a counter-demonstration to the KKK march, and things turned violent, resulting in the death of a Klan member named Abbott. They tried to hang an Irishman named Patrick McDermott for Abbott's death, but he was found innocent.

And when World War II came, my mother's two oldest boys went off to fight in Asia. The country under President Franklin Delano Roosevelt needed her boys, and while difficult, that was part of the gift of being in this country. She gladly gave back.

We had an understanding between us that required few words. She told me one day that she did not need to go to my baseball games like she did for the others. She said I didn't need it, and I smiled. She was right. I liked baseball with contact. She would not have approved of that behavior. But one time she did chase large Gordon Willard around the ball field with a frying pan to defend me.

The only time I saw my mother cry was when President Roosevelt died. She used to make us thank President Roosevelt out loud at the front door when the social security checks for the four youngest children arrived in the mail at the end of the month. Later in life, when Amnesty International asked me who I was in my first interview, I answered, "I'm the son of John L. Lewis, Franklin Delano Roosevelt, and Jesus Christ." I was not kidding—those were the men I considered my fathers and I was proud of them.

Over the years, our family had won and had lost. With my dad gone, winning again did not come easily. To me, that was my job, and I knew I could deliver. I was determined not to let the coal mines of Eastern Pennsylvania and steel mills of Western Pennsylvania produce another round of something terrible. I knew I would make things better for my mother.

My mother liked kids. She used to say that just because kids were small, it did not mean that they did not know or did not matter. They were full people, complete people—just small. Words, actions, and behavior were just as important around them as anyone else.

It was this respect for children that led me to practice the only real talent God gave me: speaking. When I was five I started giving speeches to my mother. Eleven children can't fit in one car, and on errand day when it was my turn to stay home, I would march to the curb and give a five minute speech on why she should not go on her errands without me. She would roll down the window and listen to my entire speech. My siblings, my forced audience, would scream, "Tell him to shut up! Get him outta here! Pump the clutch, let's leave without him! Here he comes again to give one of those speeches!" But mother listened each time.

Strength often comes to women when their husbands die. God does that. My brother Mike and I slept in the attic, which was hot in the summer and cold in the winter. In winter, when my mother came to wake us up, I would poke my feet out so she could put my socks on. I knew she felt badly that her babies lived in a cold attic, but this kindness made it okay. We went down to breakfast smiling every morning.

Mike and I walked a mile to and from school four times each day. He always looked out for me. He was big and tough, and nothing sent him into action faster than a big kid trying to do me in. He was much taller than me and was a natural athlete. If I learned a new skill in baseball, I'd be his teacher for about an hour and then he would surpass me. I was small. I could not use brawn, so I learned to rely on brains, ideas, vision, and speed to solve problems. This gave Mike and me parity despite our size difference. It was important to have parity as a young boy and the pursuit of it has never left me.

Being Irish, we did not speak of our bond, but it was solid. Hints in Irish families are important—if you miss the hint, you miss the love, the affection, the direction and the flow of the family. Quickness with hints is necessary in big Irish Catholic families, and I was quick. I'd watch my mother for hints, even very small ones. How she'd look at me, at other people and things. I'd read body language. I learned to trust actions and body language more than words. Most people pay attention to words, and, in my opinion, they shouldn't. There is more reality in what people do than in what people say. Trust comes from action; distrust comes from inaction. The sermon is always better than the preacher.

First my family went to church, and then we went to the beach. L–R, Mike, mom and me at the beach.

Below her calm and ease, my mother possessed a steely, rare toughness. "If someone pushes you, you push back," she said. "You're not my boy if you don't push back." So if someone pushed me, he got pushed back pretty damn fast. It was good training that prepared me for life. She often told me that she did not bring me into this world just to survive, but to do something.

When I was fourteen years old, I won a $500 raffle at school, and my sister Naomi brought the money home.

"We won $500!" Naomi proclaimed.

"Oh, good," my mother replied. She grabbed her hat, put it on her head, and announced, "We're going to Florida."

That was the day I discovered my mother was a nomad—she just had never had a chance to go anywhere. So the four of us still at home—Mother, Naomi, Mike, and I—jumped in Naomi's car and drove to Florida, just like that. She didn't think about luggage or maps or anything at all. Of course, motels and restaurants were too expensive for us. Instead, we ate apples and oranges and stopped at the Mennonite watering holes.

After what felt like seven years in the car, we finally got to Florida. My brother Mike and I were excited about going to the beach, when my mother asked, "Where is the Church?"

"Oh, no," we moaned under our breaths. "We just got to the beach and we're looking for a Church!"

Catholic Florida was not to be found. We hunted for hours. We finally spotted a Church, and of course, she wanted to stay within walking distance from it, which was about seventy-five miles from the ocean. But her rule was, *God first, fun later.*

With mother, it was always Church first, everything else second. *God is, and then we are, too.* That was the order of things and *that* was *that.* Her God was an Irish God, giving special protection for widows, orphans, workers, and the poor. No one was to make fun of anyone, especially the kids with real problems. For them it was special prayers to special saints. There are a lot of "specials" in Catholicism, and she rode them all for all of our souls.

Her Catholicism was magical. It was soft and included everyone. I learned more about religion—real religion—at my mother's knee than in all my years in the seminary and monastery. Her faith got to universals, not to bigotry, divisions, and anger. She prepared me for differences and gave me a curiosity that has never stopped. People were people and *that* was *that,* with a reminder that some of the Irish were the worst.

We were always on time for Sunday Mass. We never missed it, ever. One Sunday an ice storm came to Pittsburgh, and the city came to a halt. Ice had formed on everything. We thought for sure God would let us out of Church. And God would have, but not my mother. We slid her to Church on a sled with all of us slipping and sliding and falling behind her. *God first, fun later.*

> **I learned more about religion—real religion—at my mother's knee than all my years in the seminary and monastery.**

And of course, she wrecked our ball games with rosaries, novenas, masses, and extra masses. When the clock struck 6:55 p.m., we all fought for the bathroom to avoid the daily recitation of the rosary at seven o'clock. We were always glad she said the rosary facing in on her favorite chair, because we would sneak away or get off our knees, or not pray too much. Looking back, I think this was a half-time break for her to think, to pray, to be by herself, and to ask God to take care of us all because it was clearly a bigger job than she felt she could do. We always prayed for the conversion of Russia. Later, when communism collapsed without so much as a bullet being fired, I thought about all of her praying. Somehow it worked.

In traditional Irish families, if the grandmother was alone, the family would send the oldest daughter to live with her, and my mother was the oldest. So when her grandfather died, my mother was sent to live with her grandmother. This time shaped her views to her grandparents' era. She learned to say the rosary in Gaelic from her grandmother, and as I discovered later, the Ireland she talked about was the Ireland of the 1860s. It was as if her grandmother was speaking through my mom's words.

My mother was half-Druid. Her Ireland of leprechauns and Druids came from her grandmother as well. Along with her Catholicism, my mother read tea leaves, cards, and numbers. Itchy hands meant you were getting some money. A bird in a chimney meant someone was dying. She knew all the Druid beliefs and practices. The Catholic priests would tell her to stop doing those things, and I did too. I realized later that I should not have. I learned that St. Patrick and the early Christians in Ireland melded the pre-Christian Irish Druid and Celtic religions with Roman Catholicism, creating a distinctly Irish faith. The Reformation shifted all of Ireland into a new kind of Catholicism. I now have a lot more respect for our true religion than I did at the time.

Her faith gave her the best, but to my mind, it took too much, too. We knew that her faith held her back and brought a fear too deep for its own good. But it also gave her clarity about how to treat people. My mother kept driving me to values, concepts, and clear statements. All of that came through her faith, her Church, and her Irishness. Humility and being good were moral imperatives—and that was that.

My mother's Catholicism led me to the seminary and to my becoming a priest. Those years lifted her; she wrote me a letter every single day for thirteen years. I was ordained in 1966. I did my job for her, and in that effort, I gave myself the education, training, and focus I would need later.

I once asked her if she was ever scared.

"I was scared the night I looked up and saw twenty-two eyes staring at me after the funeral of your father," she said, "and then I realized I had a job to do and I just moved on."

In the struggle of my early teens, she bugged me regularly about being a man. She wasn't talking about macho stuff but of truth and of helping and fighting for what one believes.

Taking without giving steals the soul and leaves acidity in the body. –Mary Healey

I finally said in anger, "When will I be a man?"

"When you learn to walk the highways and byways of life," she said, "and learn to listen to the weeping and the wailing of the poor, then and *only* then will you be a man."

Lord, I thought, I will never ask her another question.

The day my father was killed, July 21, 1940, changed our family's finances and my mother's accounting. The big paychecks stopped coming, and there was no money in sight with eleven children to feed, house, and clothe. She spent most of her time at the wash basin in the cellar, or in the kitchen over the stove. We learned that it was never a good idea to ask her for financial aid when she was busy at either of these places. Plotting her schedule away from these two places became an art. After prayers was the best time to ask for a dollar or two, though none of us was ever successful at getting the big money. She just didn't have it. Or so we thought.

One time I asked her, "What am I getting for Christmas, mom?"

"The roof over your head," she replied.

For three days I stared up at our roof. Then I realized, *I'm not getting anything for Christmas. She knows the roof is a gift.* And there was no apology either. There was a lesson somewhere there. *Okay, I'm tough,* I thought. *I don't need a present.* But as soon as I got a dime, she got a present. That's just the way it was. Flowers were never passed on the way home without being snatched. She liked those "gifts."

The same was true for other holidays and our birthdays. She didn't apologize either. In time we learned that this was fine, too, because we just wanted her time, her presence. At night, we often snuck into her room to kiss her goodnight, and we savored the moment, feeling safe and secure. Most of us learn to like our mothers any way they come to us as long as they are there, with or without goodies. We learn to appreciate what life has to offer besides material possessions.

My mother was not afraid to avoid unwanted expenses. Whenever we were pulled over for speeding, my mother, from the back seat, would lean forward out the window and start telling the cop about how her husband died and how many children she had to feed. She would tell him every sad story that ever occurred to her, and the poor cop would be weeping by the time she was done. In the end, he would be apologizing for stopping the car. She wanted no part of that ticket.

Fashion was never a high priority in our house, either. When my sisters were little, they would ask her, "Mom, how do I look?" Mother would be reading, and she would reach over and feel the material without ever looking up, and say, "It's fine." She just made sure it was wool.

And when I would get dressed, things didn't always quite match. "Mom, I have two different socks on," I'd tell her.

"Who'll be lookin' at your feet?" she replied. "No one's lookin' at your feet." After that, I never wore a matching pair of socks. I figured if no one is looking at my feet, I'd just put on any damn socks.

In eighth grade, I went for my first overnight stay at my friend Dick Krause's house.

When it came time to get ready for bed, his mother asked me, "Where are your PJs?"

"What are 'PJs'?" I asked.

"Pajamas!" she said.

I told her I forgot them, but actually, I didn't know what they were. We never had such things.

When my mother went shopping, Mike and I used to meet her when she got off the streetcar at the bottom of the hill and across the bridge from our home in Oakwood, in zone five of Pittsburgh. By the time we reached mother on the bridge, her hands already had deep creases from the four heavy grocery bags she carried in both hands. There were many times we didn't meet her, and I wondered how she actually got up that hill carrying all that food. She never complained about having to carry those bags; she just worried about how she was going to pay for them. She worried her way through life.

We never really knew what problems my mother would decide were hers. She sometimes decided that certain things did not apply to her. She'd tell us kids, "Don't get sick on my watch, because there is nobody here to take care of you." And somehow, we just didn't get sick. We all had perfect attendance records at school. If one of us woke up feeling bad, she'd give us a nudge and say, "The fresh air will do you some good. You'll feel better by the time you get to school."

When I was thirteen, I smoked my first cigar, and I was sick as a dog. I came in the house and landed flat out in the front room. I heard my mother come in the room. She took one look at me and said, "He must be on drugs." And she turned around and left the room. Lucky for both of us, I wasn't on drugs, and I didn't like smoking cigars, but it was not going to be *her* problem.

My mother did not like to pay medical bills, either. When Mike and I were in eighth grade,[1] Mike broke his leg playing football. Father Lonergan, this big half-Irish, half-American Indian priest who coached the football team carried an injured Mike into our house.

"Father Lonergan," my mother began, "Why would you be bringing him into my house? I do not fix bones. He broke that leg on your property! Take him to the hospital!"

Father Lonergan carried Mike back out to his car and took him to the hospital, and ended up paying the bill. This widow was having no part of that problem, even though it was her son.

I thought to myself, *This lady is tough.*

She had her own remedies when we got hurt, to avoid taking us to the doctor. When we came home with a gash or a cut, she'd put a great big wad of bread and milk on the wound and wrap it up. I didn't know what it was supposed to do, and I never asked. As I sat there with milk running down my leg, I always wondered if it was doing any good.

One winter day when Mike and I were sledding, he bashed his head on the bumper of the car and got a big cut on his head. My mother looked at him and then turned to my brother-in-law and asked, "Would you mind sewing that up?" Mike and I looked at each other with fear and horror. She was having no part of that medical bill, so my brother-in-law stitched up Mike's head right in front of us. No medical bills that day, just a light scar for Mike.

In my second year of high school, I broke my jaw playing football. I was an 88 pound guard. The only thing the coach said was, "Take some aspirin." I walked home with a broken jaw. Later that night I had to be taken to the hospital, the pain and swelling were so bad. I was out of school for several weeks, and then the hospital bill came in the mail to our house.

"Jackie, you have to take that bill to the school," she said to me.

"Take it to school? Who do I give it to? There's no one at the school to give this bill to," I explained.

"I'll take it to the school," she told me, so she dragged me along to see the principal. When we got to the principal's office, my mother explained the situation to him.

"My boy was playing football for you when he broke his jaw," she said. "We're not having this bill."

The principal didn't know what to say, so he took the bill and paid it.

Banks had collapsed in the Depression, and she was never secure with them after that. When she died we discovered that she had $18,000 in cash in her room. We smiled at this because we knew what she would say: "I made it to the end for you and for me. I made it because we all made it." To her, the goal in life was to have dignity at the end, and all you needed to do was make it to the end with enough to end well.

My mother taught us about giving by enforcing a strict rule. She was like the IRS: everyone got taxed. Each person living in the house had to kick in money from whatever jobs they had, no matter how much they earned. The amount was not as important as the act of contributing. My sisters earned most of the money that came in, though each of us gave what we could. Mike worked at a beer distributor down the street, and I moved boxes at a local store for five dollars a week. And the tax woman arrived for me, too. Our mother made each one of us grasp the value of the home by adding to it. Prosperity for all of us came from contributions by each of us.

In most cases my mother was clever about avoiding the bill collectors, but there were times when there was no getting around them. It was then that we all had to share the burden of paying them.

One fateful day, it was my turn to find some money to pay an unexpected bill. This adventure would teach me one of the most important and enduring lessons of my life.

One night along Banksville Road in South Pittsburgh, some guys from the neighboring town of Beechview jumped my brother Mike. One of them tripped him, and the second held him down so that the third could get on top of him and sucker-punch him in the face. They had knocked out three teeth by the time a policeman strolled by. The policeman helped Mike to his feet but did not bother chasing after the three boys. Maybe he'd recognized them as sons of members of the powerful Pittsburgh mob that was close to much of the police force. Maybe he just didn't care.

By the time I got home, my mother had managed to clean up Mike and assess the damage. As the mother of eleven children, she was used to dealing with bloody noses, scraped knees, tears, and fights. But this afternoon was a little different. Mike was missing three front teeth, and my mother could not fix him with an ice pack and some Band-Aids. When my mother and Mike came home from the dentist, she asked me to sit with her in the dining room. Quiet as usual, she pulled out a chair and said, "Jackie, I don't have the $300 for your brother's teeth. You'll have to go get that money for me."

Me, 9th grade. It was this boy who took on the mob.

I looked at her and thought, *You've got other kids…why me?* But I didn't say a word. She knew I could talk and talk and talk, and this was a time for action. This job was mine, and that was fine.

I jumped on a streetcar headed to Mount Washington where the police officer who handled the case was stationed. Mount Washington overlooked Pittsburgh, which, when I was young, was impossible to see because of all the soot from the steel mills. But on that day I could see Pittsburgh clearly, and the city was beautiful.

I found the Irish cop who broke up the fight and asked his advice on how to find $300 for Mike's teeth.

He shook his head. "You'd need the best lawyer in Pittsburgh to get a cent out of those families, so just get out of here, kid. You have no idea what you're getting yourself into."

The thing is, I did know what I was getting myself into. I just had no choice. My mother had asked me to fix this. If I needed the best lawyer in Pittsburgh to handle Mike's case, I would find the best lawyer in Pittsburgh. The fact that I did not have any money, or that he might need to be paid in the first place, didn't occur to me.

From the streetcar back to downtown Pittsburgh, I noticed the menacing jail up ahead. Lawyers go with jails, I figured, so I got off at that stop. I asked the same question to everyone I passed on the street: "Who is the best lawyer in the city of Pittsburgh?" They all pointed to the brownstone a couple blocks away and said one name: Charlie Maloney.

The building directory pointed me to the third floor, so I slid into the building with a uniformed deliveryman. I was a scruffy kid dressed in my older brother's oversized pants and a dull yellow button down shirt, which had belonged to at least one other sibling—it must have been immediately clear to the secretary that I was not their typical client. From behind a large wooden desk, she mumbled, "Can I help you?"

"I'm here to see Charlie Maloney."

She must have been on to me, because her next question was, "What time is your appointment?" I did not let that deter me.

"I need Mr. Maloney to represent my brother's case. You see, my brother was beat up by some ferociously ill-tempered but well-connected local kids. They whacked his teeth out and our family needs the money from their families to repair his choppers," I said, trying to appear as cute, well humored, and as innocent as possible.

As I spoke I could see the secretary biting her lip to hold back her laughter. Then she stopped smiling, lifted a pencil from her desk and pointed at the door. "Get out of here kid."

Folding my arms, I declared, "Not without an appointment." A staring contest ensued.

Little did I know that Charlie Maloney was waiting in the doorway listening to our whole conversation. At that moment, he must have realized that he would have to intervene to defuse the standoff.

"So you want me, Charlie Maloney, to take on the case of some fighting schoolboys?" he asked, turning to the secretary and laughing along. Charlie was a handsome and imposing man who spoke with a tone of confidence that made him impossible to ignore. Embarrassed, I turned around to leave the office.

"Hang on kid," he called after me. "I'll do it."

A few months later when my mother, Mike, and I walked into the courtroom with Charlie, even the judge stood up.

"What are *you* doing on this case?" asked the judge, shocked to see Pittsburgh's best attorney on a case about a few kids who got in a fight. The accused kids' fathers were standing behind them in the courtroom to remind the judge that the boys had the power of the Pittsburgh mob behind them, literally and figuratively. Lucky for us, those mobsters were small potatoes compared to Charlie.

"What are *you* doing on this case?" demanded one of the men.

Charlie stood up tall and put his arm around Mike. "I only come to court for one reason: to win."

The fathers began whispering furiously. Before proceedings began, one of them walked over to my mother and handed her an envelope with $300 inside. "Case closed!" said Charlie cheerfully. "Jack? Mike? You all want to go get a hamburger?" Charlie Maloney had coffee at our home every Monday for the rest of his life.

> Quietly, she was training me in justice and the pursuit of good over evil, and her message was, "No matter the odds, you get going."

I learned a valuable lesson from the incident. Those who rule by using wealth and power to intimidate others are only as powerful as everyone else lets them be. Those without the guns and capital have morality as a weapon to strike fear into the hearts of the powerful. The coercive power of the Pittsburgh mob melted away when faced by Charlie, who gained power from his reputation as an upstanding person who was genuinely good at his craft. These were the type of people that I wanted to surround myself with. For the rest of my life, if I wanted something done, I would look for the best, and I would try myself to be the best at my crafts.

I also gained confidence. My mother trusted me with a need. Sometimes mothers just want an all-out effort by their kids; mine wanted a victory. Her boy had been hurt, and she was not walking away. I was small and insignificant until I listened to her plea for justice and restitution. She wanted to face that family that hurt her boy. Quietly, she was training me in justice and the pursuit of good over evil, and her message was, "No matter the odds, you get going."

I learned that even without power or money, I could solve a problem. This truth was one of my mother's immense contributions to the rest of my life. It still works for me today.

If I spent most of my time at home sitting quietly in the kitchen or laundry room helping my mother, I spent most of my time in school making life as difficult as possible for my teachers.

I had always been skinny and smaller than my classmates. My sister Naomi started me in school a year early so my mother could have some quiet moments. The fact that I was also cross-eyed and wore enormous glasses did not, as I'm sure you can imagine, help my social life much. It was what had earned me the nickname Bug, not exactly a kid's dream come true. This was not too big a problem in elementary school, because I was fast on the baseball field and the track, and because I was not afraid to fight.

But by my freshman year of high school, being fast and quick with a sucker punch was no longer enough. I was pretty much invisible in the halls of my high school, the youngest of the Healey kids and not a standout on the sports field or in the classroom. My reputation changed the day I met Jack Bear. Six feet four and 190 pounds at age fourteen, Bear towered over the rest of us. The first time I encountered him he was standing in the middle of the hallway blocking a smaller kid and dangling a cigarette menacingly. Jack's usual trick was to drop his still-lit cigarette into the cuff of another kid's Levis. The victims would walk away not realizing they were smoking from their ankles. Most of us had burn holes in our jeans by the end of that year.

That day Ray was the victim. He began hopping around like crazy, shrieking like a 10-year-old girl. I laughed, and it did not occur to me that perhaps I could have done something kinder than laugh at Ray, who had progressed to taking off his pants to find the offending cigarette. Bear heard me. He stood up and looked down at me, and I shut up, fast. We stood in the middle of the hallway, staring at each other in silence, other than the high-pitched shrieks coming from Ray, still jumping around behind Jack. "Hey...so, do you come here often?" I finally stammered.

He just looked blank, and I panicked. What had I been thinking, I should run now, he was going to come for me next. Bear repeated, "Come here often? Come here often? To school? Bug, you are crazy. What's your real name, man?" From then on I was no longer Bug. I was instead known as "the bug who hangs out with the Bear." Definitely an upgrade for a freshman.

It was the Bear's idea to steal hubcaps. We would steal the hubcaps from a car, and then go a few streets over, find some poor schmuck who had had his hubcaps stolen by some other boys looking for beer money, and sell the hubcaps to him. When we were not out extorting unfortunate car owners into buying back hubcaps every time they went to the grocery store, we found other fun activities to keep us busy.

Bear figured out that it was possible to climb the dumpster in the back of the movie theater, disable the fire alarm, and crack the back door so the rest of us could come in. Soon, just breaking in for the double feature didn't provide enough excitement. We started getting together in groups of 6 to 10 kids, and scattering ourselves throughout the dark theater. We would wait for the climax of the movie— during that moment the hero is just about to get attacked, or the moment you are pleading for the girl not to go into the dark basement alone because of course the bad guy was down there. At that moment, we'd all yell at exactly the same time. The entire theater would jump, shriek, and then call for the ushers.

When we got bored with this version of the game, we'd step it up to the next level. In those days, the movie screens were just large pieces of cloth. We would get 4 or 5 boys and squeeze in behind the screen before the film began, then wait until that perfect moment in the movie. Then, in unison, we would jump out from behind the screen and run toward the audience, yelling at the top of our lungs.

This game infuriated the ushers. It was almost impossible to execute without a few of us getting bloody noses or slapped around as we were dragged out of the theater usually with a chorus of "I told you last week not to come back here, you little scoundrels."

The girls in my grade somehow did not find my friends or me particularly amusing. For a while, this was not much of a problem for me, but then it mattered for a reason: Marcie Stinner. Marcie was, hands down, the prettiest girl in the freshman class and maybe the entire high school. She was one of those girls who managed to be beautiful without seeming to hold it over others. Naturally, as a result of her looks and her kindness, she was asked out on more dates in the fall of freshman year than I have been on in my entire life. She turned them all down— the football players and the smart boys, the basketball players and the greasers, the oddballs and the sons of Pittsburgh's elite. She was very polite, with a very firm, "No, thank you. No."

One day, when her parents were out of town, she threw a party. It seemed the whole school was there. Those who identified as "greasers," with slicked-back hair and tight jeans, as well as "white bucks," with loose jeans and big sweaters, perched in different corners with their own cliques. I arrived with my usual crew of riff-raff: Jack Bear, Sal Gaetano, Ed Schroth, Ray Santomo, and T. Malley. With slicked back hair, tight jeans, and "hard" attitude, we were solidly of the greaser subculture. We spent most of our time sitting around a card table making fun of people and playing black jack. As a prank, Jack Bear decided that he was going to try to jump over our classmates like a gymnast leaps over a horse. Although very tall, Jack was not nearly tall enough for him to clear even the shortest of those present. Instead he would take a running start, then leap, sending them hurling to the ground. As usual our classmates were amused, but in a slightly condescending manner. After a few good laughs I decided that I had had enough and it was time to leave by myself.

I walked around, giving the usual *good-bye* high-fives. Then I noticed Marcie, standing by the front door with a bow in her hair and a smile across her round face and my heart palpitations grew to quick thuds. Suddenly, I felt a bit of courage come over myself. I approached the door and glanced around to make sure no one else was looking.

"Marcie," I mustered. "May I give you a kiss goodnight?"

She leaned her head forward and puckered her lips. I pressed my mouth up against hers, and the four seconds that our lips touched seemed to be the most marvelous of my life. I walked out of the party, coolly, like it was the type of ending that I expected most evenings. The second I was sure everyone was out of sight, I skipped the whole way home.

That kiss changed me. It shattered an invisible barrier not only between Marcie and me but between me and all girls. I had gained acceptance by the other gender. I crossed a social bridge with a sure and steady friend, and it opened up the other half of the world to me.

Marcie and I became fast friends. She would pick me up on the way to school. We would sit next to each other at lunch, pass notes in class, and walk home together. This drove the jocks—who felt they were most worthy of Marcie's attention—crazy. While they were bending over backwards to get her to notice them, I had her undivided attention. All of a sudden, all those guys who had always ignored and looked down on me wanted to be my friend. Now, I was cool even for them. In one night, I had risen up the social ladder at Dormont High School so quick that I could barely remember what it was like to be at the bottom. My shyness began to melt away.

To this day, I am still not sure why Marcie even bothered to speak to me. I do, however, have a suspicion that it was because of the way that the other students treated her. Beauty is a mixed blessing. People fear and envy beautiful people. Beautiful girls are often ridiculed behind their backs by envious classmates, subjected to endless awkward conversations with nervous boys, and held to impossible standards by teachers and parents. I think Marcie just appreciated my sincerity and that I did not treat her with the fake reverence—and hidden disdain—that many of the other students did. Later in life at Amnesty, I would find myself surrounded by celebrities who others treated with similar reverence and disdain. But I always remembered my experiences with Marcie, Dormont High School's local celebrity, and how treating her the same way I treated everyone else was the best way to get to know her.

For a while, I was doing okay in high school. I'd wrangled my way onto the football team my freshman and sophomore years. I was an 88 lb. guard and without a doubt the scrawniest guy on the field. I was hanging out with Marcie Stinner and getting into only a manageable amount of trouble with Bear and the boys. And then, one afternoon on the football field it all came apart. I slammed into the fullback's knee hard, much harder than I'd meant to hit him.

It wasn't until we filed into the locker room that anyone noticed I was injured. I stumbled into the locker room, and crawled my way to the bench. I could tell that my nose was bleeding, but I could not seem to come up with the proper way to address the problem. I could barely sit up. Then I saw Buzzy Goldberry standing in front of me. He kept saying something over and over again, but I couldn't hear him over the ringing in my ears. Finally, he hauled me to my feet and dragged me out the door and towards home.

My mother, ordinarily calm in the face of bumps and bruises, nearly passed out when I walked into the room. My sister Naomi grabbed the car keys, and the three of us fled up the street to the emergency room.

The doctors at Mercy Hospital could see that my jaw was badly broken. They decided to reset the bone right then, without the use of an anesthetic. I was strapped to a hospital table, kicking and shouting as the doctor jerked the broken bone back into place. We heard a loud snap that signaled that the bone had been set. The pain was intense, and I went into shock. When I woke up, I had a helmet-like contraption over my face. Apparently it was to stay on for 6 to 8 weeks. I asked the doctor how many hours a day I would have to wear the giant helmet. "Well," the doctor said. "You will wear it all day and all night."

I never really missed having a television before. But as I spent my days lying on my back staring at the ceiling, I wanted a television so badly. I was bored and humiliated. When I finally returned to school I discovered that my class had moved on. *Moby-Dick* was covered while I recuperated. When my teacher asked me what literary tool Melville had employed by not killing the whale, I drew a blank. "What whale?" I asked, as my classmates tittered.

In algebra, I turned my parabolas into doodles, only to have them torn up by my irate math teacher. In biology, I failed two quizzes in the first week on the anatomy of the frog that had been dissected in my absence. By the end of my first week, I decided that trying to catch up was a useless endeavor.

As usual, Jack Bear had some ideas. On Friday that first week back, Bear and I passed a note around class with two words scrawled on it: BOOKS—12:07. At exactly 12:07 that afternoon, twenty minutes before the start of our lunch break, forty large geography textbooks hit the linoleum floor, causing Mrs. Callahan to shriek and drop her chalk.

"Both Jacks—out in the hallway, right now," she hissed. The next day, when 12:07 came and went without incident, Mrs. Callahan looked relieved. At 12:09, the entire class stood up, pointed out the window, at nothing, and screamed. Without a word, she looked at us and pointed to the door. Bear and I spent the rest of the period behind the gym. We decided to shoot for 12:04 the next day, just to mix things up a bit.

In the past, any trouble I had gotten into had taken place pretty much under the radar. Despite the many times we had been chased by cops, we had not been arrested. I was often sent to the principal's office, but I had not been suspended or expelled. The principal called me a barbarian. I took that as a compliment because I thought the Barbarians had won!

As early as my second day back at school, I started lying to mom. Over dinner she asked me with concern how I was adjusting.

"It won't be long until I am caught-up," I said, slopping some potatoes into my mouth.

When my mother smiled at the news, the guilt from lying gave me knots in my stomach. But I saw no other way.

Report cards were an unanticipated problem; they bore the unmistakable record of my new apathy. They came four times a year. The first one had been delivered before my jaw was broken and the second was issued while I was laid up. So, I was in the clear for those, but there were two more that my mother would be anticipating.

Not joining makes a single drop; joining makes a river.

Mike tipped me off as to when the first one was due to be sent home. Every day I tried to intercept the mail. Finally, I intercepted the 5x6 manila envelope that exposed my lies. I tore it open and hid the evidence under my mattress. To my surprise, mom never asked for it.

A few months later, I hid the final report card under my bed as well, but that one was not as easily forgotten. Mom knew it was due and began to get suspicious. The morning that I was finishing my eggs and she asked me if I had seen it, I knew my charade was up. I fished the report card out from under my bed and reluctantly handed it over.

I remember standing there, watching her read it. Her expression did not change, and she didn't say a word, but somehow, I knew that things were going to be different.

A few days later, mom called me into the kitchen.

"You have three choices: reform school, military school, or seminary."

Though terrified, I was also relieved that there were ways for me to start over. Frank Ciprianie, a rotund, quiet kid from my football team, let me know about a retreat for high-schoolers interested in seminary life. Understanding this would probably be my best option, I asked if I could join.

The retreat was sort of a soda-pop and dine for Pittsburgh schoolboys, as we spent most of our time playing baseball. In the mess hall, the fresh food straight from local farms was the best I had ever tasted. A 27-year-old priest, Father James, and I bonded instantly. We chatted about sports and getting into mischief in Pittsburgh. Father James had amazing talent for seeing potential in others. He was such a put-together man that his confidence in you gave you confidence in yourself. Toward the end of the trip he took me aside and told me that I was too smart to be keeping up my nonsense.

When we got back he joined my family one night for dinner. My mother was elated to have a priest in the house. He spoke a lot about kids needing discipline and how much he loved being a priest. I could tell my mother was smiling because she was imagining me in that position ten years down the line.

In those days, everything was changing around me. Our high school must have had some kind of coordinated effort to expel mischievous kids because that year we were all being sent away. Jack Bear left for military school. A number of Catholics went off to Catholic school or Kisco, a boarding school in PA. The city I grew up in was also changing. Jobs were getting harder and harder to find as the steel mills were closing. The loss of employment meant more frustrated parents, a rise in alcoholism, and domestic violence. Though I rarely witnessed such vices firsthand, there was a tangible feeling of decay in the city.[2] I was ready to go.

Father James suggested that I attend a three-week Latin language camp being held later that summer.

At Latin camp, the priests taught us using strict memorization. Nothing made sense to me. All the new vocabulary seemed to float in my head for only a few moments before disappearing again. At the end of the day it was as if I had learned nothing. Frustrated, I left after only one week and returned home.

When my mother saw me walk back in the door, the look of disappointment on her face was unbearable. At that moment, I knew I had to go back.

The Healey clan in 2010 at Dr. and Lisa Manning's wedding. Photo by John Madia.

CHAPTER 2

The Seminary years: 1953–1962

K EITH'S KNUCKLES SLAMMED INTO THE BACK OF MY HEAD before I'd gotten a chance to shake his hand or introduce myself. For a split second, I considered letting it go and not engaging in a fistfight on my first day at the seminary. I could give my mother a chance to drive out of the parking lot before she was called back to hear about me fighting. But Keith taunted me with threats of future punches. So I turned around and punched my new neighbor directly in the nose.

Blood spurted out across his pressed shirt, onto the white sheets of his neatly made bed, and onto the floor. As Keith and I watched the blood's movement, Father Patrick walked into the dorm to see if I'd gotten settled in my little alcove. Father Patrick looked at us. No one said anything. The priest calmly put one hand on each of our shoulders and escorted Keith to the infirmary and me to his office.

The Capuchin-Franciscan order is extremely strict. The priests take vows of chastity, poverty, and obedience. They are expected to spend their lives dedicated to the Church and training the next generation of young men. Certain things, such as smoking, speaking out against the Church, or knocking someone out with a swift uppercut to the nose, were simply not tolerated. The prohibitions are so strong that anyone that didn't get the message—me, for example—faced expulsion.

As I sat in Father Patrick's office, with its crucifix and photo of Pope Pius XII and the oppressive silence, the prospect of a call to my mother, and of returning to Pittsburgh having failed at this, as well, was not appealing. I wanted to make my mother proud, not embarrassed.

Father Patrick, a short, bald, very Irish 60-year-old, sank into his seat, put his fingertips together, and asked me in his calm, quiet voice why Keith was currently bleeding in the infirmary. He patiently explained to me that it was the policy of the seminary to expel anyone involved in a physical altercation. He understood that I had failed out of high school and said that he wanted to give me a chance, but I was making it a little difficult.

"He hit me first!" I burst out, stung by the injustice of it all. The fact was that Keith, that coward, had waited until my back was turned to hit me.

Father Patrick put a hand up. "Christ," he said. "Christ did not hit back. Not when he was spit on, stoned, attacked, crucified. Christ did not hit back. Do you understand that?"

I opened my mouth to suggest that perhaps Christ had not met Keith, but Father Patrick was not done. He looked at the ceiling as if seeking advice from above. Finally, he spoke. God was calling on him, he explained, to give me another chance. One more fight and I'd find myself in the back of my mother's car headed towards home—or maybe prison, if I continued on my present path.

The seminary and monastery are all about silence. Grand Silence begins at 8:00 p.m. every night and lasts until class begins the next day. No outside communication is permitted in the seminary. There is no music, no radio, no newspapers, no television, and no magazines. Routine is sacrosanct. I sat next to John Petruha for meals three times a day, every day for 12 years.

We rose at 5:45 a.m. every morning to the bell which, unfortunately, doubled as the fire alarm. At 6:00 a.m. we appeared in Chapel for Mass and meditation, kneeling with our heads bowed until it was finally breakfast time. We walked to breakfast in a single-file line, organized in age order. Many mornings we were required to eat our peanut-butter toast in total silence. After that initial conversation with Father Patrick, I lived in fear of being expelled, so I lined up behind John Petruha every morning, ate my toast in silence, knelt in chapel and stayed silent during meditation. I behaved.

As strange as it might seem now, seminary was basically a normal way to grow up. We were a bunch of young guys who played ball together, lived together, studied and worked together. It was very much like a boarding school with a Catholic touch. Overall it was a good way to spend our teen years.

Our school covered the usual high school curriculum: biology, English, and math. The first year was fine because I'd already completed almost two years at Dormont High, but my sophomore year did not begin well. The first biology test (I never understood what was so important about knowing where the frog's endocrine system was located) was an unmitigated disaster. I was only a third of the way through when Father Roch, my teacher, collected our papers. I had studied for a week, I knew where that endocrine system was, I could probably even pinpoint it on one of those frogs the Bear and I used to put in people's lockers. But I had failed the test. Father Roch called me to his office and I sat, hoping that he would not call my mother. Father Roch, though, did not say anything about my mother.

"Would you mind telling me how Gregor Mendel conducted his first pea experiment?" he asked, putting his feet up on the desk and leaning back in his chair. I started talking about peas and Punnett squares, chlorophyll, and the vascular system of a green, leafy plant, and how it was different than that of a tree, until finally I ran out of breath. Father Roch wanted to know why I had failed the biology test when I knew all the material.

"Dyslexia is a learning disorder characterized by difficulty reading due to problems identifying speech sounds and learning how they relate to letters and words. Also called specific reading disability, dyslexia is a common learning disability in children."
Mayo Clinic

Father Roch didn't have a name for the reason that I had failed the test. But he understood that I knew the test material. He did not have the prescribed "variety of educational tools" that can be used now to help treat dyslexia. So he came up with his own.

He began giving me extra credit assignments that allowed me to answer questions verbally. He spent time after each class asking me what we had learned. He called on me to answer questions in class, and I began to get the answers right. Soon, I was raising my hand to talk about Plato, telling my classmates about the connection between God and science, and explaining what St. Thomas Aquinas was referring to in a particular paragraph. I was participating in debates about the way justice should be enforced in society, the relationship between equality and liberty, and challenging Father Roch on what, specifically, defines a democracy.

All this extra work could not have been easy for Father Roch. He had to figure out how to help me learn and then had to convince the other priests to do the same. He would sit patiently every day and quiz me verbally. He was especially kind to do all this extra work for a kid who was basically there to avoid being sent to jail. He was one of those amazing people who not only practiced what he preached; he believed in it. He believed that I deserved forgiveness, patience, and a chance to succeed. Father Roch and the other priests recognized that my struggle to read and write did not reflect my ability. They taught me and treated me with the respect that children with learning difficulties often did not receive.

For two of the summers that I was home from the seminary, I worked at Safeway Steel scaffolding company. The regular staff consisted of nine men and my boss, George Grazorchalk. I scraped off cement, repainted steel equipment, cleaned up the place, and helped move scaffolding on and off of trucks. Once in a while, I would even go to an outside job putting scaffolding up the side of a building. I loved the job and the people.

The warehouse was on the south side of Pittsburgh, across the river from the main part of the city. The Southside was what we Irish called the hunkies' part of town. Slavs from Eastern Europe populated the area. In Pittsburgh, at that time, if you knew where someone lived, you knew what nationality and /or what church he or she belonged to. I would go bounding over to the business area each day for a sandwich and soda. Each time, I was asked to bring back sandwiches for everyone. Finally I asked George, "Can't someone else go? I do it all the time."

George said, "These guys cannot get served over there." I was surprised and upset. I went home and told my mom. She said, "I know. It is common, prejudiced, and wrong." Those trips for sandwiches heightened my walk.

The steady decline of steel in the 1960s and 1970s turned to an almost total shutdown by 1983. In January of that year, unemployment ranged from 17%-27% in the region.[3] Closed factories left behind pollution and huge tracts of empty land along the river. Unlike other such Rustbelt towns, Pittsburgh didn't have to move people in order to develop its waterfront. Pittsburgh as a city was able to rebuild itself. Crucial to the rebuilding of Pittsburgh was the pride the town shared in its sports teams, the Steelers and the Pirates. Each was rebuilt along with the city, all to the great pride of its citizens. To me, Pittsburgh's transformation has been an affirmation of the possibility of change.

The Steelers owed their revival to the dedication of their legendary owner, Art Rooney. He and I spent time together in the halls and waiting rooms of Mercy Hospital when both of us were visiting relatives there. Art was very Catholic and liked his clergy. His brother was a priest, and Art always gave the church half of any sum he won at the track. He used the other half of his winnings to buy the Steelers. I asked Art what he did for his parish at Christmas and Easter. Art said he handed them a blank check. "Write in any amount you want, Father," he would say. I asked why he did this. He answered, "I know my priest. He writes in a lot less than I would." Later, as a priest, there were many times that I wished that Art was one of my parishioners.

The Pittsburgh Pirates, in those days, were Roberto Clemente. He came to life for me in the middle of a game against the Dodgers in my late teens. It was my awakening to what a real ball player looked, acted, and performed like. I witnessed Clemente swoop up a hard hit into right field as the hitter streaked for third base. His throw from right field was so hard and so straight and so strong that the crowd in Forbes Field just stood in awe and cheered. No one believed me for years, and I thought I made it up until I read the book *Clemente,* by David Maraniss. It confirmed that day in the stands.

Clemente brought a new language—he spoke in Spanish when he won the Most Valuable Player Award—and a new era to Pittsburgh. His hitting and fielding skills won him a place in 15 all-star games and earned him 12 Golden Glove Awards with a lifetime average of .317.

Clemente embodied Pittsburgh's resurgence. He had talent graced by poise and kindness. Once a year on his days off from the ballpark, Clemente would drive 35 miles north of Pittsburgh to our seminary, jump out of the car, and throw the ball around with us for a while. He was educated by our Order in Puerto Rico, and he came to give back.

Once on my way from New Bedford, Rhode Island, to the ferry to Martha's Vineyard, I told the Puerto Rican taxi driver this story. He pulled the taxi over to the curb, turned around and said, "Tell me everything again." Clemente was a source of pride in both his original home, Puerto Rico, and his adopted home, Pittsburgh.

Art Rooney and Roberto Clemente rebuilt Pittsburgh's spirit. Both men had integrity, a spark, a fire and a sense of victory that they passed on to our city. In many ways they personified Pittsburgh. Like Rooney and Clemente, Pittsburgh did not fail its people. Old Pittsburgh was centered on the steel industry. It held a position of pride and was arguably the most important city during WWII. Then when steel failed, Pittsburgh transformed itself into a medical, education, and research hub. Alone among the rust belt cities, Pittsburgh was able to climb out of its depression and make it in the new economy.

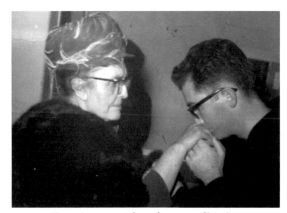

Honoring my mother after my ordination.

I set the direction of my life the moment I chose the seminary over a military academy. For 13 years, I followed a path of faith and study. It was a choice of solemn meditation over teenage pranks. It was the right decision for me. It was most especially the right move for my mother, who was determined that I grow up to be a man who cares for other people. She visited me faithfully every month, and I decided to stop the acting out that could have led to more serious problems. I moved through high school and into college for two years.

Years before, in the seminary, my first Latin teacher had been Father Dan. He was a big guy even freshmen knew to watch out for because he could be tough. He was a great teacher and it wasn't his fault that I studied Latin for 13 years but still knew basically nothing. I could not read, write, or understand it, although some classes were totally in Latin, and of course, the prayers and Mass for all those years were in Latin.

In college I had Father Dan as a teacher again, this time for English literature. I knew in seminary and then in college that Father Dan was an alcoholic. I liked Father Dan a lot, and I wanted to do something that might help him. So when assigned to write a short story, I wrote about a hobo on skid row who continually washed his hands but did nothing else. At the end of the three-page story, he dies and his brother, a fellow priest, offers Mass at his funeral, telling the funeral crowd that the hobo was a good guy gone wrong with booze. The only dignity he had retained was his respect for his long ago ordination, so he continually washed the hands that had been consecrated. My short story received an A plus, the only one I ever got. I tried to warn Father Dan, but he died of alcoholism a few years later.

In 1959, after my sophomore year of college, I joined the Capuchin Order in Annapolis, Maryland. I began wearing the brown robes of a Franciscan in 1960 and took the new name of Barnabas to mark the beginning of a new life. I returned to St. Fidelis Seminary for two more years silence, meditation, and study as required to earn a BA in philosophy.

During those two years, I lived a hidden monastic life. These were my only years of serious scholarship. While we weren't supposed to talk to other people, the difficult concepts of philosophy struggled against the isolation of my own thoughts. The questions of life being raised in my coursework needed a voice, and I needed to act. My view out the window was of a cemetery, and I felt dead. The only comfort was finding the Papal encyclicals that covered labor rights, living wages, strikes, the labor movement, and the priest worker movement. A copy of the newspaper *The Daily Worker*, written by Dorothy Day, sparked my passion. Those two years were the longest of my seminary years.

The standard procedure for leaving the seminary was simple. Guys simply disappeared. One hot afternoon, in the middle of a soccer match, Brother Davis passed out in the center of the field. He had lost so much weight as a result of stress, the silence, the regimented diet, and the lack of human contact that his heart was not functioning properly. He was taken to the infirmary, and simply vanished. We knew he was no longer in the infirmary, but he did not return to the monastery. We were given no information, and we knew not to ask questions.

A few weeks later Brother Gabriel collapsed on the way to meditation, and he, too, did not return from the infirmary and simply disappeared. A person was just there, and then not. I wondered if this would happen to me.

I was ready to disappear. I was ready to be done with sitting at desks and repeatedly discussing the same texts until we sucked them dry of new material. We were talking about ancient philosophy and history and ignoring the present. I felt the days wasting. For thirteen years, I studied the charity part of the gospels. But I felt Jesus's words—*Remember My Chains*—calling me to action. *Get moving already.*

I was going through my awakening as the nation as a whole was stirring. It was the 1960s, and a societal revolution was taking place. It was the years of the sit-ins at Woolworths that I found out about by reading the newspapers my mother wrapped my care packages in. We were not allowed newspapers, but my mother, remembering how I loved to read the paper, displayed a bit of her own defiance of authority.

The sit-ins were straight out of the pages of the Gospels: men and women standing together to protest injustice. While we studied the Book of John, and ate our morning peanut butter toast, we slept and woke in silence. Much of the rest of the country was coming closer to living our faith, fighting for equality and freedom, just as the Gospels described a world of long ago fighting in the name of the Lord.

I didn't put this thought together until the third floor toilet clogged one morning in March during my novice year in Annapolis. If the toilet had not clogged, if the plumber had not been called, maybe those final two years in seminary would not have felt so long.

Father Peter was a calm and formal man of about seventy who could silence a room of 20 year old boys with one sharp look. But on the day the toilet clogged, he was almost bouncing with excitement as the plumber hauled equipment up and down the narrow staircase.

"You know," he said to the plumber, "the last time I was in the world, Eisenhower was considering making peace with the Soviets. Can you imagine that? Peace with the Soviets. Has it worked?"

The plumber, who was about fifty and balding, just looked at him, shook his head and kept working.

"How about the Yankees? The last time I was in the world, they were winning the World Series. Are they still winning?" Now Father Peter was nearly shouting to be heard over the noise of the electric plunger, squeezing into the bathroom behind the plumber. "What's going on with Hungary? Are they still protesting over there? The last time I was in the world..."

The plumber stood up abruptly and turned around, shutting off the electric plunger, which sputtered into silence. "What in the hell do you mean 'when I was in the world?' Where in the bloody hell do you think we are now, Father?"

As I listened to the plumber and Father Peter, I knew that I did not want to become Father Peter. I was a nice, celibate 21 year old in the wrong place. I'd been sheltered in the seminary. The urge to leave came and went. When I took my simple vows I made an additional vow to myself: I was not going to leave the world. But I would stay to be ordained.

I graduated from St. Fidelis College in 1962 with my mother proudly looking on. Next I would begin graduate studies at Catholic University in Washington, D.C. As a child I had gone to Washington with my mother, my sister Elaine, and my brother-in-law, Skip Manning, on the only trip I ever took with my mother without all of our usual numbers. I instantly loved the beauty of Washington, D.C. I was enthralled by the architecture. Skip Manning and I flew paper airplanes out of the top windows of the Harrington Hotel.

CHAPTER 3

I Begin To March: 1962–1966

1962 WAS AN AUSPICIOUS YEAR TO ARRIVE IN WASHINGTON. That year everything seemed possible. Pope John the 23rd had called for the second ecumenical council of the Vatican, seeking to "open the Church windows and let in fresh air" to align the Church with the progressive changes of the time. The seminary was brimming with pride because America had elected its first Catholic president, a prime subject of cafeteria chatter. If you wanted to make new friends, it was always a sure bet to bring up the Catholic President.

No one I knew was more excited by President Kennedy's election than my mother. Though she was enthusiastic about his platform (he had run as "an FDR Democrat"), she was much more excited that he was Irish. A few days after Kennedy defeated Nixon, I received a letter from my mother stating, "The Irish will never be second class citizens in America again." When I read it, I laughed out loud. My mother was an Irish American, and I was a dream of Irish descent.

The new president carried with him the hopes of many traditionally marginalized groups. He had campaigned on issues of civil rights and was embraced by anti-segregation activists, including singer Harry Belafonte, who referred to President Kennedy as the civil rights candidate. There were high hopes about positive changes to come. A certain progressive-nationalism was in the air, and why not? The past two decades had appeared very good for America. The country had helped defeat fascism, war spending had pulled millions of Americans out of poverty, and for the first time the country had an expansive middle class who lived in one-garage houses and dreamed of sending their kids to college. History was moving forward, and it seemed that there were two choices: to be on the side of progress or the losing side. I wanted to be part of this tide of change.

At Catholic University there was a large group of progressive priests and seminarians involved in the Civil Rights Movement. During the first week of school they held a meeting for all incoming students interested in getting more involved. My entire seminary class showed up, and we were immediately put to work advertising an upcoming talk by Reverend Walter Fauntroy, a civil rights minister who worked with Dr. King in the Southern Christian Leadership Conference (SCLC). I spent hours that weekend hanging fliers on every available post on campus. After that I was hooked. The group spent a lot of its time on popular education, hosting speakers such as a pair of anti-war priests named the Berrigan brothers, Dorothy Day of the Catholic Worker Movement, and Rabbi Heschel, who had marched alongside Dr. King in Selma.

We brought a culture of activism to campus, hosting parties called hootenannies after-hours in the campus dining hall. Hootenannies were an important, but not often written about, part of civil rights culture. Groups of folk musicians traveled around the country with acoustic guitars, violins, snare drums, and a few bushels of hay (to be used as stage props). Hundreds would gather in the campus dining hall to watch the bands play songs akin to the folk music of Woody Guthrie and Joe Hill. Students would stomp their feet and holler along to the songs that always carried messages about civil rights and social justice. These events helped give me the feeling that I was part of a movement that was much bigger than me. I was eager, however, to take some more direct action.

My first action with the movement was the most iconic of my life. Titled simply "The March for Jobs and Freedom," it showed the strength of our movement and built momentum for the passage of a proposed "Civil Rights Act." The march was organized by a coalition of groups called the Big Six, including Dr. Martin Luther King, Jr., to build public pressure to pass civil rights legislation designed to end the Jim Crow laws still prevalent in the South. President Kennedy had helped to draft the legislation, but it had stalled in Congress. Dr. King, among others, decided to get people—lots of people, hundreds of thousands of people— to march on Washington in support of that legislation. My classmates and I did simple things to publicize the march: hang posters, campaign door-to-door, and hold discussions with seminarians and leaders of other faiths.

The poet William Butler Yeats wrote, "Education is not the filling of a pail but the lighting of a fire." Dr. King's voice was the clarion call of my generation. He lit the fire for human rights advocacy in me.

On the morning of the March on Washington, August 28, 1963, our group of Franciscans, dressed in black suits rather than our usual robes, began the three-mile trek to the national mall. We were about a mile away when we hit the tail end of the crowd. It was a deeply moving sight. There were thousands and thousands of people standing shoulder-to-shoulder, walking arm in arm, all together. Blacks, whites, men, women, children—friends, neighbors, and strangers—all pressing as close as possible to the steps of the Lincoln Memorial. As we walked by the White House, we wondered how the President would respond to the March.

As we headed to a better vantage point closer to the Lincoln Memorial, I saw a very young Jesse Jackson. He was about my age. *Got to get going, Jack,* I thought.

On the marble steps of the Lincoln Memorial, Joan Baez was singing about peace, love, forgiveness, and overcoming. John Lewis, the youngest speaker of the day, said, *"By the forces of our demands, our determination, and our numbers, we shall send a desegregated South into a thousand pieces, put them together in the image of God and Democracy. We must say wake up, America, wake up! For we cannot stop, and we will not and cannot be patient."*

Next, Bob Dylan was strumming the guitar, telling us to take the hand of the person next to us.

Then they all stepped off the stage, the sun was beating down, and the people passed around water and cigarettes. There was lots of good-natured jostling as we all moved closer to those white marble steps. And then Dr. King was there, about halfway up the stairs, standing in front of the Marines and next to John Lewis, raising his arms as he stepped in front of the microphone. He did not smile as he looked out at the thousands of us gathered there. The crowd fell silent. Then he began to speak, and his voice seemed to thunder from heaven itself.

Dr. King spoke to all of us and to each one of us. "The marvelous new militancy which has engulfed the Negro community must not lead us to distrust all white people, for many of our white brothers, as evidenced by their presence here today, have come to realize that their destiny is tied up with our destiny and their freedom is inextricably bound to our freedom. We cannot walk alone," he said. "Let us not wallow in the valley of despair."

And then he told us about his dream, and it was as if the dream itself was present there, in front of us, almost within reach. We could believe that black children and white children could grow up to share our country. We shouted our agreement with Dr. King from the crowd and from all over the country. *Thank God Almighty. Free at last.*

I knew I had attended a moment of history, when the promise of hope had been firmly planted on American soil.

My years at Catholic University (1962-1966) were beyond any expectation. I felt lucky to be living in an exciting time. The country was in a good place during these years. We had John Kennedy as our President. We had Dr. King working on civil rights. We Catholics had John XXIII as Pope.

I was learning about the changes sweeping the country and my church and was beginning to participate in them, if only in a minor way. My classmates and I were no longer as isolated. We walked everywhere, since we had no money for buses. We tutored at Kelly Miller Middle School, visited patients at the Washington Hospital Center, went to courts to hear criminal trials, visited Congress, sat in on Supreme Court cases, and participated in debates on campus. I was slowly testing my wings.

But there remained a large gap between what we were saying and what we were doing, or more precisely, not doing. The frustration continued as constant background noise until November 22, 1963. That day Walter Cronkite delivered the news that the President of the United States had been assassinated. He had died while riding in the back of a convertible in Dallas on a beautiful, sunny day. JFK was not supposed to die. He was the president that we had all been waiting for. He was the young, handsome Irish Catholic who we thought would change our country for the better. Our faith for the future had rested on him. Then Lyndon Johnson was sworn in on Air Force One, Jackie Kennedy had a bloodstain on her skirt, and Caroline and John had no father. The future was uncertain.

The university was silent the night of the assassination. The cafeteria was desolate. The city itself was silent; we were all in shock. The assassination and the funeral were all that we could think about.

On the day of the funeral, the Superior got up at breakfast and instructed us, in no uncertain terms, not to attend the funeral. We were to stay within the walls of the monastery and pray. The entire monastery was devastated. Later, some of us took advantage of the lunch rush to slip out the back door. We were walking down North Capitol Street, joining the crowd of thousands and thousands of people in black, when someone wondered out loud what our punishment would be. "Are you out of your damn mind, worrying about that right now?" said Joe, a Canadian. "Haven't you been paying attention? JFK is dead."

The feeling of isolation and of existing in an alternate universe got worse after JFK's death. It reminded me of the days during the Cuban missile crisis when every sixty seconds you heard a jet fly over Washington, D.C. Fright dominated the atmosphere. I thought that the country was falling apart, and all I knew to do was to get through the next few steps, get confirmed as a priest, and then try to be an active participant in change.

Following Kennedy's assassination, the country refused to wait for civil rights legislation any longer. Activists mounted a vigil at the Lincoln Memorial 24 hours a day, every day, until the Civil Rights Bill was passed. I participated in the vigil, along with many of my fellow seminarians, and Protestant and Jewish faith leaders as well. We usually took the night shift since it was our only chance to get away. Among the many people who joined us was Jim Carroll, the former Paulist and writer. He later referenced the vigil in a book he had written. We also had the dubious pleasure of the company of a crazy Nazi who would stop by to tell us about the Irish girls he hit on. I surprised even myself at how quickly I could explode. One morning in my second year of theological study, I was upset about something or nothing. I tossed my bowl of milk at Joe MacDonald at breakfast. He returned the honor and we were off, almost flipping the table over as we wrestled, upending the other monks' places and spewing cereal and milk all over. Joe sat across the table from me for all those years. Maybe we were just tired of looking at each other. We grappled and fought while forty other monks sat in stunned silence. Afterwards, Joe protected me to the Superior by saying he had provoked the fight by repeatedly kicking me, a lie that cemented our friendship. For a week after that, I ate my meals on my knees, in silence, on the hard stone floor of the dining room.

I was sent to see a psychiatrist. I thought it was nonsense, but it was required in order to move beyond the incident. I told the shrink that I didn't know why I had reacted violently. I still don't know why. But I remember his observation: "There is something wrong with your monastery."

Those words gave me great relief. I wasn't crazy after all. It was so refreshing to hear someone mirror my own thoughts. I loved the seminary. The Fathers understood my dyslexia and gave me a solid education. I learned to pray. But I was a social creature. I needed room. I was simply not built for being silent. My frustration stemmed from this internal conflict between love and honor for the church and my mother, and my own personality.

CHAPTER 4

Priesthood: 1965-1968

T HE FINAL STEP IN ORDINATION AS A CATHOLIC PRIEST IS to say Mass in your home church. My first Mass would take place at St. Bernard's, a few blocks from my home. It was October 30, 1965, and I had been in the seminary for 13 years. St. Bernard's Church was full that day, but I barely noticed. I was focused on walking my mother to her pew in the front, so that she could see her son say his first Mass. She wrapped her shaking hands in a shawl.

Parkinson's disease had struck her a few years earlier, and she could barely hold her rosary beads in her hands. But when I stood at the front of the room, and offered communion to the assembled congregation, she walked to the front by herself to kneel down and accept the body, the blood, the Holy Spirit.

I became a priest for myself as well as for my mother. I have never known which motivation was stronger. But whatever the inspiration, I will always be proud that I lifted her spirits during her long wait for me to be ordained. As usual, she was quiet, serene, and simply present for me. No words, no pats. Just truth and love. My mother didn't thrive on big congratulations. She simply said, "You set out to become a priest and you did it." She preferred delivery over promise.

Ordination. L–R Mary Healey, me, Sister Elaine, Aunt Betty, Aunt Elaine (BB) and L–Jay.

My first posting was in the Catholic diocese of Baltimore in western Maryland. I was a novice Master for brothers and a chaplain for the new Newman Center to be created at Frostburg State College during the 1966/67 school year. Frostburg State had 3,000 students, most of them from nearby

Cumberland. My boss in the monastery was Father James, my old mentor who had started me along the process years before. At the Newman Center, I was under the jurisdiction of Cardinal Shehan of Baltimore.

I did not have a church. What I had was a small conference room with white-washed walls and a sign on the door informing visitors that they were entering the ecumenical center where different faiths held religious services. It was a perfect complement to my style…simple, easy, plain.

Before I was assigned to the College, Catholic students at Frostburg State had never held a Mass or been offered communion at school. I was the first priest at the College, and the College was the first place I was a priest. They had no idea what to expect, which was good, as I had absolutely no idea what I was doing.

The first thing I did was to put up a paper sign: **"First Catholic Mass, Sunday Sept 18, 1966."**

As I stood at the front of that small room on my first Sunday, watching all twelve people file in, it occurred to me that perhaps I might have underestimated the effort it would take to develop a Newman Center at Frostburg. The sermons that I had learned as a seminarian were irrelevant. What had I been thinking in planning to quote the Old Testament to these people? These were college students.

Whenever I speak in public I always pretend to have a written speech. But the use of written material to speak from is not an option for me. I cannot see the print with my eyes, and my dyslexia would make me jump from the page to my own thoughts anyway.

So I gave that first sermon simply from my heart. I spoke about Christ, about what it means to be a follower or a peacemaker. That faith could be practiced in many ways: sitting at a lunch counter, riding a bus in the seat of your choice, or marching across a bridge that others tried to stop you from crossing. These actions, I said, were among the best examples of what it meant to follow Christ. I had hidden my talent for speaking from the Order; I do not know why I did that, but I had. My first sermon at the Newman Center showed me that God had given me a talent. Years later, Sting, lead singer of the Police, said: "Jack has a tear in his voice. And I am jealous of that."

Saying Mass at Frostburg State.

The tiny group of students in front of me became, in my imagination, throngs of people, gathered on the Mall in Washington, D.C., listening to me speak on the steps of the Lincoln Memorial while Joan Baez sang behind me, inspiring us all to walk together, holding hands. Then, abruptly, I realized where I was, and that everyone was staring. One girl had her mouth hanging open. A young man looked pale, shocked. I stopped in the middle of a sentence about the fire hoses that had been turned on the children in Selma. Perhaps a sermon on civil rights had not been within the expectations of the few students who attended Mass that day in that small, conservative college.

The silence lasted about forty seconds, which was an eternity to me as I stood alone at the front of the room. To my surprise, those twelve students seated on old cafeteria benches started clapping. It was an amazing day. Father James sent some of the monks to play guitars and drums. Some students could sing, and they joined the monks. It became a hootenanny/folk Mass.

The next week thirty students came, and then fifty the next. People came who were not Catholic and had never listened to the Gospel of John, but had heard of John Lewis and the movements for workers' rights and civil rights. Then the next week, locals were crowding in around the students on the plastic cafeteria benches, and people had to stand in the back. My isolation, along with its silence, its eerie disconnect from the world, was slowly evaporating.

To fit our growing congregation, we soon rented half of a duplex for the Newman Center, right off campus. The first brochure we created for the center still says it best: "The Center provides a place where statements such as 'if the Church is going to be Christian, it must be willing to accept identification with the world in which it finds itself situated' can be freely discussed and practiced."

On April 4th, 1967, I carried a radio instead of a pretend sermon into the Ecumenical Center. By the time people found seats or places to stand in the back of the room, Dr. King had begun his "Beyond Vietnam" speech.[4]

> *"As I have walked among the desperate, rejected, and angry young men, I have told them that Molotov cocktails and rifles would not solve their problems. I have tried to offer them my deepest compassion while maintaining my conviction that social change comes most meaningfully through nonviolent action. But they ask—and rightly so—what about Vietnam? They ask if our own nation wasn't using massive doses of violence to solve its problems, to bring about the changes it wanted. Their questions hit home, and I knew that I could never again raise my voice against the violence of the oppressed in the ghettos without having first spoken clearly to the greatest purveyor of violence in the world today—my own government."*

It was not the first time that the Civil Rights Movement and the war in Vietnam had been contrasted. It was hypocritical to demand freedom for our own citizens, while our government was using napalm and bombs to deprive the Vietnamese of their freedom and their lives. But Dr. King's speech gave me the realization that the two movements were so deeply intertwined that I could not be involved in either to the exclusion of the other.

The students and the townspeople and I started talking about the war. We learned about the Gulf of Tonkin Resolution that had authorized the U.S. led coup against the democratically elected government of Ho Chi Minh. He had apparently committed the ultimate crime by using dangerous phrases like "redistribution of wealth" and "neutrality in the Cold War." We talked about many of the major issues of the time, including civil rights, Vietnam, women's rights, and drug use. These

Frostburg College students and Brother Hillary playing at Sunday Mass.

discussions took place in the Newman Center, in the Ecumenical Center, in clergy meetings, and in Father James's office where I stopped by most nights for a drink.

The talks were an important step, but I did not want discussions to substitute for active participation. The split between the church and action was resolving itself within me, and I knew it.

The Newman Center became a center for activism. The student leadership of Frostburg State responded. People like the Kenneys, the Boyles, the Sullivans, and others joined, and eventually we had an active chapter of the Newman Center that was quickly and powerfully alert.

"Are you boys here to be social movement tourists or are you going to make yourselves useful?" Father Joe, Father Stan, and I had just gotten out of the car after a twelve-hour drive from Maryland. We stood there like idiots, blinking in the late afternoon Milwaukee sun. Father Stan started to speak, but before he could, Father Groppi rolled his eyes, announced that the copy machine was in the back of the church, and stalked off. "Copy machine?" Father Joe asked under his breath. It was Groppi's way of telling us that if we wanted to be idle machines, we should move to the back of the room.

Like many northern cities, Milwaukee was a segregated town. Although the rules written into neighborhood covenants in Milwaukee claimed that all races were welcome to purchase a home in the neighborhood (of course they were, this was the north, and not the racist south), home ownership was impossible for blacks in many neighborhoods. Black men and women were thwarted in the process of getting a loan to purchase a house. The banks simply denied housing loans to any family of the wrong color who attempted to buy a home in a white neighborhood. The practice was known as "red lining," and it reinforced an apartheid line.

For about five years, City Council member Val Phillips, from the north side of town (also known as the black section), introduced a bill to end red lining and allow blacks to move to any area in Milwaukee. She introduced the bill three times, and the bill was defeated each time. The 18-1 vote matched the racial make-up of the council.

Father Groppi was one of the few Catholic priests in Milwaukee who actively supported the Civil Rights Movement. As such, he had grown close to the NAACP membership. The NAACP youth commandos and Father Groppi organized protest walks in response to the repeated rejection of Val Phillips's proposal to outlaw redlining. Father Groppi had marched with Dr. King in the south, was a close friend of Fannie Lou Hamer of the Mississippi Freedom Democratic Party, and was one of the early proponents of bringing the fight for civil rights north. In the north, racism was seldom codified, but was no less virulent. Many Northerners who spoke out against racial discrimination in the south ignored the black ghettos and gross discrimination in their own towns.

Milwaukee, a northern, supposedly integrated city, and the entire country watched the battle on the 6 o'clock news. Father Groppi and the NAACP were using their moment in the spotlight to tackle the issue of fair housing in a major way. Father Groppi was threatened by phone and in person many times.

We attended Father Groppi's Mass and were shocked by the format. The entire parish stood in a circle around the altar and took turns reading from the Bible. We passed the chalice cup from person to person. Fannie Lou Hamer led the community in song. It was my first experience with an alternative style of Mass, and it was the first time I met this great woman of the Civil Rights Movement.

After Mass, the commandos would go to the baptistery to plan the march. Then we joined Father Groppi and his congregation on the streets of Milwaukee, singing our songs of freedom. We followed Dick Gregory, the activist and comedian, who walked with Father Groppi and led us down the streets of the white neighborhoods and the black neighborhoods to the bridge, now named after Father Groppi, that crossed the river.

We ignored the police that circled our group of two or three hundred. We walked together, priests, nuns, and lay people, black and white, men and women. There was safety in numbers because the NAACP commandos walked between the marchers and the police of Milwaukee. We thought that the more of us that were present, the less likely it was that Milwaukee reactionaries would attack.

Groppi and Val Phillips won the battle against red lining, mainly because Milwaukee could not afford police coverage for the constant marches. The battle in Milwaukee also marked the beginning of my life-changing relationships with my mentors, Father Groppi and Fannie Lou Hamer and Dick Gregory, who often led the marches.

Around the same time, I took up the habit of going shooting with Father Pete. He loved skeet shooting and generally aiming his gun at different objects, dead or alive. I went along with Father Pete because he was fun and one of the younger priests in the area. One day Pete suggested I learn to practice self-protection. That was not my style, but I agreed, figuring that I wasn't going to harm anyone.

Pete drove us to an isolated, small field up against a hill. When he went to get guns out of the truck he brought out a Thompson sub machine gun. Pete said, "It is an antique." I asked where it had come from.

"From the confessional," Pete told me. "Last winter, a guy comes in to the confessional and says he killed someone. I was shocked, and all I could think to ask was, 'Why did you do that?' The guy said he did it as a living. I told him that I couldn't offer him forgiveness unless he gave up killing and his lifestyle. We went back and forth. He finally said, 'Okay, I will stop.' I told him I needed a real sign of his decision. It was so damn serious, I couldn't stand it. Finally, he said, 'Okay, Father, I will give you the gun.' I told him that was a good sign and appropriate. I expected a pistol, but he pushed through the old red curtains and he gave me this gun."

We had fun aiming the Thompson at targets, but neither of us pulled the trigger.

It occurred to me that we had an untenable situation in Frostburg. We made this whole trip to Milwaukee to advocate for civil rights, and then we returned to Frostburg, where there were only four blacks in the entire student body: two from the Caribbean and two who had been recruited to play football. There was no official policy at Frostburg against accepting black students, just as there was no official segregation in Milwaukee. The dean claimed the admissions board was color-blind. But every applicant had to submit a photograph along with an essay, which gave admissions the ability to select the race of its incoming class. We needed some direct action at our own college to confront the admissions department.

We wanted Frostburg to integrate its student population. Dennis Kuhn and Professor Robert Gilligan had been coming to Mass since my first week at

Frostburg, and they wanted to plan a rally. We invited people prominent in the Civil Rights Movement to speak, to help us shame the hell out of the supposedly color-blind administration.

Frostburg State had never before hosted a conference like the Black Backlash Conference we planned in May, 1968.[5] We wanted the rally to be large and inclusive. We raised funds with the help of the entire parish, friends, and some of the professors like Bob Gilligan. We had bake sales, car washes, and everything else, and we plastered the entire campus with posters about the event. We invited Rev. Braxton Boyd, a Washington minister who worked in Mississippi and Alabama with Dr. King; Dan Gant of the Congress of Racial Equality; Robert Jackson, assistant director of the Neighborhood Youth Program and a community organizer of Southeast Washington; Rev. Walter Lubarski, a sociology professor at Virginia Union College; Rev. Goodwin Douglas, president of the Cumberland NAACP; and Nelson P. Guild, dean of the College at Frostburg. Speakers came in from Chicago, Cumberland, and Washington, D.C. Stan Lubarski spoke, as did Dennis Kuhn and Professor Gilligan, as well as a Protestant pastor from D.C. Student representatives came from Bowie State College, Coppin State College, Morgan State College, Salisbury State College, University of Maryland, Catholic University, American University, George Washington University, Howard University, Virginia Union College, and Mary Washington College of the University of Virginia.

We had managed to secure the necessary funds and a space on campus to hold the rally, and for a moment I thought that the rally might go smoothly. Then, the night before the event, as I was sitting in my little single, puzzling out the order of the speakers, there was a knock on my door.

It was Father James. He was pale and shaky, twisting a handkerchief as he stood in the hallway. My mother was dead. Her Parkinson's disease had become worse in the past few months, but I had somehow thought she was going to be fine. She had always been fine; she was my mother.

It had been quick and relatively painless, Father James said. I slumped down and sat motionless in the doorway. Father James was saying that I should return to Pittsburgh and prepare for the funeral. This was not unexpected, but it was still difficult to believe. I left early the next morning, and picked up my brothers Joe and Mike on the way. We drove home without saying a word.

The funeral Mass was to be held at St. Bernard's. I could stand and say the words of the Father and the Son and the Holy Ghost, but my mother would not be there in the front row. Instead, she would be lying before us in a mahogany coffin, covered in linen embroidered with the sign of the cross, just as she would have wanted. Since she would not be there, I asked Rev. John Petruha, my oldest friend from the seminary, to give the sermon.

John delivered a beautiful sermon in the church my mother had gone to every single Sunday. Despite the fact that it was awful, it was also beautiful. It was exactly how it should have been, with all of us there, and my mother finally completely at peace. Yet, all eleven of us sat there devastated. We knew what we had lost.

The Frostburg rally had proceeded without me and brought state attention to the racial disparities at the school. By the next year, Maryland Governor Marvin Mandel had appointed Pansye S. Atkinson to fix the admissions policies. She was the first to hold the new position of Coordinator of Integration, a position that quickly became Director of Minority Affairs. The governor, in fact, mandated that the same position be created at all six state colleges in Maryland.

CHAPTER 5

Awakening

"**F**ATHER HEALEY LIES! DON'T BELIEVE HIM WHEN HE tells you everyone can reach the Kingdom of Heaven. Only Catholics can reach the Kingdom of Heaven. Only baptized Catholics." I was being heckled during Mass. While Father Montgomery was right that I didn't think the gates of heaven were open only to Catholics, I was furious that he had picked my Sunday Mass to make a public display of our theological differences.

Cardinal Shehan, Monsignor Frank Murphy, and me at Newman Center.

Maybe Father Montgomery did not approve of the mixing of Jesus and John Lewis, of Ho Chi Minh and David, or maybe it was simply that many in his congregation had started attending my Mass instead of his own. I am sure that he did not approve of the reforms that had recently been instituted by the Vatican. The reforms had been designed to make the Church more accessible, by giving Mass the language of the community's population. The church also removed the altar rails that had separated the priest from his congregation and suggested priests dress in more casual clothing for day-to-day work. The visionary Pope John XXIII was not admired by most western Maryland priests who had little interest in the Church joining the twentieth century.

Father Montgomery just happened to hit his breaking point toward the end of my Sunday morning Mass on parents' day weekend. He was standing in the back of the room with his face red and his starched white collar dripping with sweat. He bellowed at me as I began the final blessing. Shocked, the congregation turned around, and stared at the balding, middle-aged priest who had committed the unheard-of sin of interrupting another priest's Mass.

I waited at the altar for him to finish. When he finally fell silent, I finished the blessings. After Mass, I considered my options. There was, of course, the violent route with a quick uppercut to the nose that would probably solve the problem. Or, more reasonably, I could call Cardinal Shehan, head of the Baltimore Diocese, and lodge a formal complaint. For once, I chose the latter. I called the Cardinal and explained what happened, and told him that if Father Montgomery pulled a stunt like that again, I would have no choice but to kill him.

At seventy years old, Cardinal Shehan was as sharp as ever. He cleared his throat and said, "May I remind you, Father Healey, that you are opposed to the death penalty?"

In 1967, Father James and I had led a successful campaign to stop the execution of Gary Miller, a 16- year-old who had been convicted of murdering a young girl, Judy Lee Ziegler. Two judges paid us a visit to challenge our position and asked us to look at pictures of the dead girl. "If you also look at the photos of the last people you hung, I'll look at your photos." They left in a huff, the hanging judges of western Maryland. Spiro Agnew, then governor of Maryland, ultimately granted a reprieve because Gary Miller was a minor.

The growing problem in the Church was bigger than just sour old Father Montgomery. The reforms, known as Vatican II, were hitting some of the priests hard, shaking up their routines and undermining values they had learned in seminary. For the Church, change was necessary to remain relevant in the 1960s. The Church could not allow itself to be extraneous. Television increased popular awareness of other cultures, and much of the world was becoming more urban and sophisticated.

Latin America had once been an unofficial laboratory for the Church's expansion of conservative policies. In the 1960s, "liberation theology" was gaining ground and, among other things, it urged direct action for the poor. Many priests, especially in Latin America, believed such action was a necessary prerequisite to being a good Catholic. Liberation theology, the priest worker movement of France, and Dorothy Day's work kept me involved with the church. To the extent that I had a Catholic tradition, this was it.

As the Superior of the monastery, Father James was in charge of implementing the welcome changes. At our monthly priestly community meeting, we sat in a circle and discussed how we were implementing the recent reforms. We shared reforms we had begun, how our congregations had reacted, and what we had learned that might help our fellow priests. The meetings resembled a social hour. We'd drink and talk freely. Franciscan monks hold friendship with one another as an indispensable part of the life. In that isolated, airless environment, the men around you are your friends and also your family. They are the only ones that understand the precise, quirky nature of the world in which you reside.

But our Order was not isolated from the ideological battles splitting families apart all over the country. The split between old and new was just as vitriolic, if not more so, within the wood-paneled walls of our monasteries and churches. Father Guy, Father Montgomery, and other older, more conservative priests hated Vatican II. They grumbled at the suggestions of new liturgy, rolled their eyes at the idea of connecting with younger parishioners, and finally, at one particularly tense meeting, Father Montgomery outright laughed at Father James's suggestion of mixing Old Testament stories with parallel stories from contemporary politics.

Father James turned crimson but kept talking to retain control of the situation. I leaned over to Father Montgomery and poked him. "Act your age," I told him, perhaps a little too loudly. Father James stopped talking, and the entire room looked at me. Father Guy narrowed his eyes. "Decorum, Father Jack," he said, shaking his head at the priest across from us.

Within a few weeks of that meeting, the conservative clergy simply stopped attending the sessions. Their open hostility and complete lack of fellowship went against everything the Franciscans stood for.

Maybe Father James had always been a drinker. But now he drank nightly in the community room where monks visited each evening. I generally joined him after the others had gone to bed. They didn't like either of us. We were progressive. The old 45 turntable spun an endless loop of "The Impossible Dream" while we discussed the pros and cons of the changes coming from Rome. We must have heard that song 10,000 times, night after night, as Father James gulped from a heavy glass tumbler of dark liquor. He would fill his glass again and again as the night wore on. I sat with him and watched as he moved the record player's needle back to the beginning again. It was not an inspiring experience for a young priest. Andy Williams and cheap whiskey accompanied our deep confusion and disappointment with the failure of the Church to stand up for Vatican II.

Father James was my mentor, and he was collapsing in front of me. He reminded me of my late professor, Father Dan, and I was worried. I watched in sadness, feeling helpless to lift the weight of disappointment magnified by alcohol, torn between loyalty to him, our joint cause, and others. He was in decline, and I did not want to follow his trajectory down. I wanted to carry on for both of us, for my mother, for the nation.

By 1968 the United States was tearing itself apart. On the night of April 4, 1968, Father James was watching television when the news came on. We had plans to eat dinner in the cafeteria together, so he came looking for me. We both were in Washington, D.C., on a visit.

He found me sitting in the garden. It was spring and cherry blossom season in Washington was in full bloom. Father James looked pale. "It's Dr. King," he said. We decided to go to the soup kitchen of our mutual friend. We served sandwiches, because we did not know what else to do and because it seemed to make sense. We worked in silence. There was nothing to say. It was one year to the day since I'd carried that beat up radio into the Newman Center so the students could listen to Dr. King's "Beyond Vietnam" speech.

While we served soup, a few miles away on East Capital Street, Stokely Carmichael, head of the Student Non-Violent Coordinating Committee, was leading a spontaneous walk, asking stores to shut down for the day in a show of respect for Dr. King. Tensions were high, and by the time the marchers hit the crossing of 14th and U Street, someone had thrown a garbage can through a window. Stokely had brought a gun in the hope of discouraging rioting. He pulled it out, threatened the assembled crowd, and told them to go home before people got hurt. He asked them to respect the memory of the fallen leader of the non-violent movement.

We heard the story later that day on the radio. The marchers had not listened to Stokely and had started to vent their anger. They threw bottles, stones, and anything else they could find. Washington was not the only city descending into lawlessness, fear, and violence. Rioting spread across the country.

By that night, entire city blocks had gone up in flames, and the mayor of Washington, D.C. went on the radio, imploring residents to stay in their homes and lock their doors. Father James and I decided to spend the night in the rectory. We were setting up makeshift beds with the television murmuring in the background. Father James burst out. "Tanks," he said. "Tanks in the middle of Washington, D.C."

Armored tanks were rolling down 14th street, past the bars and restaurants, the clothing stores, and markets. They were followed by swarms of National Guard troops, nearly 13,000 of them. Tear gas blanketed the city by nightfall, and from the Church we could hear the occasional smattering of gunfire, too far away to know whether the National Guard had killed any Americans on their own streets.

The next morning a haze hung over the city. Despite perfect spring weather, it felt as though a storm was coming. When I risked leaving the Church for coffee, two young black guys standing in the door grabbed me, slamming me up against the wall. "Go home. Get the hell out of here. This is our time," they yelled.

Back in Cumberland, miles from D.C. at a mostly white, Catholic school, Father Birne, a local priest, was standing at the front of his classroom, trying to find the right way to break the news about Dr. King to his students. He wanted to talk about an American hero who had been shot and why large parts of the country were erupting into violence. He began by stating that Dr. King had been shot and killed. The room of 18 year old boys stared at him. And then, in the back of the room, somebody spoke up. "He's dead? Finally!" Then the room seemed to break open, and some of the boys were slapping hands and cheering, while others were telling them to shut up. A classroom snapshot of a nation divided.

Father Birne walked quickly out of the room, found a trash can and threw up. He called me to help him calm down. He wanted them to understand the tragedy of the violent death of a leader who advocated non-violence and social justice. I did not know what to say. Father Birne forged on and helped his students to address these issues.

One of the worst effects of the assassination of Dr. King was the way it split the country along racial lines. The divide was also between long haired kids and short haired kids. Military and non-military. Red and Blue states emerged. Catholics split over the pill. These schisms have never really healed. In cities the already existing racial rifts expanded, fracturing the tenuous connections that Dr. King had worked so hard to create. It was as if Dr. King had never spoken; the divide he had worked so hard to narrow still existed, and his message of nonviolence seemed lost.

After the assassination, we continued as before with civil rights speakers and marches. There was an increasing feeling of urgency but also of hopelessness. We were afraid we had lost, that we were soldiers standing on a battlefield shooting at shadows in the bushes long after the enemy had won the war and gone home.

Dr. King's last project had been the development of an "economic bill of rights." The Southern Christian Leadership Conference (SCLC) carried on the project after his death. The document was intended to act as a statement of principle, establishing the right to housing, food, and education as a necessary precondition for the exercise of civil rights. Some Americans already had full access to these economic rights, but clearly, others did not.

The proposal for such a document was not new; in fact, it was first proposed by FDR, Healey family hero. After Dr. King's death, the SCLC convinced seven thousand people to come to Washington, set up tents around the capitol, and demand the passage of an economic bill of rights. They set up a shanty town called Resurrection City and lived there in tents despite the pouring rain and thunderstorms that marked the summer of 1968. Rivers of mud seeped into sleeping bags and food but they would not leave Resurrection City until an economic bill of rights was enacted.

We found housing for two busloads of people headed to Resurrection City. Father Groppi arrived in Resurrection City and helped put up tents and maintain order. He and I often met at Mr. Henry's, a bar and restaurant in the heart of Capitol Hill, and he spoke to me of the drama of 7,000 people living in such close quarters in Resurrection City. I told him about the monastery and the division with the conservative priests who now took the separation so far they had stopped saying hello. I also told him that Father James was going through a full bottle of booze every day or two.

My mentor, Father Groppi, was facing a similar divide in Milwaukee. The conservatives there had called the Archbishop of Milwaukee, demanding that the civil rights work halt and that Father Groppi go back to his regular duties and cease his unbecoming behavior. He responded that he found it more unbecoming to support a system that deprived a certain portion of the nation of life, liberty, and the pursuit of happiness purely because of the color of their skin—but he was not calling the Archbishop to complain, now, was he?

One night I confided in him. I told him I was looking for a way out. I was considering leaving the priesthood and the Franciscans. I felt we were not helping anyone while stuck in the monastery, with our careful prayers and our quiet meals, watching the country collapse around us.

He spoke slowly, measuring his words carefully. "Here's the thing, Jack," he said. "You've got a choice here. Do you want to spend your time fighting other priests or fighting this messed up system?"

Leaving the priesthood required a lot of discussions. It had taken me over twelve years to be ordained as a Catholic priest, and it would take me over a year to finalize my decision.

When I told my superiors in the summer of 1968, they asked me to pray about my decision for six months before leaving. I sought advice from friends in the priesthood. When I went to see the dean of our area, he listened to me then said, "Father, you can really preach and you are a good priest. Stay and work it out." Then he said, "I…perhaps I should…well I need to—how shall I say—explain something." He tugged at his collar. "I've been feeling rather hypocritical. The thing is, as of Monday, I'll be leaving the priesthood to become an insurance agent."

Next thing I knew, we were laughing so hard that we could barely breathe. It was just time to go. I left the priesthood on Christmas Day, 1968, with nothing but gratitude toward the Franciscan Order and hope for the future.

I did not mind praying, meditating, going to bed early or getting up early, but

I really wanted to expand beyond the walls of the Church. I wanted to see our big world and the people in it. I knew I was good in a fight, but now I was ready to take on some non-violent ones.

CHAPTER 6

Baby Steps to Out of Control Skiing

For reasons that remain mysterious, my sister Naomi decided the first thing I had to do upon leaving the monastery was to go skiing. Naomi is the kind of person with whom it is useless to disagree once she has made up her mind.

Naomi always played the role of surrogate mother to me, and watched out for me from the age of two well into adulthood. She kept me out of trouble and would often grab me by the ear and drag me out of the local pool hall. She was my watcher. So it was no surprise to see her face on the Christmas day I left the priesthood.

I had nowhere to live, no source of income, no savings and no job prospects. But we were going skiing, Naomi announced when she and my brother Mike came to pick me up from the monastery. We tossed my beat-up suitcase in the back of her Ford, and drove off the monastery grounds for the last time. After the endless conversations I'd been having that year, it didn't seem possible I could just get in a car and leave, but the Order simply said goodbye. Money had never been a part of that life. I left without a penny.

Mike, who had spent the years that I was in seminary developing a successful career in marketing, made enough to buy a cabin in Western Pennsylvania—the lucky bastard. So off to Pennsylvania we went.

I had never skied in my life, so Mike gave me my first ski *lesson*. I use the word *lesson* here loosely. Mike, despite being my favorite brother in nearly every other way, essentially strapped the skis on me and pushed. Also, I was twenty-nine years old, and pointing the skis toward the bottom and letting go was pretty exciting.

It was a little less exciting when I found myself lying face up on the snow, leg bent beneath me at a sickening angle, hearing the voices of other, more judicious skiers, all around me. "Whoa, did you see him hit the tree?" "He just went right at the thing." Next thing I knew, Mike was in the back of an ambulance with me, looking nauseated, as we sped down the mountain toward the hospital, where I was treated for a broken leg. The cause of the injury, printed in big block letters on my chart, *"out of control skiing."*

The broken leg resulting from *out of control skiing* landed me on Naomi's couch for the next few weeks. I slept, drank Orange Julius, and tried to figure out my life.

I was almost thirty. I had never had a paying job (except summer jobs), done laundry, cooked my own food, or paid rent. I felt like one of those prisoners who are released after thirty years only to find out that people now have machines that allow them to type words on a screen. I had acquired plenty of practical skills at the monastery: carpentry, plumbing, laying tile, and shoe making among them. Jobs in those fields just didn't interest me.

As I was driving down Connecticut Avenue in northwest Washington, I spotted the brick house across the park from the National Zoo where a lot of ex-priests lived. Cardinal O'Boyle fired about 60 priests on August 18, 1968, after the priests signed a petition demanding the Church change its position on birth control for Catholic women. Jane Briggs Hart, the wife of Michigan Senator Philip Hart, believed in what the priests had done. She rented them a building to live in and thus bought them the time to start a new life.

I found an apartment on the other side of the zoo on upper Wisconsin Avenue. My first home outside the seminary was a nice place with a rooftop pool. I figured all the fired priests would not fit in the Hart house, and more ex-priests were coming to town every day to look for government or teaching jobs. I hoped I could find tenants from among these ex-priests and use their rent money to keep me in groceries.

On one of those days when the rent had not covered the cost of scrambled eggs and day-old bread, I went to a soup kitchen with a friend. It was a nice evening, and we strolled through Lafayette Park across from the White House.

In the middle of the park, sitting in a big circle on the grass, was a group of maybe 50 or 60 people. It was a motley group, some in business suits, some in flowery dresses, some who looked like drifters and some who appeared to be barely out of high school. It was an anti-war meeting organized in part by Sam Brown, who would later head ACTION under Jimmy Carter. Sam and a few of his friends would devise a plan for a protest, a walk, a demonstration, or even a party, and the group would make it happen.

Although the group was in agreement that the war in Vietnam needed to end quickly, stopping the napalm, the body bags, and the dying children, the ragtag coalition sitting on the blankets often disagreed about everything else. Some, the men in suits, wanted the war to end, and for business as usual to return to the United States. Others, the men in the ragged t-shirts, hoped a Trotskyite revolution might spring from these evenings in Lafayette Park. Everybody somehow managed to agree to the extent that the protests happened, the walks took place, and the demonstrations got action. For those equally committed to partying, someone always brought weed and beer for a party afterward. This was the growth of the anti-war movement.

Elizabeth was the center of attention at one of those parties. Dressed in bell-bottom jeans, John Lennon glasses, and with flowers braided into her long, black hair, she was stunning. A friend of hers had thrown the party, concerned that Elizabeth had met no one new in the months since she left her husband. That night, I watched as Elizabeth poured drinks for journalists, activists, and politicians. As she turned around from the record player, we locked eyes for just a moment. Then we stared a little longer, and she made her way over to me.

It was a little like Marcie all over again. I was talking to the beautiful girl in jeans as the other guys in the room shot me dirty looks. Those looks got nastier when Elizabeth pulled a piece of note paper from the pocket of a nearby journalist and wrote her number on it. She handed it to me, smiled slightly, and slipped away among a bunch of guys arguing about Mao.

I called—how could I not have called?—the following Tuesday. Tuesday seemed eager but not over-eager, I thought. After our date, I was sitting on her couch, talking about her three kids that she was raising on her own. And then we were kissing, and all I could think about was that I had not kissed anyone since the ninth grade, and I had no idea what I was doing. Fortunately, she did. Then she was unbuttoning her long, flowery shirt, and I felt so lucky I left the seminary.

Elizabeth did not care that I was just learning how to live. I did not know how to hail a cab, order take-out, or date. Everything she did fascinated me, from the way she did her hair, to how she slept in some mornings until eleven, made dinner reservations and then cancelled them. I was excited every time she called, and I never said no to dinner, drinks or a party. All I could think about when I was with her was what it might be like to do this for the rest of our lives.

One day Elizabeth called and invited me to coffee in Dupont Circle at one of our favorite little cafés. As usual, I was early and ordered her a cappuccino and imagined we might go for lunch later. Elizabeth finally arrived and told me she and her ex-husband were getting back together. She was calm and direct about our break up. She just recently divorced, and she was not prepared to jump into a serious relationship. I had to have known that, didn't I?

I had not. She spoke about her husband and said he was moving back in with her. I couldn't listen. The only thing I could do was pay for the iced tea and the damn cappuccino and walk out of the café.

There was pounding on my door late that afternoon. "What is going on, Jack?" It was Sam, an ex-priest friend of mine. I told him that Elizabeth and I were not moving in together, and we would no longer be seeing one another. Sam and I sat on our wooden floor, Sam drinking a pop and explaining that this happened, at least once, to everyone. He patted my shoulder. As he was getting up to go to work, he said, "I'd give it about a year." "Give what a year?" I wanted to know. "What could possibly take a year?" He smiled. "Getting over Elizabeth. I'd give it about a year."

"What the hell, Sam?"

I drove to Philadelphia that evening to see my friend Bob Gilligan. When Bob and I worked together at Frostburg State, he always seemed to know what to say. He was often found calming the nerves of anxious college students, so I thought, perhaps, he could help me in my situation.

Bob and Barb, his new wife, were kind about my misery. This happened to everyone, he proclaimed, absolutely everyone. Bob was a psychologist. As I left, he said, "It's probably going to take you about a year to get over it." My two close friends could do no better than to confirm what Sam had told me the day before. Bob and Barb looked after me for quite a while. They were right...it took about a year.

"If you have to ask whites for your freedom, they will always have the power to take it away from you." Malcolm X, with his usual eloquence managed to express the sentiments of an entire movement in a single sentence. Many black civil rights activists believed that collaborating with white activists was no longer the right way to equality. I respected their belief, but that meant there was no longer a place in the Civil Rights Movement for a white ex-priest, and that work was all I knew how to do.

I briefly considered working for the government in the office of Economic Opportunity that President Johnson had created as part of his Great Society. I thought about working in a drug counseling program. Now that Nixon was president, he was busy eliminating every job I might have been interested in. I did some paper work to get a civil service rating in case I was hired for a government gig. My rating was low until an ex-priest challenged the process and we ex-priests ended up with a GS14 rating, way above where we were first placed.

And then one afternoon, Sam and I were again sitting on the kitchen floor drinking pop—we never sat at the table—and Sam told me he got me an interview for a job. I had been unemployed for nine months. I was tired of having other ex-priests in my place. He said the job's got something to do with walking around the world to end hunger.

CHAPTER 7

American Freedom from Hunger Foundation: 1968–1973

I INTERVIEWED THE NEXT MORNING FOR A JOB AT THE American Freedom from Hunger Foundation (AFFHF) that Sam had considered and rejected for himself. He was headed to Peru to marry a mountain woman and has lived there ever since.

Hunger was and is a pervasive issue in the United States and around the world. Lester Brown published *Man, Land and Food* in 1964, and the *U.S. News and World Report* picked up on the urgency of the issue. Brown predicted drastic world hunger by the end of the century. Drought, famine and overpopulation were all issues that needed to be addressed. In the United States, people like Bobby Kennedy shined a light on conditions of hunger, especially in the inner cities and the south, on migrant farm workers and on the many children going to bed hungry.

In 1968, former Congressman Len Wolf took over AFFHF, a small non-profit that was the United States affiliate of the Food Agricultural Organization (FAO) in Rome. The goal of AFFHF was to reduce hunger across the world. The youth arm

World Food Conference planning session for the U.S. delegation, 1970.
Photographer unknown.

of this organization was called Young World Development (YWD), and its focus was on raising awareness of the issue of hunger in the United States and around the world. High school students joined the movement and organized events, such as walks, to raise money and educate people about the food crisis at home and abroad.

YWD had chapters in a few high schools in the mid-west. The chapters organized hikes in which young people would walk about thirty miles and ask people to donate money for the number of miles walked. The chapter that organized the walk could decide where to donate the proceeds. The Congressman's only rules were that, after an allowance of 15% to fund AFFHF operations, the money raised had to go to organizations fighting hunger, and that half would fund projects abroad and half would stay in the States. Local decision making and control could make the program work. The students learned about the factors that caused hunger: war, drought, and corrupt governments. Perhaps more importantly, they learned how to analyze projects, organize large events, and communicate with massive groups of people.

It was September 1969. I was wearing an ill-fitting suit I borrowed from Sam, and I had no idea how to answer an interview question. Congressman Wolf's aide asked why I wanted to work there, so I told her I had experience with organizing students. I had been in charge of the Newman Center at Frostburg State. The interviewer said she did not give a damn what the Newman Center was. At Freedom from Hunger I would be expected to nationalize the youth movement. She told me I could start work the next day, and I better be on time.

Then she yelled into the other room, "Bryce Hamilton, get in here. We've got a new staffer who doesn't know what the hell is going on." Bryce was leaving to work on a new effort called Earth Day. Congressman Len Wolf, with his shock of black hair and red tie, ambled in. "Son," he said. "You're gonna need a passport and a suitcase."

Today the fight against hunger—to eradicate starvation, malnutrition, and food insecurity—is somewhat apolitical. The basic ideal of feeding the world's

Madison Walk for Development.

children is an idea that we can all support despite our differing political leanings. Forty years ago, the fight against hunger was inextricably linked to the ideological battle of the century. We could not seem to discuss the issue of global hunger without arguing whether the communist or the capitalist model offered the best solution. It was a life-and-death battle both for those who struggled with hunger and those who were engaged in the fight against it, many of whom risked their lives to be a part of the conversation.

My first assignment was to attend the annual YWD meeting at FAO headquarters in Rome. The goal of the meeting was to get young people who were working in the fight against hunger together in one room to share ideas and garner emotional support.

Rome was meaningful to me for many reasons. The Vatican and St Peter's Basilica are the spiritual, physical, and political center of the Roman Catholic Faith. The Order that had been my life for over fifteen years originated in Rome. There were buildings that stood before the birth of Jesus Christ. It was also a city where the bars stayed open all night and where people casually started a night out at midnight and stayed out until 5:00 a.m. I did not understand the exchange rate and aggressively overpaid my cab drivers. Everything, even the magnificent old architecture, was new to me.

Sitting in a conference room around a large table in the middle of the ancient city, we heard from young people, speaking in different languages, about hunger and food production. They spoke about land monopolization in Latin America, white minority rule in Africa and its control of resources. They told of unequal wealth distribution in Asia, and starving children in Argentina, and governments that used food distribution as a means of power, Stalin-style. The attendees came from so many places I had to run out at lunchtime and buy a map to locate them.

We discussed different models of development. These were extremely important issues to many of the participants, and because of the political situations from which they came, the conversation had to be held in complete confidence. Discussions of land reform had led to executions in some South American states.

A young woman in a blue pinstripe suit quietly entered the room and slipped me a note. It read, "This meeting is being recorded and broadcast throughout the building."

I stood up in the middle of testimony about the Brazilian government illegally *reclaiming* land from Indian tribes. I said, "This meeting needs to stop, now." I announced that the conference was being broadcast throughout the building.

Mr. Judd, the British parliamentarian who was moderating the conference, was apoplectic at my *highly unprecedented* interruption. He exclaimed, "You're out of line, Mr. Healey."

I agreed without apologizing. For a moment, nobody said anything. Then everyone was moving, whispering, and talking at once. The 18-year-old Brazilian student who had been talking about the *reclaiming* that was occurring in his hometown calmly took the microphone. Running a hand through his black, curly hair, he said if his government were made aware of his remarks at this meeting, he might be shot. Land reform protective of Indians in Brazil, as in most of Latin America, was a dangerous topic. His blood, he said, would be on the hands of the FAO, because they had broadcast the conference without consent instead of keeping the meeting closed as promised. Brazil was run by the military at the time and recorded political sessions were not a promising way to stay alive.

Mr. Judd, red faced and sweaty, approached the microphone. Banging his gavel, he attempted to be heard above the din that had broken out in the elegant room. He placed the meeting on hold until we received an official reaction from the top. As he was making his announcement the door opened, and Mr. Boerma, the Secretary of the FAO, came in.

Very quietly, as though he hoped no one would hear him, he confirmed that the meeting was being broadcast and monitored in just this building. As he stammered through an apology, I could only look at the 18-year-old Brazilian boy, standing there calmly next to the girl from Malawi. He was listening, politely, to the leader of this conference. He did not look surprised. That someone could die for expressing an opinion at a conference was a door into a new reality for me.

My first year at YWD was surprisingly successful given my complete lack of experience. We held Walks for Development in cities such as Fargo, Minneapolis, Madison, and Beaver Dam. I spoke to high school students from nine to six every day. The high school approach worked, thanks to the great young people who joined the YWD and organized marches against hunger in their hometowns and in their schools.

The first group of kids that I met with was from Madison, Wisconsin. They ran their office better than the office of any organization I've worked in before or since. Their local Walk for Development chapter was extremely efficient. Their phones were always answered, there was always paper in the printer, and nobody left for cigarette breaks and returned three hours later.

I went out with five of the YWDers to a local coffee shop to talk about their recruitment efforts in the neighboring towns and in the local public schools. They told me the walk, scheduled for the following week, had been organized over

Mike McCoy and Mark Stillman, two of the organizers of the Twin Cities Walk for Development. Mike became the 1971 International Walk Day coordinator with Fannie Lou Hamer. Photo by Mark Stillman.

the course of the past six months. They had been aiming for 50,000 students but were pleased with the 30,000 that had been signed. They were confident they would all show up and planned their route with a great media strategy to maximize the effect of the walk.

They had one big concern. "We've heard that Father Groppi, the dangerous radical, is coming to town this weekend. What if he sabotages the march?" Groppi was taking on the Wisconsin legislature as part of his civil rights work.

Four of the five of them looked grave. Milwaukee's conservative papers had portrayed Groppi as a dangerous radical, hell-bent on disrupting and undermining white communities. I told them Groppi was an old friend of mine, and I knew he would support what they were doing. I suggested we have coffee with him the next day. Groppi ordered an iced tea instead of a coffee and asked them about their project. At the age of fifteen, Bob Peterson had proven himself to be a brilliant organizer. Waving his constantly active hands as he talked, he got into the planning details and flushed with pleasure when Groppi admired their recruitment process.

Then it was the boys' turn to show admiration as Groppi described marching with Dr. King in the south and the disregard for physical danger the marchers had displayed. He recounted facing police shooting tear gas in Milwaukee. Bob told Groppi the Madison Walk would help two major causes: Freedom Farm Co-op, run by Fannie Lou Hamer, and the liberation of Portuguese East Africa (now Mozambique).

The Madison Walk in 1969 was a total success. The battles for civil rights and economic rights blended, as they maybe always should, as Groppi proudly joined the march, and walked with those 30,000 high school students the thirty miles and raised tens of thousands of dollars.

From Madison, I went to Chicago, where thirteen students had planned a walk that attracted 40,000 marchers and plenty of press. The march was planned without any organizational hierarchy, a fact that Len Wolf could barely absorb. Sadly, Congressman Wolf died from cancer soon after. These students created a process so effective that we asked them to help us in the Washington organization so other groups could imitate their process in planning an International Walk Day for 1971.

I spent Christmas of 1970 in Chicago, where the students and I wrote a manual detailing the students' method of organizing a walk. We sent the pamphlet to high schools all over the country. We let the students at each school plan their own route and decide what charity would receive the money. Sixteen-year-old Perry Muckerheide not only organized the Milwaukee walk, but he also produced the film that became our hallmark. It was set in a church and rallied students to the fight to end hunger.

Anselm Rothschild and Laurie Ferber in Buffalo chose a march route designed to pass the maximum possible number of homes and businesses. The north suburban Chicago organizers competed with the Buffalo team to be the nation's largest walk in 1971 (100,000).[6] The students taught us to keep things non-hierarchical but efficient. They had each person on their team pick a job and stay with it, holding themselves responsible and nudging along team members who proved less focused. To my knowledge, there has never been another organization that let students make the funding decisions.

Bob Peterson and Debbie Sweet in Madison combed the manual again and developed an improved strategy for getting maximum press attention. Mike McCoy and Sue Forsythe in Minneapolis; Pat Hughes in Boston; Bill Brieger in Chapel Hill; Janis Goldstein in Miami; Jerry Schmitz in San Diego; Bill Kokontis, Gerry Connelly (later elected to congress for Northern Virginia during the Obama wave of 2008), and Gloria Ciaccio in Chicago, and Schlossberg and Lutz in Fargo; Mike Seltzer ran the northeast office with Cathy Smith and Howard Berkes, who went on to become a reporter for NPR; Martha Fritts ran the Midwest office; Rosemary Rapp and Moira Sher ran the west coast regional offices.

By the end of my first year at Freedom from Hunger, we had held over 300 walks, which were organized by deeply committed kids in high schools from all over the United States. The second year there was a march in every state in the union.

Sister Corita Kent, made famous by her anti-war posters, made posters for the Walks, with words like HOPE and LOVE and POWER filling colorful canvases. We printed her designs and pasted them like wallpaper across schools and storefronts. They covered every conference room where we sat with high school students and helped make their school's plans, and wondrously, the plans were implemented. All of these successes made me see the country as connected, open, possible.

Less than two years earlier, our small organization had been sinking financially. When I started at AFFHF it was $300,000 in debt. Now it was at the forefront of a nationwide movement. We added Joe Kimmins, Kathy Desmond, and Mary Anne Mason as education officers. We had two people to oversee projects: Harvey Silver and Dave Landry. The money poured in, and we earned $12.5 million that year. Our slogan was, "Development is the New Word for Peace."

Indian nation visit and fast in Nebraska with Anselm Rothchild and Barbara Body, 1972.

We were fighting for economic security as a necessary, not a secondary, precondition for peace and a basic human right. More importantly, we were raising money and funding initiatives that provided food and food production. The walks were the means; food security was the goal. Since each walk picked its own beneficiaries, we funded a large variety of projects across the political spectrum. The St. Louis group, led by Greg Darnieder, bought a bus and drove it to Central America. Another donated to the American Indian Movement; still another chose Catholic Relief Services. It really was up to the young people who worked so hard to plan the march. Choosing a charity was part of the task.

Michelle Burke, co-coordinator with Steve Rabin of the North Chicago walk in 1972,[7] was later told they were the toughest project analysts many non-profits had ever seen. Their teams grilled applicants: "Exactly what does your budget cover? What are your outcomes? Show us the proof of your effectiveness over the past five years. We demand that every penny get to its intended recipients." When the press asked me a question at the Chicago press conference, I stepped aside to let Steve Rabin field the questions. They were finding their voices. Steve and Michelle both went on to become public relations specialists.

For our chairs of International Walk Day 1971, we chose legendary civil rights leader Fannie Lou Hamer for her Freedom Farm Co-op and Mike McCoy, a 16-year-old organizer from Minnesota.

The full impact of this movement went beyond the approximately $15 million we raised for anti-hunger projects. I have remained in touch with many of these young activists over time. Their lives have been marked by activism and service. Their life choices have made me see that perhaps the greatest impact of our movement was on the young people—those who organized as well as those who walked year after year.

Greg Darnieder, who ran the St. Louis walks, later became the mentor to thousands of young people living in Cabrini Green and is now part of the Obama administration's Department of Education. Laurie Ferber became a Wall Street financier. Bill Brieger went into third world health and was a part of the team fighting the Ebola crisis that broke out in 2014.

I recently reread an old letter written by my friend Michelle Burke (Foster) to one of her teenage friends in another school. She started by giving very serious instructions on how to organize a walk: "Reach out to businesses. Have them supply water trucks for the walkers, get first aid tents, ask stores for free fixins for the thousands of peanut butter sandwiches you'll be making. Development is the new word for peace. You must tell the students we have to end hunger!" The letter then seamlessly switched to teen talk of her most recent boy crush before ending with the news that she'd spoken to Presidential candidate George McGovern earlier in the day and he had thanked the students for all their work to end hunger. They were normal teenagers…but also passionate young people who had found their voices.

I didn't notice Beckie when she started working for Freedom from Hunger as a part-time accountant. Then she joined our group after work for drinks, and I was drawn to her beauty and grace. One Tuesday I walked with Beckie after happy hour at McFadden's, and she leaned over and kissed my cheek. She suggested we get a drink. I can remember staring at the plastic necklace she was wearing, at her short red hair, opening my mouth to say no (so far I had dated a grand total of one person, if you don't count Marcie Stinner) and instead saying yes. I guess my year of grieving was officially over.

We went out for drinks, then dinner, and began seeing each other every day. She was smart, good looking, and kind. We talked about everything: our lives, our work, and our goals for the future. We went to parties where people had to shout over the din to announce the location of the next street demonstration and where we would all discuss the best place to buy cheap bread and cheese, because none of us had much money. We would walk downtown holding hands for blocks and blocks and kiss next to the monuments.

And then we were standing together at the wedding. Beckie was wearing a yellow sundress. I was wearing a suit that I borrowed from Sam. Her father and mother sat together, the latter dabbing her eyes, mostly out of disappointment at the utter lack of niceties at the ceremony, and we were married. We rented a cute house a few blocks from the capital. It was a new life.

The Walks for Development were not a radical form of protest or agitation for change. They were not extreme or revolutionary, especially in comparison to the more violent protests of the time, such as throwing bombs at little girls in churches in Selma or destroying buildings on campus.

Perhaps the mainstream nature of our organization was what prompted the recognition we received from President Richard Nixon. Before his name became synonymous with the Watergate scandal, he was seen as a symbol of the endless war that was spreading death throughout the jungles of Vietnam and much of the rest of Southeast Asia. The administration was trying to reconnect with Americans—especially young Americans. And so, in the aftermath of the wildly successful Madison Walk for Development planned by Debbie Sweet, the administration sent her a letter of congratulations and invited her to a ceremony at the White House to receive the Young American Medal for Service. She asked me to accompany her and her parents.

Nixon, I thought, did not know what he was getting himself into with Debbie. He probably thought that Debbie would be thrilled to receive the medal. She was young and from the Midwest; she appeared harmless. Debbie and I made a pact in the car on the way to the White House that we would behave ourselves. Her parents liked the idea of the award. The ceremony was also important to the FAO and to Robert Nathan, Chair of our Foundation. We agreed Debbie could burn the photo afterwards, give away the medal or throw them straight at 1600 Pennsylvania Avenue. The plan was to get in and get out of the ceremony with dignity.

The President entered the room, said a few words about how pleased he was to be there, and started pinning medals on the recipients. Nixon stopped as he reached Debbie and paused to say, "The good kids are in here and the bad kids are out on the street."

That was too much for Debbie, who had behaved with perfect decorum until then. As the President started to pin her medal, Debbie said, "Mr. President, I simply cannot trust you until you end the war in Vietnam." The President stepped back, his dark eyebrows shot up. The leader of the free world glared at Debbie, opened his mouth, and nothing came out. He turned and walked out, followed by a bevy of anxious-looking White House staffers, cabinet members, and congressmen, including Senator Tom Dodd, J. Edgar Hoover, Senator Strom Thurmond, Richard Gordon, and Richard Kleindienst—a lot of corrupt folks juxtaposed with a principled 16-year-old. And then the immoral ones called the moral immoral. I thought, "If you cannot handle one anti-war teenager, how can you run a war?" Debbie walked out to a massive press conference and when she landed in Madison she was met by a cheering crowd.

Debbie used her voice to speak truth to power as few before or after did.

Part of my job at AFFHF was visiting funded projects to ensure money was being spent properly. By the time I got to Saigon, I had visited project sites in a number of countries. They were beginning to run together in my mind—a blur of project managers, cheap hotel rooms, and amazing spicy food. Saigon was different—so different that I still remember exactly what it felt like to stand in the middle of its windy streets, where it was hot and sticky and the motorbikes could barely make their way through, it was so crowded. I remember the feeling of walking into a bar and seeing 18- and 19-year-old American GIs, raising shot glasses and blowing kisses to petite Vietnamese women dancing on tables. Young women wearing too much make-up offered anything for a few dollars.

American helicopters provided a continuous background noise that drowned out all other sounds, even on a busy street in the middle of the day. The first few times I heard the helicopters and saw them blowing up dust, I stopped and looked up. Then I realized I was the only one looking; no one else noticed the helicopters anymore.

I was in Vietnam to close a chapter of the International Volunteer Service (IVS), because it was being expelled by Vietnam. IVS volunteers had signed a petition calling for the ouster of South Vietnam's President, Nguyen Van Thieu. IVS's policy was that projects could not be involved in politics. But this line was hard not to cross when it was clear that the U.S. government's policy of propping up the regime was causing devastating poverty, hunger, and despair.

Since Nixon had given Thieu his "absolute assurance" and sworn to support Thieu's government against aggression by North Vietnam, an American NGO calling for his ouster was, at the very least, embarrassing. Thieu was furious and demanded the immediate removal of the organization, and the Nixon administration was more than happy to comply.

I showed up at Saigon's IVS headquarters not knowing what to expect. It was my task to tell a bunch of passionate and courageous American volunteers they had lost their jobs because they had signed a petition with which I happened to agree. There was no doubt that Thieu's government was corrupt and that ordinary Vietnamese citizens were being denied access to food, jobs, and clean water at the hands of this government to which we had given our "absolute assurance."

The office was small, hot, and humid. We sat on plastic chairs around a card table that overlooked a rice paddy. I felt awful about my mission. The volunteers already knew the Vietnam program had been cancelled, they all would get air tickets home, and they would have to find jobs.

They opened up to me, explaining why they thought it was crucial for them to sign the letter to Thieu. Many IVSers stayed in Vietnam even without IVS support. Many became journalists who could speak Vietnamese, French, and English. Their goal was to assure that accurate news made it home to the United States. Many of them had used their time at IVS to gather information on American war crimes in Vietnam, including the slaughter of civilians, rapes, and the burning of homes. They were passing most of the information to reporters, saving some of it, hoping that when they got back to the US, they would be able to get the news into the mainstream press.

After explaining their true mission, they asked me what to do with all the leftover equipment. There were thousands of dollars worth of basic medical supplies that AFFHF had bought in addition to home building tools and agricultural supplies. I smiled. "Give it away to people who can use it," I said. They looked happy to hear this. We shook hands, and I walked out, past the rice paddy and onto the potholed street. I have no idea where all that equipment ended up.

I had a few days left in Vietnam after that meeting, and I wandered the streets of Saigon, chatting with vegetable vendors and eating pho. I was eating at a pho shop when I met a couple of U.S. soldiers from Texas and California who had been in Vietnam for over a year. When I told them the organization I worked for, they asked me if I knew anything about the anti-war movement. In retrospect, it may not have been the most judicious move to identify myself as an anti-war activist while chatting with a couple of American boys risking their lives in the war effort I opposed, but we were all happily eating pho, and I had not spoken to any Americans in a few days. So we bought each other Cokes and kept talking.

Another American soldier walked by and asked if it were true that some hippies tried to levitate the Pentagon. I explained that I had, in fact, been there when the crowd of thousands of people surrounded the Pentagon, linked hands, tried to translate collective thought into action. This young soldier found it hilarious, but he finally stopped laughing long enough to buy another round and join us. He suggested that I visit the local GI hangout with them and explain this hippie talk to his buddies.

This was not a set up. It was simply a bunch of American GIs who wanted to talk about the war they were fighting. We walked the few blocks to their hangout, a large, open room with giant ceiling fans and throw pillows all over the floor. It had once been a teashop, explained my new friend, as we picked our way through the roughly 60 soldiers sitting on the big, plush pillows. I started coughing. There was so much marijuana smoke in the room, from the fifteen or so huge glass bongs being passed around, that I got high just from breathing. I felt reassured. I was fairly confident that the majority of them were so high they would not notice our little parade.

My friend stood at the front of the room, and waved his arms to get everyone's attention. A few guys looked up sleepily. Someone at the back of the room started laughing as he gave me a little push, nudging me to the front of the group. "This dude is gonna talk about the anti-war movement going on at home," he said.

A few people sat up and looked at me blearily. I talked about how the anti-war movement had begun as a "hippie movement" and was rapidly spreading across the country and into the mainstream. Marches and demonstrations had occurred in almost every city. College campuses were often on strike. I told them after the police massacred four student protesters at Kent State on May 4th, 1970, more people had joined the movement. The Crosby, Stills, Nash and Young song about the egregious abuse of power had gone to number one on the charts (Tin soldiers and Nixon coming/Four dead in Ohio). I spoke about the release of the Pentagon Papers by the *New York Times* and the *Washington Post* that had disclosed U.S. involvement in Vietnam since 1945 and proved that the White House had repeatedly lied about the nature of U.S. actions in Vietnam. Kent State, the Pentagon Papers, and a general war-weariness had convinced much of the U.S. that it was time to leave Vietnam.

I told them of the polls that showed the vast majority of Vietnamese civilians wanted the U.S. out of Vietnam. The Vietnamese wanted to be left alone to sort out their own affairs. They were tired of being used as a pawn in a global struggle for hegemony. I expressed to them the anti-war movement was NOT an anti-military movement. I relayed my own family's service history in World War II and explained that most protesters recognized that the soldiers were also unwilling pawns of Nixon's policies. However, they knew and I knew that this was not always the case back home.

I asked if they had any questions for me. Initially the weed smoke-filled room was silent, the stillness broken only by the click of lighters and an occasional smoker's hack. Then a guy in the back of the room tentatively raised his hand. "Are all anti-war protestors Maoists?" He heard we were planning a communist takeover of the world and wondered why I believed Maoism was the way of the future. I told him that was just nonsense.

And then somebody else raised his hand, and then two more people had questions. By the end of the afternoon, my voice was hoarse and there were no more questions. As I left, they stood up and applauded.

I walked out onto the street, got a taxi, and climbed in. I sat and thought about the afternoon's conversation. It was tragic that those boys had so little information about their own country and the war they were fighting. This same awareness has followed me through too many wars in the past fifty years. Our brave soldiers rarely know the full story of why they risk their lives. I was so lost in thought that I did not notice the police car pulling up alongside the car. The car cut in front of us and then stopped abruptly, forcing the taxi driver to slam on the brakes.

Four Vietnamese officers got out of their car and approached the taxi. They gestured for the driver to roll down the window. My driver, an American, turned around and said, "let us switch passports." When the policeman asked for my passport I handed him the driver's passport. The policemen stood with their hands on their guns demanding something. The driver reached into the glove compartment and handed them a document. They glanced at it and then the driver shoved some bills out the window. They continued to stand there, so he offered more bills. Finally, one of the officers shrugged and said something in a low voice to his companions. They went back to the police car that was sitting in the middle of the street, holding up traffic. The cab driver rolled up the window and cautiously put the car into gear.

I asked him, letting out a breath that I did not realize I had been holding, what had just happened. "They wanted to know about your talk back there," he said, in clear English, laughing. "They were not so pleased about it."

He had saved me time and who knows what unpleasantness. He said he could get another passport. I never found out the name of the man who got me safely back to my hotel. When I got out of the cab, I gave him all the money I had on me and thanked him again. My guardian angel waved me off, smiling, and sped away down the narrow street.

I left Vietnam with a renewed conviction that the U.S. had to stop its part in the war and leave this battered land. It was crazy to use U.S. money to feed people when that same money was used to kill so many. The U.S. was dropping thousands of tons of bombs, more than all sides had dropped in both theaters during WWII. The war was causing malnutrition and starvation, and the chemicals the U.S. dropped were killing, burning, and maiming the population. In addition, we had destroyed vast crop fields and destabilized nearby Laos and Cambodia.

My trip went on to Kenya, Zaire, Nigeria, and Algeria where I met under trees with the Masai and advised on projects. None was as interesting or as compelling as Vietnam. But in Kenya, I got to see Serengeti Plain with all those beautiful animals.

After I returned, Groppi and I decided to go spend time with Fannie Lou Hamer at her Freedom Farm in Ruleville, Mississippi. Fannie Lou was a pioneer and soldier of the Civil Rights Movement. When Fannie Lou finally was able to register to vote, after countless attempts, she went home to find she and her husband had lost their jobs and their home. She endured jail, beatings, and hatred in her battle for civil rights. In 1964, as she was fighting, unsuccessfully, to get an integrated delegation from Mississippi seated at the Democratic National Convention, Fannie Lou had authored the line, "I'm sick and tired of being sick and tired."[8]

That summer of 1973, the Freedom Farm was a busy place. Fannie Lou Hamer's project had gone from a subsistence farm to a profitable organization. Profits were returned to the community through donations to food charities, scholarships for local children, and funds to create affordable housing. The goal was to make the farm blossom into a charitable community comprised of wooden houses, vegetable patches, and arable land. The Farm had been partially funded by many of the Walks for Development.

Fannie Lou lived in a small clean brick house set on cinder blocks. Her home was always brimming with people coming and going, eating, drinking, and talking. It reminded me of my mother's home, when my mother never seemed to leave the kitchen and people were always at the table. I felt an affinity with her since she was one of 13 children and I was the last of 11.

Fannie Lou put Groppi and me in the spare room and announced that while it was lovely to see us, everyone who stayed at the farm had to work. On the first day, we worked in the vegetable patch near her house and met some of the other workers. It was late by the time we finished working and ate. About an hour after dinner, we heard a loud thud against the outside wall of the house. We did not pay much attention to it. Our muscles ached; it was probably not important.

The next morning, Groppi and I were standing in the walkway to Fannie Lou's house admiring her small sitting porch, a popular feature in Mississippi at the time, when Fannie Lou came out the front door. She walked over to a large, broken glass bottle. We examined it and found a long, string wick inside, and saw that the bottle had been recapped. Obviously, someone had thrown the bottle, and though it had broken, for some reason it had failed to explode. We were lucky, extremely lucky. The homemade bomb had been constructed so poorly that it merely flamed out, hurting the grass and nothing else.

Fannie Lou had faced death threats before. She had known and worked with James Chaney, Andrew Goodman, and Michael Schwerner, all of whom had been killed while working to register black Mississippians to vote. She walked with a limp because the state troopers hit her so hard when she was in jail that they had damaged her kidneys. She displayed no surprise at the glass bottle and the charred grass.

As Groppi and I were examining the bottle, a large white car pulled up. Two men in stiff, black suits and sunglasses, looking as though they had stepped out of the Matrix, got out and approached us. "Mrs. Hamer, we are FBI agents, and we heard there was a bomb thrown here last night," one of them said. The second nodded, pushed his sunglasses onto his forehead, and arranged his features in a show of concern.

Fannie Lou stood back from the bottle and crossed her arms against her chest, perhaps in unconscious self-protection. She told them that no one had called the police, "so that was probably you." And with that, she turned and walked calmly back into the house, pulling the screen door shut behind her.

Visiting Fannie Lou reminded me of the strength and bravery of the people in the Civil Rights Movement. These people had been attacked physically, financially, and psychologically but refused to give up their vision. I left the farm, went back to D.C., and told AFFHF that I was quitting. Our walk strategy had been absorbed by literally thousands of other organizations, and they no longer needed our leadership.

CHAPTER 8

Next Steps: 1974–1976

ONCE AGAIN, I HAD NO IDEA WHAT I WOULD DO NEXT. Washington, once the vibrant center of the movement, felt stagnant. The promises of the 1950s and the 1960s, including the social programs and safety nets that had sustained my childhood, were disappearing. Slowly, and without much notice, progressive income taxes were being repealed, the Great Society programs were being chipped away, and idealism was fading. The high school students who ten years earlier had boycotted their prom and donated the money to charity were taking limos to country clubs in fancy tuxes and dresses. I did not know whether the Civil Rights Movement would continue, or whether we would ever leave Vietnam, or what I could do about it. I began to question my own role and place in the movement for social justice and peace.

It was in that weird, nebulous state that I first met Dick Gregory, although I had seen him years earlier during Groppi's marches in Milwaukee. Dick was a huge celebrity, and I never expected to meet him in person. Dick was ironic, clever, and funny. He worked as a comedian and had been doing a stand up routine in nightclubs all over Chicago. As a black man, he only worked in black clubs until Billy Eskstine told Dick to get over to the new club owned by Hugh Hefner, called the Bunny Club. Dick was so nervous he got off the subway a stop too early. Once on stage in front of a white crowd, he began to burn the rug.

Hugh Hefner was not easy to impress, but that night he said he laughed so hard he cried. This was how Hefner explained his decision to book Gregory as the first black man to perform as a comedian at the Playboy mansion. After that start he played his uniquely bold routines to mixed audiences, appeared on the Jack Paar show (the first black person to be invited to sit with Paar after a routine), and wrote his autobiography, *Nigger*, in 1964 (Headlam, 2009).

A year and a half after he appeared at the Playboy mansion, Dick's annual income had risen from $1800 a year to over $3 million. Dick decided that if he was in a position to be making $3 million a year, it was time to become a major participant in the Civil Rights Movement.

Dick liked to tell the story of walking into a segregated restaurant and taking a seat at the counter. When the waiter told him that the restaurant did not serve colored people, he replied: "Really, don't worry about it, sir. I actually prefer not to eat colored people. Just bring me some chicken."

His activism was obvious from the nature of his comedy, but it did not stop on the stage. Dick was one of Dr. King's closest confidants; he marched alongside Dr. King in Birmingham, and spent five days in a jail cell next to King after they were arrested. He chartered a plane, along with the Student Nonviolent Coordinating Committee, and flew to Mississippi to deliver food and water to the residents of a county that had been denied welfare checks in retaliation for registering to vote. Even though he was a number of years past his prime as a college athlete, where

Dick Gregory and I protested at the White House to demand a reopening of both Kennedys and MLK assassinations.

he set records, Dick ran the entire distance from Detroit to Washington to raise awareness of the importance of a good diet and adequate nutrition.

I met him at the end of that run at a small park in D.C. My first afternoon with Dick in 1973 I learned that he was a good friend of Father Groppi's. We started talking about Groppi, what he had been

doing lately, how hard he had been working—the usual. At the end of the night Dick scrawled his phone number on a piece of paper and suggested we get together sometime soon.

We developed a close friendship. Dick was a frequent visitor to our townhouse and stayed with us when he was in town. One morning over coffee at the kitchen table, he threw his newspaper down. "Across the country," he said, as if we had been having a conversation. I looked at him somewhat blankly. "I'm going to run across this country to end world hunger," he said. And with that declaration he resumed reading the *Washington Post*.

I said, "Dick, let's steal the bicentennial with the Dick Gregory World Hunger Run across the country." We decided that his run would end in New York on

July 4th, coinciding with New York's planned Bicentennial Independence Day celebration. New York's holiday was being marked with the arrival of the so-called "tall ships" in New York harbor. The ships were supposed to represent the ships that the original settlers from Europe had sailed to North America.

Dick pointed out that one of the ships was from Chile, and its prior use had been as a prison where prisoners were tortured. The ships were also replicas of the ones that had sailed to North America with hundreds of thousands of kidnapped Africans. The Africans were taken away from their homes and families, shackled to the hulls of ships only to die on the rough seas, or sold into slavery and a life of backbreaking work. Our nation's economy and so much of our history was built on the backs of those slaves.

Dick's goal for his run was to stop and visit every mayor, governor, church, synagogue, school, and politician along the route, as well as soup kitchens and programs of people feeding people. The kickoff date was April 23, 1976, at Mayor Bradley's office in LA.

Charles Mingus was an African-American jazz musician, civil rights activist, and arguably the best bass player of all time. He played with a number of big jazz acts, including Louis Armstrong, Charlie Parker, and Duke Ellington, before forming his own record company and jazz ensemble, Jazz Workshop.

Mingus and Dick Gregory were friends. It was not uncommon for Mingus to visit Dick's immense, beautiful house in Plymouth, Massachusetts, and stay for a couple of days. Usually, these trips were prompted by Mingus's desire to gain control over his eating habits. Dick would advise Mingus on nutrition and get him back on the right track. Then Mingus would go back to bingeing. In the summer of 1975 I was staying at Dick's house, working on the plans for his bicentennial run; when Mingus arrived with his wife, Sue. Mingus was down in the dumps and needed cheering up.

Mingus said, "Dick, tell me every joke you know—especially the anti-white ones." Dick expressed his sympathy and

Dick Gregory leaned into me and said, "Jack, you better call Danny Sheehan, my lawyer. I think that guy is about to arrest me."

agreed to entertain Mingus. He offered to have his driver, Big Mike, drive Sue back to the airport. Dick added to Mingus, "Why don't you jump in the front seat there, see her off to the airport. The ride's on me."

Mingus said he thought that was probably a good idea. As Mingus was about to sit back in the car, Dick hollered: "You'll take anything for free!" Mingus bolted out of the car in anger, and I looked on in shock, as did everyone else around. Mingus's temper was obviously about to boil over. Then he saw that Dick was laughing. Dick could pull a line out of even the most dire of situations. The tension broke, and we all laughed.

Dick sent Mingus and I down to his large boathouse on a beautiful inlet. After the scene outside, I did not know what to say. Finally, after a very long silence and some uncomfortable tiptoeing around Mingus's volatile personality, I asked him, "What do you do, Mr. Mingus?" I had been so sheltered in the seminary. I wasn't even sure what instrument he played. Mingus turned on a radio, "You hear that? That bum bum bum bum? That's what I do. I have a whole orchestra in my head."

I said I wasn't quite sure I had anything in my head.

Mingus said, "Yeah, and when you were born you thought you were better than me, too." Surprisingly, this started a conversation. We talked on and on about mortality, philosophy, and human rights as we ate dinner. By the end of our meal, Dick still hadn't shown up. Nobody was surprised since he was often late. We decided to call it a night and went to bed.

In the middle of the night, Dick woke us up. Dick sat Mingus in the chair and told me to stand in the corner and watch. I understood. It was Mingus's night. Dick turned on some of Mingus's music and began a monologue that lasted until dawn: "I am going to run for the Presidency. I am going to win the Presidency. And I am going to paint that White House." And it went on from there. Dick went through his entire repertoire that night.

Finally, the sun came up, and Dick finished. Mingus said, "Thank you, Dick. I am ready to die." It was an incredibly moving scene, shared by two of the most talented men of the twentieth century: Dick Gregory and Charles Mingus.

Dick knew everybody. He called Stevie Wonder from Beckie's office. He asked Stevie to set up a concert in New York City and perform on July 4th. Dick planned to have Stevie Wonder close the concert just as he ran into the stadium. "While they have that tight ass party in Manhattan, with their thousand dollar fireworks, we'll be dancing in Giants Stadium," Dick said to me, grinning as he put down the phone.

I did advance work for the run, and my friends Bill Davis and Danny Sheehan from the Jesuits and Margie Tabankin of D.C.-based Youth Project helped me raise over $90,000 to start. Oxfam, through its representative, Nathan Grey, worked with Dick as well. We needed money for events Dick planned to have in each city he ran through. The money that we raised during the run would be donated to organizations working to end food insecurity and hunger in America.

At one point, Dick asked me to go over to Richard Pryor's house and get $75 from him. I picked up the check for $75 and gave it to Dick, who looked at it incredulously. "$75,000, Jack, I asked for $75,000!" When I returned to Richard Pryor's place he had a $75,000 dollar check for me and a huge grin. "I thought I was going to get away with saving some money," he said.

Every comedian in LA at the time showed up at Mayor Bradley's office for the kickoff: among them, Richard Pryor, Soupy Sales, Shecky Greene, and Redd Foxx. Foxx rode up in a dune buggy sporting what was for him a normal outfit—a bright red velour running suit.

Also present were Tommie Smith, who had made the famous clenched fist salute during the Mexico City Olympics,[9] and Big Mike, Dick's go-to guy and driver. The *LA Times* and *San Francisco Chronicle* came. They all stood around the mayor's office and watched Dick do jumping jacks and stretch. Dick chatted with the photographers as though he were preparing for a casual five-mile loop around the neighborhood.

Dick pointed his feet in the direction of New York and started running. In every city, he visited the local high school, stopped by the offices of a few non-profits, and talked with the local politicians. He publicized the fact that hundreds of thousands of Americans were suffering from malnutrition and food insecurity. Some lacked access to enough food

George O'Hara, Ali, and me on the day of the Jimmy Young fight outside of D.C. Dick Gregory suggested that I ask Muhammad Ali to join him on his national run for hunger. Mr. Ali did join the run.

to keep their families going. He proclaimed this was not a truly free country if people were starving or living hand to mouth and falling ill as a result.

At first, there were photographers and journalists in every city. There were students lining the sidewalks, mothers with babies and men in business suits. Unfortunately, about halfway through the run, somewhere around New Mexico, attention started waning. Americans had other things to worry about.

Dick called me from a coffee shop, where he was drinking his usual giant glass of water. His diet for the run was limited to water, fruit juice and a vitamin-enhanced drink he had developed. I had just been on the phone with the press. They had not been interested in where he was going next. I was worried—seriously worried.

Dick reassured me through the phone. I heard him take a gulp of water. "Go see Muhammad," he said. "Muhammad always helps me out when things get like this."

I was surprised. Dick knew my background. "I'm Catholic," I said jokingly, "and I pray to Jesus. And I don't think Jesus does publicity runs."

Dick laughed. "Jack. Muhammad Ali. Go and see Muhammad Ali before his fight with Jimmy Young in Landover, Maryland." It was April 30, 1976. "Just go over. I will send George O'Hara from Chicago to help you. When Muhammad wins, he will speak on national television about the run. Get him to run with me for part of the run and announce it on national TV."

I said, "If Ali is fighting Jimmy Young I can never get in." When Ali was on TV after winning a fight he was the biggest event going. He was at the top of his game…this was a big deal. I had no idea who Jimmy Young was or whether he could fight, but I had to hope Ali would win so he would get the mic after the fight. Ali spoke to the world, not just the United States.

"Don't worry, man. He'll win," assured Dick, clearly amused. Because it was Dick and because he was usually right, I agreed to go and try to see Muhammad Ali, king of boxing, and the most well-known face on the planet in his prime. I picked up George O'Hara at the airport, and we went to Ali's hotel. It was a mad house, but we got in. Dick's wife, Lil Gregory, had called ahead as she always did for him, to set it up for us.

George and I managed to make our way into Ali's suite about six hours before the fight. He was sitting at an ornate desk at the front of a large room. He was wearing black silk pajamas, through which you could see the outline of his muscular shoulders, his powerful forearms. He was declaring, "I am the greatest and I will destroy Jimmy Young tonight." There was a very long line of people waiting to see him: reporters, photographers, fans, and assorted others. I slipped into line behind someone with an enormous camera. Nobody seemed to notice. The atmosphere in the room was odd. Around the champion it was very quiet, while everywhere else it was madness.

Ali saw me and immediately came over and reached for my hand. He graciously welcomed us to the room and to the fight. "You're with Dick Gregory," Ali said. He waited politely for me to say something.

For an endless few minutes, I was completely tongue-tied. "I'm here, Mr. Ali, to ask if you would consider joining Dick Gregory on his run across the country to raise awareness of the problem of hunger in the U.S. and around the world. We need you in New Mexico to get us an extra kick of publicity." I blurted this out all at once. Behind us, a photographer stamped his foot impatiently.

Ali said, "You want me to pee blood for two weeks, fly out at my own expense, and go running in the desert?"

I stammered, "Yes, sir."

Ali smiled, "Okay," he said.

That night, Ali beat Jimmy Young after fifteen contentious rounds. Surrounded by hordes of sports reporters and TV cameras from all the major networks, he simply ignored the reporters' questions about the fight and looked straight into the camera. "I'm headed to New Mexico," he said. "I'm going to join Dick Gregory on his run across the country to fight hunger in this country and the world." This was a moment that was watched by millions, and it is impossible to overstate its impact. Thanks to Ali, the nation rediscovered the run. Ali ultimately joined the run after his fight in Germany.

With Muhammad Ali on the run, we were back on the front pages. The two of them made quite a sight as they ran into a city. Dick was in his beat up running suit, Ali was running in tennis shoes—which he refused to exchange for running shoes, no matter how many companies offered to make him personalized shoes. The run was once again filling city blocks with

Giving the opening speech for Dick Gregory with Tommy Smith for the World Hunger Run, L.A., 1976, Mayor Bradley's office.

people, drawing out high school students, businessmen, and local political types.

I felt like I was fourteen, standing in that courtroom with Charlie Maloney again. All we had to do was ask, and someone stepped up and threw themselves wholeheartedly into the cause.

A few months after the run, Dick Gregory called me. He asked me to be his representative at a luncheon in Virginia organized by Chip Carter, son of the new President. The lunch was designed to bring together a number of people and organizations that were dedicated to alleviating world hunger. Harry Chapin, the singer, was there along with a number of people representing various organizations. Don Greene represented Sam Brown, the new head of ACTION, which included a number of agencies for seniors, volunteers, and the Peace Corps. I asked Don to set up a meeting for Dick and me to meet Sam.

Dick wanted to secure a good position for the great civil rights leader, John Lewis. Sam assured Dick that John was already his deputy. Sam was anxious to learn Dick's opinion about what ACTION could do for the country. On our way out, Sam asked me to join him at ACTION. I knew that I could not work in political Washington and said, "No, Sam, I am no bureaucrat." But I told him that I would take a posting for the Peace Corps if it were Lesotho. Lesotho was an independent country located in the middle of South Africa. My friend Jerry Brady had told me about Lesotho and how much potential influence the Peace Corps could have there. I wanted Lesotho because of its location inside the apartheid beast, South Africa. A few interviews later, I was offered the post. Dick Gregory, Mary King, John Lewis, Sam Brown, and I went out to celebrate.

CHAPTER 9

The Peace Corps Years: 1977–1981

ONCE I ACCEPTED THE PEACE CORPS POSTING, I DEVOTED myself to learning everything I could about the political situation in Lesotho and South Africa. Father De Soto, a Jesuit priest, stopped by to help me pack, and he told me that Julius Nyerere, then President of Tanzania, would be giving a lecture in D.C. the following week. The lecture would cover different issues in Africa, but its true focus would be apartheid.

The talk was not only about the effects of apartheid on South Africa but its harmful effects on the region in general. Nyerere wanted support for the fight against apartheid from the United States. The lecture was surprisingly informal and personal and not at all the speech I had expected. When he finished, Nyerere stayed to chat with the attendees. I told him I had just been appointed director of the Peace Corps in Lesotho. He squeezed my shoulder. "You, my friend," he said in his low, lilting voice. "You are going into the belly of the beast itself. Be sure to give them some indigestion over there."

Me, with friends Dick Gregory and John Lewis, when accepting appointment to Peace Corps Lesotho.

My first day in Africa was September 25, 1977. That was also the day Stephen Biko, anti-apartheid activist and hero of the black consciousness movement, was buried.[10] Biko was among the principal organizers of the massive and powerful Soweto uprising in 1976, for which the South African police arrested him.

He was a member of the Bantu tribe and had coined the phrase "Black is Beautiful." Although mundane today, in the fall of 1977 in South Africa, it was a radical statement.

Biko's death was officially attributed to the hunger strike that he had been on in prison. The beatings with clubs were not recorded on his death certificate. The true cause of his death was revealed much later. He died in a police van due to police brutality and neglect.[11]

Thousands of people, including leaders from all over the globe, showed up in South Africa for Biko's funeral. His coffin was passed from person to person in the streets as mourners shoved their fists in the air, singing, marching, crying, and chanting.

Years later, Biko's words were combined with the music of Peter Gabriel to become one of the most moving parts of the concerts I did for Amnesty International. Biko said, "We have set on a quest for true humanity, and somewhere on the distant horizon we can see the glittering prize."[12]

I entered the Peace Corps with a wave of other Americans that had been active in the social movements of the 1950s, '60s, and '70s. For example, my colleague Reg Petty, director of the Peace Corps in Swaziland, had spent a year in Mississippi registering voters with the Student Non-Violent Coordinating Committee. Norman and Elsa Rush, who directed Peace Corps Botswana, spent some time in federal prison for refusing to fight in the Korean War. The first time the four of us met was amazing. I remember this energy in the room, a feeling of hope similar to my days marching for civil rights. We were there to continue the struggle for justice for all that we had started at home. This goal never changed, but we would soon find out that our methods had to be altered.

When Beckie and I arrived in Lesotho, our books, clothes, and chipped dishware were moved into the Peace Corps house reserved for the director in Maseru. Beckie set up her office from which she would work as a freelance accountant. Though we lived and worked in Lesotho, we were directly across the river from South Africa. The only fertile region in Lesotho, and the area where most Basotho lived, was on the border with South Africa. This proximity meant that most people crossed the border frequently to get the many necessities that were unavailable in Lesotho. Traveling on the roads of Lesotho was extremely dangerous. There were a lot of accidents and no ambulances. You kept close to home when you could.

My first effort was to post a "Boycott RSA" (Republic of South Africa) sign on the volunteers' message board. I asked them not to spend money there if they could avoid it. The volunteers, of course, were free to go where they wanted, but I wanted them to be conscious of apartheid as a system that damaged everyone it touched. Within 24 hours, the chief of security from Bloemfontein, the heart of the Boer farming power structure, met me as I was on the way to the local store in Lesotho to pick up the newspaper. He identified himself and welcomed me to South Africa. He told me the volunteers were still welcome in South Africa, even if I did not want them there.

My fellow Peace Corps directors and I were not naive about conditions in Africa. But our knowledge was spotty, and we were left with more desire than ability to help the population with change. We decided we could do something to prepare the Peace Corps volunteers for their time in South Africa. That, we would work on.

An example of how tactics that might have been effective in the U.S. were inapplicable to Africa was the Line. It was the Line from Hell, and it formed at the border between South Africa and Lesotho. My experience of traveling out of Lesotho was simple. I'd drive up to the window of the concrete building and hand the border agent my passport. The gates would open, and I would drive our little VW across to South Africa.

Basotho entering South Africa had a different experience. They could not drive up to the building as I did. They were forced to stand in a separate line for blacks composed almost entirely of women shopping and miners trying to find work. This line could entail a full day's wait, as the white South African border guards took coffee breaks, cigarette breaks, and lunch breaks while slowly, casually examining the passport of each black person who went through.

I had seen the tactic of civil disobedience work in the U.S., and I wanted to try the same strategy. So on my first visit to Pretoria, I joined the black line. After about three hours, I reached the window and approached the guard who was engrossed in lighting a cigarette. He saw me, reached up, and slammed the window shut. He shouted into a megaphone that the border was closed for the rest of the day. "Get out of our line," someone shouted from behind me. It echoed again and again, up and down the line, which stretched for hundreds of people.

The miners behind me were enraged. My efforts had left them with no income for the day, and I had in no way improved their status. Civil disobedience, of the type I was familiar with, was apparently not going to work in South Africa.

Minority volunteers, whether black or brown or Asian, were at serious risk if there was ever a need for medical attention in that part of the world. Lesotho had a reasonable hospital for minor emergencies, but people with serious illnesses or injuries were sent to South African hospitals where trauma level care could be provided. However, about 15% of our volunteers were minorities. We knew if one of these volunteers needed care we would be faced with three terrible options. One option was to try gaining entry into one of the 'whites only' hospitals in

In Lesotho, the Mountain Kingdom at waterfall, 1978.

South Africa. Even if admitted under pressure from me or the ambassador, these patients would likely be ignored or mistreated. Or we could take our chances at one of the deeply inferior black hospitals and pray for the best—like the blacks in South Africa had to do every day. The third bad option was to hope an American jet could fly from Frankfurt, Germany and transport the patient back in time to save his/her life. I was fortunate not to face this dilemma during my tenure, but it weighed heavily on me every day.

These challenges became topics of discussions held in our evening office—Fat Alice's Restaurant. Issues were argued, events were planned, and ideas were explored over supper at Fat Alice's. Fat Alice was an Israeli-run African deli where diamond dealers met mercenaries and U.S. Peace Corps volunteers met volunteers from other countries. Bishop Tutu frequented the restaurant. He'd smile when we called him *macaw* because of the colorful clothes he wore while dining with his wife. It was a spot to meet. An African salon.

At first we sat around, drank coffee, bounced ideas off one another, and got excited about what we could do to help. Within a few months, we sat around, drank more coffee, and decided to redo the training program in David Levine's back yard at Peace Corps headquarters in D.C.

In addition to our own difficulties with apartheid, we realized that in some ways our work supported the institution of apartheid. We were providing volunteer teachers to villages, bringing agricultural experts to struggling farmers, and expanding medical care outside of the townships. None of these activities threatened apartheid. At the same time, the American government was actively supporting the Republic of South Africa and therefore supported their ability to maintain the apartheid system. The U.S. government paid our salaries and set our mission while simultaneously supporting an apartheid government politically and financially.

The potential problems still awaiting South Africa were brought home to me one day when I was dining with a group of friends. We noticed two lovers quarreling at another table. Suddenly the girl stood up and slapped her white boyfriend and walked out. As the young man headed for the door, he caught us staring. He snarled at us, "What are you staring at?" One of our team replied very nicely, "If you can't handle one little white girl, how will you handle all of us?"

We were functioning in a gray area. We were complicit, but we were trying not to be complicit. The Basotho parents wanted the Peace Corps volunteers to teach their kids math and science in the schools. This was some of our most valuable work. The boys who learned math and science would go get jobs in South Africa. Girls learned the same math and science but still became domestic workers. We were trying to do the right thing by educating students in Lesotho, but young graduates went to find paying jobs, which were only to be found in South Africa where they also economically supporting apartheid. Strangely enough, Lesotho's largest export was human blood, taken from the miners as they came and went through Lesotho.

The mission the Peace Corps had given me was development. Development can mean many things, but to us it meant that we tried to make the communities we worked in a little better. Non-governmental agencies joined with the United Nations and tried to implement improvements for Lesotho. It was rarely effective. Countries like Lesotho were accustomed to western nations coming in and then changing their agendas every few years. Our mission in the Carter years was to provide for basic human needs. Despite our resources, money, personnel, and experts, we were ill-equipped to effectuate real change. American aid could bring in tractors and build roads and dams. Inevitably, a few years later, there would be no gas for the tractor, no upkeep of the road, and the dam would leak. There was no point to funding development unless provisions could be made for future needs.

An example of the failure of aid agencies to understand the people they purported to aid was NGO rondovals. Rondovals are the historic thatched roof homes of the Basotho. A few mountains and valleys away from our home in Maseru was the small isolated town of Thaba-Tseka. Thaba-Tseka was made up of many small rondovals in which people lived four or five family members to a room. If you kept driving through Thaba-Tseka and up the bumpy dirt road for a few minutes, there were a few beautiful thatched roof homes with no one in them. I asked Sam, my Peace Corps driver, why nobody lived in these rondovals.

"That home is too high and has a window," he said. I looked at him blankly. It turned out that no one, not the Canadian engineer who built the rondovals, nor the NGO that had financed them, had bothered to ask the Basotho whether they actually wanted a high window.

I learned that the height issue was about the children. "They would climb up and hurt themselves, and there are no doctors around," Sam told me. Further, Sam said, "we Basatho hate lightning. It kills us all the time. We do not want to look up in that big window the Canadians put in. None of us will live there. I know they meant well, and they thought to provide heat since a big bucket in that window will absorb heat and warm us at night. But the children might fall, and we cannot take that risk."

The misguided attempts at helping were not a reflection on the volunteers. My respect for the Peace Corps volunteers was enormous as I watched how they interacted with the people, endured being separated from loved ones, and struggled with new cultures and languages. As in all my previous work, I saw young people as the hope of the world. These young people came to another world to give of themselves. The people they worked with were very grateful, and I was proud of the volunteers in Lesotho.

Across the border in South Africa, with a clear vision of what they wanted, some were fighting hard to end the apartheid system. People like Nelson Mandela, in charge of the African National Congress (ANC) and its armed wing, Spear of the Nation (MK), were constantly and unflinchingly challenging white supremacist rule in South Africa. Unlike the Civil Rights Movement back home, where *nonviolence* and *dignified struggle* were the keywords, the anti-apartheid movement was violent. It was a world of AK-47s and homemade bombs and kissing your wife or your husband goodbye every single time you left home, even to go around the corner and buy a jug of milk.

Me with Nelson Mandela in 1993.
Photo by Anthony Allison.

The ANC practiced civil disobedience, but it was disobedience bolstered by guns. The slogan, chanted at rallies and whispered by black families, was simple. The goal was to "make the country ungovernable," and keep it ungovernable until Africans of all colors were entitled to equal rights and equal treatment under the law.

In retaliation for their work, Mandela and many other leaders of the ANC were locked in small, cold cells in a prison on Robben Island, a small rocky island off the coast of Cape Town. Mandela's home was an isolated, desolate place surrounded by ocean and great whites on all sides.

In spite of the absence of many of its leaders, or perhaps because of anger at the injustice of depriving the movement of its greatest minds, the anti-apartheid movement continued to grow in size and power.

In 1993, years after I had moved from Lesotho, I had the opportunity to meet Nelson Mandela. President Carter and U.S. philanthropist Dominique de Menil, a lovely woman who had worked in the Carter administration, presented the Carter-Menil Award to Nelson Mandela. I was invited to the award ceremony.

The usual rush and commotion around this hero of the world made it difficult to converse with him. I did get my photo op as one of the many he graciously permitted. My opportunity to meet him came when both of us got stuck in a bathroom. A camera crew had set up right outside the entrance to the men's room, so Mandela and I had to wait together. I tried my minimal Sesotho on him and told him I had been in his hometown in the Transkei. He nodded kindly. I asked him, "What would you have done if there were no apartheid?" His answer was quick and easy: "I would have been a boxer." I smiled and left him alone with his thoughts.

The great anti-apartheid and religious leader Archbishop Desmond Tutu lived in Lesotho during my tenure at the Peace Corps. As the Episcopal Bishop, he walked a very fine line, neatly and skillfully. Tutu spoke at Episcopal churches around the region—some built with brick and marble and others that featured a cross under a thatched roof and open-air seating on the reddish dirt. He told his congregations that they could not lose hope. He told them the struggle was succeeding, and it was imperative they keep at it. It was written not in sand but in stone, he said, that the blacks would succeed. I met with the Archbishop Tutu regularly to place Peace Corps volunteers in the Episcopal school system in Lesotho.

Another great anti-apartheid leader living in Maseru was Chris Hani, who was in charge of the military operations (MK) of the ANC. Sadly, Hani was assassinated on April 10, 1993, right after Mandela was released from jail. I would often run into him on the street. An unusual man of great kindness, he had a youthful look that belied the military man he was. He was well educated, and we talked about Chesterton and Belloc and John Henry Cardinal Newman, which gave away his Catholic background. Phyllis Naidoo and I met with Chris Hani at small closed events. I wanted to learn from both of them about their movement. Phyllis came at apartheid as a mother and activist. Hani came at it like a philosopher-soldier—not angry, but steady and sure. His funeral was one of the largest in African history.

At one point, I needed to hire a lawyer to deal with a hiring dispute within the Corps. I had no understanding of the legal system in Lesotho, and I asked Chris Hani for a reference. He referred me to Khalaki Sello, a radical anti-apartheid fighter and a brilliant attorney. Sello was wanted for murder in South Africa. His cellmate in South Africa had been Joe Quobo, who was executed by the South African secret police in Zimbabwe.

The legal system in Lesotho was modeled after England's, so we needed a barrister as well as an attorney. Khalaki called Denis Kuny to be our barrister. Kuny had defended everyone in the movement from local activists to Nelson Mandela. Mandela, facing the death penalty for sabotage and conspiracy, stood in the courtroom and bravely proclaimed that the establishment of a multi-racial democracy, "the ideal and democratic free society," was an idea "for which I am prepared to die." Denis Kuny, as a young barrister, was part of the team led by George Bizos that defended Mandela. The lawyers' eloquent arguments and evidence underscored the David and Goliath nature of the struggle. Mandela was convicted as had been preordained by the government, but he was spared the death penalty. I was honored that Denis would represent me. He and Sello thought it highly amusing to be paid by the U.S. government.

Denis often held dinners in his home for me with anti-apartheid poets, journalists, and activists. Phyllis Naidoo[13] worked with the MK in South Africa until she received so many death threats that she escaped to Lesotho. She introduced me to Father John, an Episcopal priest, who was both a political radical and a reliable and devout priest. Phyllis recruited me to help with the work. She was the heart and soul of the work. Phyllis, Father John, and I made a habit of sitting outside chatting and enjoying the cooling African nights. Denis introduced me to his favorite habit: eating lychee nuts. Denis spoke about the legal issues of the ANC and the MK and the endless uphill struggle against apartheid. David McAdams of the United Nations Development Program often joined us for card games at the Chief Justice's house and we would play all night.

I was with people who were among the best and bravest human rights activists ever. For me, this was the equivalent of Paris in the twenties for American artists. We had fun and serious talks, lots of laughter intermingled with moments of sadness. The air was heavy with unfulfilled expectations. There was just so much to hear and to be aware of every day. As the Persians say, I fell back in the honey. These folks helped me get a layman's Ph.D. in South African politics.

Father John always maintained his composure during our long, rambling conversations. One night he uncharacteristically quieted a heated discussion about the role of third-party governments in supplying weapons to rebels. He was frustrated and was finally showing it. "Jack," Father John said, "you can't really do much to help here. It's not your fight, you know that. All that you can do is to support the people the fight belongs to and, for heaven's sake, listen to those people when they tell you what to do." He was right, and I vowed to follow his advice.

I began by asking the refugees from South Africa what we could do instead of deciding for myself how we would help. One thing they wanted was help with hospital visits. Hospitals in Lesotho did not provide patients with nutritious food—this was up to family and friends to supply. The hospitals were under the constant watch of the South African Defense Forces, who had a nasty habit of picking up family and friends of hospitalized ANC members and making them disappear into a labyrinth of jail cells. My Peace Corps friends and I began delivering food to injured ANC members.

Phyllis Naidoo and Father John ran an organization that supplied blankets and clothes to political refugees from South Africa. The clothes and the blankets were mainly from East Germany, sent in packages decorated with exotic stamps. One afternoon Phyllis and Father John were sitting in Phyllis's rondoval that also functioned as their organization's headquarters and mailroom. Father John picked up a small, brown package like any other, complete with German stamps and duct tape. Phyllis was standing behind him folding blankets into a neat pile. She did not see Father John cut the cord that set off the bomb in his hands.

By the time that Peace Corps nurse Faith Merick arrived at the scene, Father John was unconscious. Phyllis had pieces of metal shrapnel lodged in her lower back. The folded blankets and the furniture were stained red with her blood. Phyllis's eardrum was permanently damaged. Father John's hands were dripping with blood, there was shrapnel in his chest, and a testicle had been blown off. Faith stabilized them both as best as she could, helping Father John, who was white and British and therefore able to get health care, into her car. Someone drove him to the nearest good hospital, 20 miles across the border in South Africa. But Phyllis could not go to South Africa for treatment without risking arrest. No decent hospital was available to her.

Faith found an IV needle, and in the dusty, blood-spattered office, she put Phyllis on a morphine drip. Then, working slowly and carefully, she pulled the shrapnel out of her back and cleaned and then bandaged her wounds. We crossed our fingers and prayed for Phyllis, Father John, and Faith. And when both patients, thank God, recovered fully, we thanked the universe for Faith's healing hands. When Phyllis years later joined us for the Amnesty concert in Zimbabwe, I prayed the audience understood the hero they had in their presence. Later, Phyllis turned down political jobs in favor of removing the death penalty in South Africa.

Chris Hani and Phyllis Naidoo led the anti-apartheid movement in Lesotho. Going to Lesotho was the fastest and easiest way out of South Africa for those under threat for being members of the African National Congress. Many refugees came, some damaged already from torture. These folks, along with Chris and Phyllis, had to practically change lodging nightly in Maseru, Lesotho's capital. Quite often the raids by South African forces hit the wrong rondovals in these illegal, cross-border incursions, and the citizens of Lesotho were killed as well as the ANC members from South Africa.

Lesotho's government was at times as tough on their dissidents as the South African raiders. Citizens of Lesotho were often found dead along the highway. One victim's cause of death was discovered by the lawyers Khalaki Sello and Denis Kuny. The police would not say how this gentleman died, but the lawyers discovered he had been shot on the top of his head, and the wound had been covered up to disguise how he had died. No one knew how many people died or who killed them. Was it a South African raider hit or a Lesotho police hit? The raids by the South Africans were not challenged by the Basotho police, and thus we assumed there was cooperation for getting in and out of Lesotho. Lesotho would blame South Africa and vice versa. Finding the truth of who killed whom was impossible for us expats.

Phyllis Naidoo was the mother image; she took care of people. She held their hands and solicited and received clothing for the incoming refugees and donations for medical care. Phyllis was South Africa's Fannie Lou Hamer, in my mind. Many years later, Naidoo was the official designated representative to the 1988 Human Rights Now! tour in Zimbabwe. In that role she thanked Bruce Springsteen and Sting for their contributions. Much like Fannie Lou Hamer, Phyllis was sort of forgotten by her movement.

Chris Hani was a military leader trained in the Soviet Union. His 30ish face was like a teenager, youthful and full of energy. Bombs were not dropped every day, but they were not infrequent either. Many of them were aimed at Chris and Phyllis. I remember one at the German embassy and another where Chris Hani was aiding the dying man who was probably the culprit of the bomb. Another bomb went off when I was having supper with Joe Lelyveld of the *New York Times* and author Allister Sparks. We went to the scene of the bomb and got as close as we could. We were questioned and detained for a short time. Getting information from the police was impossible. Phyllis Naidoo was the source to go to for any real evaluation. She was the mother of the anti-apartheid movement in Lesotho. Chris Hani's job was to make South Africa ungovernable. Naidoo and Hani did their jobs and survived the apartheid state—memorable people for sure.

I got a call from the Peace Corps asking me to go to Sudan to attend a meeting about Africa. Crossing South Africa from Lesotho on a Sunday required police consent. Boers were forbidden to travel on Sundays. I stopped in a little town in the Orange Free State and went to the police station to ask permission to buy petrol. "No…we will not permit you to buy petrol," was the answer. The policeman in charge thought President Nimeiry of the Sudan was a communist. It took me two hours to convince him that Nimeiry was not a communist. He figured since Sudan was in another part of Africa, it had to be communist.

My plane took me from Lesotho to Mauritius to Dar es Salaam to Sudan. It was a slow trip, but beautiful. I knew that John Lewis—'Saint John,' as we called him—was to be there as well. The presence of a living monument to decency and the power of an individual to effect change made me so happy that I didn't mind attending yet another conference. Due to overbooking, I got to room with this legend. John and Dick Gregory helped me get the Peace Corps job in Lesotho, so I had met John before, but I did not know him well. One of the best honors I ever received was when John said "okay" at the front desk when they asked him if he would mind sharing his room with me.

In the next three days, I witnessed his love for his wife Lil. I kept telling John to "quit calling her. She does not want to hear from you. Quit calling her." I do not remember much of the conference. But being with a legend was great fun.

As we struggled with apartheid in Lesotho, the anti-apartheid movement was gathering momentum in the United States. The movement in the U.S. started with the TransAfrica Forum, a small non-profit dedicated to fighting apartheid from within the U.S. The Forum had joined with the Congressional Black Caucus, and together, they were making a national human rights struggle into an international one. Randall Robinson was the inspired dreamer and motivator of this enormous effort.

Desmond Tutu, now the Archbishop of South Africa, speaking from the Cathedral in Cape Town, asked for the world's help in fighting apartheid. He asked companies wherever they were located to oppose apartheid by refusing to do business with the South African regime. It was a grassroots sanctions movement, and many people boycotted companies that continued to sell lumber, oil, food, and other products to the South African government. Many also protested against South Africa, and protests and arrests at South African embassies increased regularly.

The U.S. government was obsessed with the notion that the ANC had ties to the South African communist party and to other leftist organizations. The U.S. continued hosting politicians from South Africa and sending them money and business in an effort to prevent South Africa from becoming a communist domino in the war of ideologies. American politicians used the ANC's communist affiliations to avoid taking a stance against apartheid. As my friends in the ANC were constantly reminding us, the best thing Americans in Africa could do was to convince our government to stop supporting the regime.

When my first term of two and a half years was up, I begged Peace Corps director Dick Celeste to let me stay in Lesotho. He made a special exception to the usual rules to allow me to stay. I was delighted.

The State Department called during my third year in Lesotho. Sandy Berger, an old friend from D.C. and President Carter's deputy policy man at State, and later National Security Advisor to President Clinton, wanted to visit Lesotho on one of his trips to South Africa. I was asked to show him around. Sandy arrived dressed in khakis and a rumpled shirt. He proved willing to try anything. I liked Sandy enormously. He told me that he wanted to see the area up close, more of a native tour than an official visit. We drove around Maseru and to the mountains, including Thaba-Tseka, where Sandy laughed at the clean, empty, ill-advised rondovals, and ate dinner downtown.

I set up meeting after meeting for Sandy. The arrangements could be difficult, because it was absolutely forbidden for me to set up a meeting between a U.S. government employee and an African National Congress (ANC) member. When I invited Sandy to Khalaki Sello's home to meet some young ANC members who might be seen as communist activists, I told Sandy only that they were active in the anti-apartheid movement, and that they could give him the real story of what had been happening in the jails of South Africa.

Sandy brought a few young fellows with him. The fellows and many of the ANC activists were about the same age. The Americans listened intently to the young activists. One young man made an emotional appeal that gave Sandy and the fellows a look into the torture chambers of South Africa. It riveted the young people. The activists spoke in great detail against apartheid and what happened to them in torture chambers and how U.S. support for the South African regime was undermining their work. As they spoke of torture one young man began to look ill. He was about twenty-two, handsome, but sweating heavily.

His empathy was evident. He stood and said, "I can't, I can't…as an American. I can't work for the U.S. government when it's supporting this type of regime. This is wrong. I am not sure of my traveling now with this delegation." The young American had been deeply rattled by what one of the ANC members had to say. Sandy and I were speechless. The fellow was right about the U.S. government. Sello asked the young man to step outside with him. Later, Sello told us that he had told the fellow that "the ANC is multi-racial always," and "no one is permitted to insult Jack in his home. He is with us, and you should join us too. If you can do so, come on back into my home and the meeting." They entered together.

With the help of Dick Celeste and David Levine in the D.C. office, Norm and

Elsa Rush, co-directors in Botswana, Reg Petty, and I developed a training seminar for new Peace Corps recruits. We held our training sessions at an international hotel. Our staffs were African and found places to make things easier for all of us. The seminar started as soon as they arrived. We taught the history of the region, its colonization, and specifically about apartheid. We compared it to the Jim Crow laws in the U.S., which our volunteers were familiar with through their high school texts.

We invited representatives from embassies, the UN and, of course, the anti-apartheid movement, to speak at seminars. We addressed directly the issues raised when black and white volunteers were treated differently, and we warned them that this would happen. We also talked generally about what they could do to help, here in Lesotho or in Swaziland or Botswana. Senator Helms of North Carolina challenged this program, as did some Peace Corps volunteers, but Dick Celeste and David Levine stood behind us, and we were able to continue the program.[14]

After our initial correspondence from Jesse Helms, the first few letters were polite. They asked if we were hiring ANC "communists" to train our Peace Corps volunteers in violation of U.S. law. We explained we were not, but the letters increased in numbers and became more strongly worded. First they asked us to change the training program, and then they accused us of being communist collaborators.

We were visiting the U.S. embassy on a regular basis to explain to our ambassador that we had no way of knowing who worked for the ANC, nor did we care, and that we needed the freedom to hire the best of the best to train our volunteers. We were lucky that so far we had friends at the State Department, beginning with Sandy. We were also lucky that the Carter administration valued the Peace Corps and considered the organization an important part of its foreign policy. Dick Moose, the Assistant Secretary of State, was a supporter as well. We became increasingly nervous. The political climate was complicated, and we couldn't be sure what was coming next, whether the administration would support us or cut us loose.

We were sitting around on my porch one night when Reg slammed down his beer, making all our glasses jump. "I'm going to quit," he said. I started to protest. He explained, "I'm going to quit if one of you gets fired. If they want to fire one of us for what's going on and for what we're trying to do here, they're going to lose all of us." And so we made a pact. Though Norman and Elsa Rush were not there that night, Reg and I figured the pact would sit fine with them. If the government fired one of us, then we would all quit in protest.

Congress had passed a law forbidding Peace Corps employees from giving information to the Central Intelligence Agency. To avoid any potential conflicts of interest, I stopped visiting the embassy except to pick up cables and to attend the ambassador's requisite weekly meeting. These meetings were attended by the director of Voice of America and the director of USAID. I was present to report on the activities of the Peace Corps.

I kept in strict compliance with Peace Corps rules. My reports were meticulously bland, recording the number, background, education, and sex of new recruits. I would write about the number of schools that the Peace Corps was now operating in (and the number of classrooms and what color we had painted the new office) and in a real sleep-inducing report, the budget. I could, I found, go on for as long as I needed to about the budget, and eventually everyone would stop paying attention.

What I did not answer in those endless meetings were questions about the demonstrations and bombings. Or, what is Phyllis Naidoo like? Why does the prime minister like you? When I was out jogging they had noticed that Prime Minister Joseph Leabua Jonathan would stop his car and talk to me. I think Leabua liked me because he found out about my family's history in coal mining.

The first ambassador I worked with, Ambassador Norland, found my refusal to discuss politics merely irritating. He would ask about a bombing. I would ask what bombing he was referring to. He would bring up Phyllis. I would explain that I bumped into her occasionally. He would roll his eyes and get on with the agenda.

Ambassador Clingerman replaced Ambassador Norland in 1979, and he found my silence infuriating. One particularly unpleasant exchange was over a July 4th celebration at his home. I found out the embassy hired a South African caterer to cook the July 4th hot dogs. The Prime Minister always came to this event, so I told the Ambassador that I was not going. He asked why, and I told him that the Basotho could cook hot dogs. I did not want a South African hot dog. I wanted a Basotho hot dog. He explained to me that July 4th was an important day to show that I was a part of the team. I went to the barbecue.

The longer we spent in Lesotho, and the more the political situation heated up, the more difficulty Beckie and I had in our relationship. Beckie had been an incredibly good sport about the move to Lesotho. She traded her job and the culture of a city for freelance work and tall mountains.

Beckie and I took a great trip to Southwest Africa, now Namibia, to see the lions, giraffes, springbok, and elephants, but were also witness to the South African army at work against The South West African People's Organization (SWAPO). One day on the bus, we saw people from Latin America in SW Africa to celebrate Hitler's birthday. SWAPO later won, and Sam Nujoma took over as Prime Minister.

During my days at AFFHF, some of the walks had funded a hospital for the Frelimo people in Mozambique. We invited Sharfuddin Khan, who represented the Frelimo people and the project, to speak at one of our YWD conferences. Now that we were in Africa, Beckie and I were excited to visit him. Few Americans were permitted into the country at that time. After a short meeting, Mr. Khan excused himself. He was worried about being seen as "too western" by being with us. My reaction was instant. If this is the left, I want no part of it.

For two years we had learned what we could eat, whom we could talk to, where we would go, and even where to buy blankets for the fifty degree nights. Slowly, our relationship had disintegrated. She was tired of me being distant, distracted, and overly independent. I was away almost all the time, caught up in my life with the Peace Corps. When I was home, I spent the night entertaining and participating in conversations in which she was becoming less interested. She missed seeing or even being able to call her friends, her family, or her home.

This time there was no discussion over an ill-advised cappuccino, or locking myself in a bathroom, or even Sam around to talk sense and laugh at me. The dry season came, and the wild grass turned brown, providing fuel for an occasional brush fire. I went home one day to find Beckie packing. She was crying. She did not have to explain; I understood. We did not talk about our marriage. We just packed.

After Beckie left, I started traveling on the weekends to Johannesburg to spend time with Denis Kuny. I went to the swamps of Botswana, where there were snakes, alligators, giant worms, and crayfish. I drove a Land Rover down the rocky South African coast—almost drove it off a cliff once and kept going. I went to the long, wide beaches of Port St. John where I waded into the clear, blue ocean, which stayed shallow forever. I rode horses through the bright green mountains of Swaziland, camping, making fires, and sleeping under the stars. Beckie and I wrote to each other less often and the expensive phone calls became shorter.

The political climate in the U.S. changed again. Jimmy Carter had failed to free the hostages in Iran, and soaring interest rates during his presidency undermined his domestic policy. He had not convinced Americans that the global fight for human rights was worth their attention or their taxpayer dollars. His successor, Ronald Reagan, barely mentioned civil or economic rights in his campaign. Instead, phrases like "supply-side economics" and "competitiveness" in economic policy dominated the national rhetoric. Deregulation, once a dirty word in Washington, was being negotiated over coffee in Dupont Circle and Adams Morgan.

Reagan's presidency focused on cutting federal programs and easing regulations on large corporations. Reagan's policy toward South Africa was dubbed "constructive engagement." The White House expanded the financial and political ties between the South African regime and the U.S. I am certain that it was constructive for "supply-side" economics and the diamond trade to strengthen trade relations and to export more goods to South Africa. In addition, Reagan could assure the

Republicans in Congress and the American people that the godless communists—in this case, the African communists—were never going to win.

U.S. policy was less constructive for Reg, Norm, Elsa, and me. We did not buy into the portrayal of Nelson Mandela and the ANC, including Phyllis Naidoo, Khalaki Sello, and plenty of other people as communists. My days on the porch in Maseru eating lychee nuts with Dennis Kuny were going to end and probably soon.

One afternoon, I was wandering through Lesotho's Peace Corps headquarters, and I noticed a flier stuck over somebody's desk. It pictured a burning candle surrounded by barbed wire, with the notice, "AMNESTY INTERNATIONAL SEEKING NEW EXECUTIVE LEADER." I had been donating small amounts of money to Amnesty International for a while, but I did not know much about the organization.

My only prior exposure to Amnesty occurred one afternoon during my fourth year in Lesotho. I stopped by the Hilton Hotel and saw a very long line of South African and Lesotho men and women snaking out the doorway and around the block. They were waiting to talk to a man sitting at a table holding a notebook and pen. He was impressively dressed in a linen suit that defied the brown dust of Lesotho. He was very much the British gentleman.

It was a dangerous line for any South African or Basotho to be seen in. The man was David Soggot, and he was on a mission for Amnesty International. He had come from London to record individuals' stories of torture at the hands of the government. Just being in the line could easily bring about an arrest, a brutal interrogation, or death. And yet people waited patiently in the brutal heat, eager to share their stories despite the grave risk.

Soggot asked very thorough questions, took extensive notes, and then dabbed his forehead with a carefully folded handkerchief. Khalaki Sello and I invited him over to talk and see if we could help him. He surprised us that afternoon over tea. He knew a lot about South Africa and Lesotho and had a lot of information we did not know. Amnesty, I figured, must be doing something pretty incredible back home. I was surprised to discover that whenever I talked about it to friends from home, the name and work of Amnesty International was unknown to them.

I stuck a copy of my resume in the mail to the Amnesty office in New York City. Beckie called about three weeks later to tell me that Amnesty International had asked me to interview, and they offered me transportation to the U.S. At that point I had not been home in a long while, and the free flight was an additional incentive to go interview.

My interview took place in Ramsey Clark's office in Greenwich Village. The questions were difficult and made it obvious I did not know as much about Amnesty as I should have. The questions were: who are you? How would you improve the effectiveness of the organization? What is your background? What makes you qualified for this position? My answers were basic: Son of Jesus Christ, John L. Lewis, and FDR; cut programs that are not working; Irish Catholic and poor; struggling against injustice in South Africa and also the U.S. After I answered a question, the eight interviewers seemed to be waiting for me to say more. When I was silent, they would glance at one another then write something down. I left unsure of how the interview had gone, but I was relaxed, with an understanding that I would probably never see them again.

I went to see Beckie in Washington. We sat in the backyard and talked about the mortgage, the parts of the house that were falling apart (probably because we had traded beer and not dollars for home repair), and the bills that we needed to pay. We discussed how Beckie could tell me if I got the Amnesty job. She couldn't just forward the letter because there was little chance that letter would reach Lesotho anytime in the next decade. We knew that the South African intelligence service listened in on our calls, and we did not want to give them or the Reagan administration advance warning that I might be leaving the Peace Corps. My starting salary at Amnesty was $34,000—a $20,000 decrease over my salary at Peace Corps.

Beckie suggested that if she called and told me that we were at war that would mean that I had gotten the job. If she called and said that we were not at war, it meant that I had not gotten the job. A few days later I packed my bags and returned to South Africa and Lesotho. I tried not to think about the last time that I landed in South Africa, when Beckie and I had gone together.

I got back to work with the Peace Corps volunteers, who continued teaching and farming and building bridges. They followed the rules and treated their students with respect and showed up as required at our meetings. We had contributed grants and farming techniques and reliable teachers who taught English and math and were not abusive to students. I was proud of their achievements and happy that, as expats and volunteers in Lesotho, we had made things a little better for the Basotho.

Two of the volunteers had fallen in love and planned to get married in Lesotho where they met. My house in Maseru West had a great backyard, maybe the best in town, so I offered to host a backyard wedding during the dry season.

The wedding was untraditional, messy, and lovely. Tons of people packed into the living room and onto the deck and spilled out into the backyard. Everyone made a speech about our time in Lesotho. The speeches grew longer and longer as the night went on, as more of the strong beer and South African wine disappeared. There was lots of food, and everyone was barefoot.

The party was still going on when I decided to go to bed. I grabbed a meal and a brownie from a tray and headed to my room. I was lying on the bed with no idea how I had gotten there. Everything was liquid, heavy, and slow. The ceiling was spinning around the fan. The fan was perfectly still. The patterns on the peeling paint were moving slowly around me, fascinating in their complexity, in their connection to one another, and to the rotating ceiling. It occurred to me, after about a half hour, or five minutes, or possibly two years, that maybe the brownies were pot brownies. Eventually I realized that I was high, out of my mind, and I was totally losing it. I laughed and could not stop laughing. I was completely stoned.

I was slipping in and out of sleep, with dreams that were vividly colored and included lots of fabulous people, when the phone rang. It was Beckie, calling from Washington. "Jack," she said. "Jack, war!" Furious, I demanded to know who we had gone to war with, why I had not heard about it, what the hell was the Reagan administration thinking involving us in yet another war, and what were we supposed to do in Lesotho?

Then I realized that obviously it was not Beckie on the phone. The phone had been tapped. The South African government was pretending to be Beckie in an attempt to get to me. I had to hang up immediately or the house might be bombed. I threw the phone as if it were a poisonous snake and then I climbed safely back into bed and passed out.

The next day, after we had cleaned up from the wedding and thrown away all of the baked goods, I called Beckie to ask about a mortgage payment. Beckie wanted to know why in the hell I hung up on her on Saturday. She also wanted to know why I was turning down the position of Executive Director of Amnesty International. Had I lost my mind in Lesotho? Finally, I realized that it was Beckie on the phone using our code for the job. I explained what happened, and then both of us were laughing hysterically on the crackly long distance call, maybe the only laugh we had shared in the past two years.

As soon as Beckie and I hung up, I called Amnesty headquarters and formally accepted the job. I apologized, profusely, for not responding immediately, but did not explain this particular lapse in judgment.

Every Peace Corps director who leaves a posting is given a farewell party hosted by the U.S. ambassador. Among the volunteers and people in town that I invited were Khalaki Sello and Phyllis Naidoo. They found the idea of attending a fancy dinner at the U.S. embassy faintly ironic, but they agreed to come. After a lovely dinner including lots of fancy imported wine, the time came for toasts. Khalaki stood and clinked his glass for attention.

He spoke briefly about our friendship, our nights on the deck, meals at Fat

Alice's restaurant, and the many volunteers he had met through me. Then he added, "I am a fan of Jack's. The thing that I'm not a fan of is the U.S. government's policy regarding apartheid—the greatest struggle of our time." He spoke eloquently of the horrors of the apartheid regime.

He went on to detail the abuses of the regime, his voice clear, spreading through the big room, commanding the attention of every single person. When he finally sat down, raising a fist in the air, the ambassador's sigh of relief was audible.

That night represented the jarring coming together of two sides of a contradiction that I balanced my entire Peace Corps career. On the one side, my job was to promote understanding between peoples and provide skilled labor to countries that wanted it. On the other, I was the representative of a government that promoted policies that resulted in quite the opposite. Though my Peace Corps experience was invaluable, I knew the U.S. was the place I needed to be if I wanted to make large-scale change. I knew a single vote in Congress would go much further towards changing the wretched conditions that my friends in South Africa were forced to live in. It was frustrating to feel so far from where actual decision-making was taking place. I had enjoyed my Peace Corps experience as well as my time with the volunteers. However, in my next role, I wanted to raise the consciousness of the American public to the perils of U.S. support for apartheid and other similarly restrictive systems at home and abroad.

No matter what the politics, Khalaki spoke eloquently of the horrors of the apartheid regime. When I left Africa, Khalaki Sello's strong voice went with me.

A few years later, I discovered that 2400 shock batons had been sold to the Republic of South Africa by the Reagan administration. I visited the manufacturer in Florida, and they told me they were cattle prods, not weapons of torture. In LA I visited the chief of police, Darryl Gates and suggested to him that he buy the prods for his work in LA. "I would not use such a thing on human beings," he said. This sale was hidden from Congress for a while. To me, it meant a slap in the face of all the anti-apartheid folks I had met.

CHAPTER 10

Too Small to Win: 1981–1994

GENERALLY, I AM UNCOMFORTABLE IN SUITS, AND IT DID not help that the sweat, which had collected on my collar while walking down the humid Washington, D.C. streets, had become sticky in the stale air that circulated through the State Department building. I kept thinking about what I was going to say when we got into our meeting. Distracted, I handed the guards my library card.

"Sir, this building requires a photo ID."

"Right, right," I assured him as I searched my wallet for my driver's license.

While I was fiddling, Patricia placed her ID on the desk and strode through in one graceful motion.

"That's why you run the Washington office, and I'm up in New York," I joked.

I could tell she was fighting the urge to roll her eyes, but it did not matter. We had to have our game faces on because we were about to confront a very unsympathetic audience.

Short, with his hair neatly parted to one side, Assistant Secretary of State Elliott Abrams met us at his door. We were there to talk to him about a soon-to-be-released report on the human rights record of the Sandinista government in Nicaragua and the U.S. backed Contra rebels with whom they were at war. It was a sweeping document that we could have started with the 1823 adoption of the Monroe Doctrine, the official beginning of U.S. interference in the region, but Amnesty's style is to focus on more recent history.

Nicaragua in those days was violently transitioning after a revolution. Longtime U.S. ally General Somoza, whose family had ruled Nicaragua for over forty years, had been overthrown in a popular coup by the Sandinistas. The Sandinistas pledged liberal benefits, multi-party elections, and an end to exploitative business contracts with the U.S. These contracts were unpopular in Nicaragua because they caused over-mining of natural resources and depressed grain prices by dumping subsidized grain on Nicaraguan markets.

Washington was divided between those who believed that the Sandinistas represented a Marxist takeover of Nicaragua that would adversely affect the balance of power, and those who saw the Sandinistas as legitimate representatives of the Nicaraguan people. President Carter sided with the latter group and he did not intrude in Nicaragua. Then about three years after seizing power, the Sandinista government announced they would be nationalizing various U.S.-owned mines.

This was too much for U.S. business interests. In 1980 President Carter authorized the CIA to give advice to the Contras, and by the time Reagan took office in 1981, Washington had turned against the Sandinistas. They were viewed as an existential threat to the United States, its global standing, and its local and foreign markets. Reagan sent U.S. military advisors to Nicaragua to train rebel groups to overthrow the Sandinistas. With the help of the experienced U.S. military, a mixed group of rebels morphed into a well-organized group that became known as the Contras. The U.S. then began sending guns, surface-to-air missiles, and ammunition to the Contras. Human rights did not appear to be a major objective in this effort. By all accounts, the Contras did harm to anyone in their path.

The Contras waged a devastating war against the Sandinistas. The American public, largely uninformed about politics and developments in South America, paid little attention. The *New York Times* and a few other publications reported that the Contras were employing tactics that included kidnapping, rape, and bombing schools to weaken popular support for the Sandinistas.

As awareness of the war and its atrocities grew, pressure on the administration to stop supporting the Contras grew with it. In 1982, and then again in 1984, a bipartisan majority in Congress passed the Boland Amendments (I and II), which barred the U.S. from providing any more weapons, money, or military training to the Contras. The administration did not let anything as insignificant as the law interfere with its policies. Reagan treated the struggle against the Sandinistas as essential. No longer able to use taxpayer dollars directly for the Contras, a new plan was devised.

At that time there was an arms embargo against Iran resulting from its capture of American hostages. The arms embargo, originally designed to force Iran to free the American hostages, left Iran without the weapons it wanted and with no spare parts. The Reagan administration entered into a secret deal to sell weapons to Iran in exchange for cash. They were even able to overcharge for the weapons because Iran was restricted by the U.S. arms embargo. The influx of money from that sale gave the administration money that Congress, and especially Representative Boland, did not control.

Cash from the sale of weapons slid into Nicaragua and into the hands of the Contras. The newly enriched Contras were able to continue running training camps and, once again, to buy weapons for use on Nicaraguan citizens. The plan was partly the brainchild of Elliott Abrams, and when we met with him at the State Department, the whole arms for cash deal and America's covert support of the Contras were still secret.

Our meeting started out as banal as any other run-of-the-mill business meeting. We were all very cordial, breaking the ice with some pleasantries about the weather before jumping into discussion about the report. We went through it in detail. There was one aspect of the report that I wanted to make sure he would understand; it had to do with the report's focus. The first 32 pages dealt with the human rights abuses of the Sandinista government, but only four pages addressed the abuses of the Contras. The report was explicit as to why this was the case.

Amnesty International's policy was to condemn the killing or torture of captives by both government forces and those of opposition groups. However, Amnesty took action only with respect to governments, since they are the entities bound by the international legal standards that Amnesty International upholds.[15]

I pushed this point to Mr. Abrams. Then I reiterated to him that the report's attention on the Sandinistas did not mean they were engaged in more human rights abuses than the Contras. It simply reflected Amnesty's focus on the human rights abuses of governments. I remember him nodding and telling me that he understood Amnesty's position.

I pushed more, asserting that all available evidence seemed to be that the Contras were involved in far more terrorist acts than the government and a harsh U.S. statement condemning the Contra violence could do a lot of good because of the administration's ties. At this point I was expecting him to explode, but the anger never came. He simply restated to us the administration's position on the matter, that while the administration was concerned about the Contras, it was more concerned about the spread of Cuba style communism.

I left with mixed feelings: somewhat satisfied that Abrams had listened to me, and slightly uneasy, feeling that little would change. I was not at all prepared for what happened next.

Elliott Abrams was discussing U.S. Latin America policy with some members of the press who had gathered in the hall by his office. Nicaragua's revolution was on everyone's minds. I watched him chat, hoping that our meeting had some kind of impact on what he would say. Any mention of the human rights abuses of the Contras would have been a victory. As allies of the United States, the Contras would surely take Washington's criticism to heart.

About halfway through the conference, Abrams turned to a reporter who pressed him about his vocal support for the Contras. He told the reporter that Amnesty International had released a report about the ongoing war in Nicaragua. I was eager to hear what he had to say next.

The report, he noted, had only four pages detailing the abuses of the Contras, while it contained over 30 pages on the Sandinistas. Nobody should question the severity of the communist threat or the valor of the anti-regime fighters.

I was completely shocked. Abrams had ignored what I said entirely and was using Amnesty's work to support his claims that the U.S. should continue to bolster the Contras. The idea that politicians spin stories to their own advantage was nothing new to me, but it was unnerving to experience it in such a direct way. Once an official with Abrams's stature makes such a comment, it can become very hard to counter in the media. In newsrooms, where fast turnaround is key, critiques of U.S. foreign policy are often viewed as too difficult to substantiate and not worth the time and money. Because of the need to get the news out quickly, U.S. government sources like the Pentagon and State Department are granted a certain benefit of the doubt that most organizations outside of the government are not.

I began to feel that lobbying the administration on behalf of human rights was a waste of time. State Department officials knew what we knew—they were just looking for ways to use our work to forward their own arguments. The pressure for change had to come from an angry and informed citizenry. This would not be easy—Amnesty would have to find a way to be in the media as much as the government. That way, the human rights side of the story would get out just as strongly.

How was I going to get Amnesty to be listened to with the same frequency as the institutions that we were trying to critique? There was little to improve in terms of standards of research. Our research department was already held up as the gold standard for human rights abuse reporting by many of the world's top academics and policy members. What we lacked was people power. We had to turn our voices into thunder and turn our candles into bonfires so the government could not ignore us.

I had been at Amnesty for a while when the Abrams incident occurred. Initially my goal as Executive Director was to raise the profile of the organization and make it a familiar presence within the United States and around the world. After our encounter with Abrams, I knew we had to change the power balance in the media. The way to combat this type of information manipulation was to make Amnesty so well known that we did not need to use politicians to get information into the public forum.

Amnesty was created in 1961 as the brainchild of English barrister Peter Benenson, who had written an opinion piece in the *Times* of London about the illegitimate arrest of two Portuguese students in fascist Portugal. Benenson had appealed, in his writing, to the people of the world, begging them not to 'let this injustice pass unnoticed."

He broke new ground in establishing the importance of people caring for people. This crucial work could not be left in the hands of governments. A rare man, a rare thought, and a rare action.

It was one of those rare times when journalism inspired the community and became a catalyst for immediate and tangible change. The essay sparked a rally in Tottenham Square in London that attracted activists and students. As seen by recent history, it seems that the first step in creating any type of social revolution is to find a proper town square. Those who gathered chanted a phrase that represented both idealism and realism. "It is better to light a candle than to curse the dark." It may not have been poetic or even original, but it sure as hell was powerful.

Amnesty had its origins in this initial small protest and began operations with a tiny, all-volunteer staff. Benenson began his fact-finding missions to uncover human rights abuses in Haiti and then expanded his research to much of the world. Under his direction, Amnesty International grew in size and mission.

Twenty years later, Benenson's vision had been bureaucratized. Amnesty USA was stagnant and demoralized. The original founders had moved on to other jobs, and volunteers were few. Reports of human rights violations took six to nine months to produce. The volunteer board and the professional staff did not get along to the detriment of the entire organization. That conflict continued for decades.

At that time, the U.S. chapter of Amnesty had about 35,000 dues-paying members. The average member was over forty and the annual budget was about $3 million. There were ten staff members at the New York office, five in D.C., four in San Francisco, and one each in Chicago, New Orleans, and Los Angeles. The London office was responsible for research; our U.S. offices were supposed to focus entirely on increasing our influence in Washington, spreading the news of human rights abuses, and energizing and building the movement. Nobody knew, in or out of the organization, what Amnesty was trying to accomplish. Amnesty was making itself irrelevant in a time of need. Ronald Reagan, trickle-down economics, and military buildup were gaining momentum, and opposition was badly needed to counter its effects. Deaths in Central American dictatorships and military juntas had to be addressed, and apartheid needed to go.

It was time for Amnesty to undergo an overhaul. I dismissed the law firm, CPA, and fundraising firms that had been on retainer. I hired Craver, Mathews,

Smith, and a dynamic law firm, Hogan & Harston, where my friend Sandy Berger worked. These were two of the best decisions I made at Amnesty.

In prior years Amnesty branches "adopted" a political prisoner. Members of an "adoption group" wrote letters of protest to the government holding that prisoner. The groups met once a month and they sent a dozen letters to offending governments. This was a start, but letters about each prisoner were limited to the size of the branches that had adopted him.

We implemented a new campaign to increase the volume of mail. Once a month each Amnesty donor received three pre-addressed letters in their mailbox. The letters were addressed to leaders of different countries from all over, including India, Thailand, Kosovo, and Iran. Each letter contained a description of a political prisoner with their name, personal information such as whom they were married to, the name of their children, maybe, and a detailed explanation of the facts behind their imprisonment. The letter had space for the Amnesty donors, who might be from a large number of different backgrounds and locations, to write letters of protest to the governments that imprisoned these individuals demanding their immediate release and the restoration of their civil liberties. The result was a huge increase in the volume of mail about each prisoner. We hoped these letters would have some effect on the governments receiving them and keep Amnesty donors feeling involved in the human rights process.

A trade unionist in Guatemala had been in solitary confinement for years. After the first 200 letters demanding his release arrived from around the world, the guards had given him back his shirt and pants. When the next 200 arrived, the prison director came to visit him. Then when the next 400 arrived, the prison director's superior came to visit his tiny cell. When the letters reached 3,000 and could no longer be contained by the mail bins at the prison, the President of Guatemala invited him to his office. How, the president asked him, how on earth could a trade union leader from a small town have so many friends all over the world?

I was in Washington for yet another Amnesty board meeting. I called Beckie, and we met for a coffee at a place near our house. We sat and attempted to have the conversation we had avoided for the least three years. We left the coffee shop and stopped at a nearby bookstore. As we browsed through the books, Beckie stopped and held up a small, tattered book.

How to Get Divorced, the front cover read. Her sad gesture let me know that we had both accepted that our marriage was over. The book turned out to offer extremely good advice about ending a marriage and moving on with life. My salary at Amnesty was only $34,000, so we had very little to split up. Beckie kept the house, and I bought an apartment in New York. We were both happy with this arrangement. I went to see a therapist, Dr. Philip Luloff, for three years, and I was grateful I did. It may have been him who let me know I made a better priest than husband.

I was in Boston to speak on a panel at Harvard University on "the spread of democracy around the world." I would be appearing with, among others, a representative from a conservative organization named Freedom House that released an annual index ranking countries based on how "free" their governments were. The criteria for a country to be ranked as "free" were very narrow. White, Christian, European countries were continually ranked as the most "free," while no African nation had ever been ranked higher than a five, the lowest score. These criteria caused a lot of friction among human rights organizations.

I sought out Noam Chomsky for support, and he kindly offered to have dinner with me. His ability to marshal facts and stories to bolster his cause was impressive. I resolved to try to acquire a similar ability. His invaluable advice to me for both the conference and for my tenure at Amnesty boiled down to: pay attention to the research, stick to the facts, and you'll be fine.

My initial plan for my talk at the conference had been to offer a few suggestions as to how the criteria could be made more inclusive, to go easy on what I thought was a nonsensical way to view the world. But then their representative began the event by launching into a long monologue about the advantages of their ranking system, the ways it could change the world, and on and on. I decided I was not going to allow this philosophy to go unchallenged.

When it was my turn to talk, I asked the Freedom House guy what, exactly, he meant by freedom. "Does that term carry with it any cultural baggage? Why is it that only white middle class countries seemed to do well as judged by his organization's criteria?" The audience began paying attention. Comments, arguments, and time flew by. The Freedom House representative became noticeably angry. At the end, I asked him how dividing the world along racial and cultural lines was going to make it freer. The audience roared its approval, giving me a standing ovation.

Later that year, Ginetta Sagan, one of the founders of Amnesty International USA, arranged a supper for me with Steve Jobs in the fall of 1982. After the appropriate niceties, Steve let me know he did not like charities much. He said charity work was too inefficient and slow. The many board members guarantee confusion and stagnation. I did my best to debate this very smart man who did not like my line of work. Since I am not a money chaser, I was not a brick and mortar type in the priesthood either. I did not care whether he gave to Amnesty. I was after memberships of young people at $25 apiece. Depending upon the rich is not my game, either. I knew clearly what my intention was: I would use membership funds to try to free political prisoners. But, money alone cannot solve human rights abuses. It takes people. Human rights without a constituency is a river without water.

A few years later I was at a reception that Harry Kraut, Leonard Bernstein's manager, set up in the hall where Leonard had conducted the San Francisco orchestra. Steve came over and nicely said to me that he had not changed his thoughts about charity but was happy to see me and to come to the event. Years later, Steve and his public relations firm hired U2 as the poster child to sell a new iPod. Rob Schwartz of TBWA created the campaign that worked for Apple.

I never wrote Steve, but I was waiting to run into him so I could say, "You paid a lot to use U2 at the turn of the century. Amnesty International, our inefficient, stagnated non-profit, had U2 in 1986 free of cost for two weeks." I kept myself entertained with that thought.

On the other hand, Steve made a good point about efficiency. We had 11 chairs during my dozen years at Amnesty and went through more than 140 board members in that period. I once calculated that I spent a full 365 days of my 12 years as director in board meetings.

Human rights reports focus on moments of torture or statistics about deprivation. It was my conviction that such slices of truth are not enough. To create a movement, you need something that captures people's aspirations. Music, especially live music, has the unique ability to inspire people, moving them physically, intellectually, and emotionally all at the same time.

When I had first arrived in South Africa with the Peace Corps, people were singing protest songs in the street. Long after I'd forgotten other details, the music stayed with me. The music brought the crowds together, and the music carried their message with more strength than words. I was intrigued by the power music could have and wondered how we could use it to advance human rights.

I am an Elvis fan. His songs and charity work awed me. At 14, he woke me up with music. What struck me most was his energy. My epiphany was, "Music generates energy. If we attach music to our message, it will

With Steve Jobs at Leonard Bernstein event for Amnesty International in San Francisco, 1983. Photographer unknown.

help create the interest and excitement that is necessary to move people out of inertia and into activism."

That led me to realize that artists—musicians, painters, writers—make the best activists. In every culture, they, not the politicians, are the highly visible, prophetic leaders telling the culture what's coming, capturing and conveying the emotional state of society and questioning what is right and what is wrong. Goya's *Third of May 1808* or Picasso's *Guernica* are examples of artistic works that allow us to see with new eyes.

I was not the first to exploit the symbiotic relationship between music and message. The iconic Odetta Holmes—singer, songwriter, and human rights activist—was known as "The Voice of the Civil Rights Movement." Harry Belafonte, Bob Marley, John Lennon, Joe Strummer, Bob Dylan, Jackson Browne, Joan Baez, and many others had harnessed music to serve the Civil Rights Movement. The songs that arose spontaneously from the crowd filling the National Mall were as powerful as any of the speeches given. Activism followed the artist.

Desmond Tutu said upon accepting his Nobel Peace Prize, "Most of God's best collaborators and partners have been young people." I committed to bringing in young people, because in every struggle in the world, whether it's South Africa, Latin America, or Burma, it's the kids, the babies, who are in jail. The soldiers are babies. The demonstrators are young, as in the 1960 Sharpsville Massacre in South Africa. The young girls being raped are babies. They're 10, 12, 15 years old. They're seldom over twenty. So I wanted to bond those who were struggling for justice with those who struggle for justice in the United States, because they're the same age. isn't for older people to save the young. It's for the young to save the young. The youth deserve to be supported by us. This was my belief and my intention.

But I needed somehow to make it happen. I had to. Sello, Kuny, Hani, and Gandhi were in my ear.

The first opportunity to use music as a voice for human rights came with a concert in May 1983, featuring the Modern Jazz Quartet. Kita Taylor and John Morris coordinated the event. We took a risk, not knowing if there would be interest, if we could raise funds, or if musicians would even participate. The concert cleared $10,000 for Amnesty. This early success in the face of significant risk bolstered my confidence that music could work for us.

Twice before, in the spring of 1982 and then again in 1983, Amnesty had sponsored the concerts entitled "The Secret Policeman's Ball" in London. Sting had performed as a young musician. The music had been lovely, and the concerts received some airtime. Amnesty even made some money when Harvey Weinstein acquired rights to sell the movie of The Secret Policeman's Ball for HBO.

Leonard Bernstein performed in San Francisco for a Bernstein fund in honor of his deceased wife. Cellist Yo-Yo Ma performed for Amnesty. Emmanuel Axe performed in Chicago. The music was lovely, but nobody under the age of fifty paid much attention. I wanted to find the music that would draw young people to the fight.

I went to see Barry Fey in Denver to get some ideas. One of our ideas was to create an anti-torture train to go across the U.S. flying the flags of nations that sanction torture. If a country stopped allowing torture, we would take their flag off the train. I would still like to do the train idea.

We did need something that would attract notoriety. We needed the type of music young people flocked to. I flew to San Francisco in late 1981, where I managed to set up a meeting with Bill Graham, a renowned promoter of the best talent in the rock business. He was a legend; he had represented major rock groups including the Rolling Stones and the Grateful Dead. He was also a German Holocaust survivor, an orphan of the gas chambers of Auschwitz, and he owed his life to the networks of people who risked their lives to spirit Jewish children out of Germany. His total and complete commitment to the human rights struggle may have had something to do with his background; I would not presume to know.

In the 1960s Graham managed a radical mime group. The group performed street theater and protested the War in Vietnam by wearing fatigues and acting out scenes of attacking Vietnamese villagers. Their stage was the sidewalks in the middle of the towering office buildings in San Francisco. They would put somebody in shackles, and they would pretend to beat him while men and women with briefcases hurried by on their way to work.

Eventually some musicians joined the mime group. At first, they were just people with guitars and the desire to do something to stop the war. When the Grateful Dead joined, the performances moved from the dirty square in the middle of the business district to Golden Gate Park. Chet Helms's ideas for concerts caught on and Bill made them work. Eventually Bill started a new business organizing shows for people like Allen Ginsberg and Jefferson Airplane through contacts he had made in the square, back when they were putting people in shackles and none of the people walking by in business suits were paying any attention.

Bill's office was large and sunlit and no longer in Golden Gate Park by the time I met him in December 1981. Bill knew about the original Amnesty protest but had not followed Amnesty after that. I told him about my plan to extend Amnesty's reach with thousands of people and the kind of music you can dance to, a sort of explosion of the Golden Gate Park idea for human rights. He was twirling his pen, nodding along, but he did not express any interest.

I thought about Charlie Maloney. "Come on, Bill. I know you care about this stuff. At least, you used to care. When you and the guys were playing around in Golden Gate all summer, all year long? And now you're here in this office in this big building and you don't care, all of a sudden? I mean, do you know what we are doing here? We're fighting for human rights. This isn't some teenybopper concert where we can just sign up some talent and call it a day. We need you, Bill."

Graham kindly explained that he did not take orders from arrogant assholes, even if they were supposedly the heads of human rights organizations. "Then prove me wrong, Bill." That really pissed him off. The staff gathered outside the thick mahogany door listening to what was quickly becoming a shouting match. Bill was pounding the desk.

"Fine. Fine. But Jack, I'm not Superman. These things take work. You have to get the talent. If you can do that, I'll run the damn show…Yes, okay, yes, Jack; that is a contract. It's a solid contract. Now get out of my office."

Radio City Music Hall was gorgeous, with high ceilings and red carpet and recently re-upholstered leather chairs arranged so that the stage was visible to the entire audience—no need for pushing, shoving, or crowd surfing. But the first time that U2, the Irish band led by Bono, played at Radio City, people climbed up on top of those chairs. They stood on those chairs, and fought to see the stage, and we thought that a mosh pit might break out.

I found myself at that December 3, 1984, concert as a result of a check for 10,000 dollars—which was even more generous in those days than it is today—that Amnesty had received from U2. The check was accompanied by two tickets to the show at Radio City Music Hall which I promptly passed off to my secretary, Claude Isakov, because I had no idea who Bono or U2 were. Claude's friend couldn't make it at the last minute, and she burst into my office and told me she needed me to go with her because she was simply not willing to miss U2 live. So I went.

Two minutes into the song "Bloody Sunday," I was shouting along with the rest of the crowd. The lyrics were about truth and human rights, justice, freedom, and power to people who have been denied access to power. There was a picture of an American Indian and Dr. King on the back wall of the concert wall. That sealed it for me. I had found our band.

I believed, and still do, that there are two causes that the United States must understand and come to grips with: the taking of land from Native Americans and the issue of slavery and racism in the United States. Bob Peterson, our Madison Walk coordinator, then sixteen, spoke at the World Food Summit in 1971. He said, "We stole the black man to work the land we stole from the red man." Bob ultimately went on to become a union leader in Wisconsin.

The next year, when I headed to the annual worldwide Amnesty Conference in Finland, I flew through Dublin. I arrived in Dublin Aug. 23, 1985, with the plan to recruit U2 and get the blessing of Sean MacBride, the worldwide chair of Amnesty for its first thirteen years. We landed in Ireland just as the morning fog was lifting. Every time I land in Ireland, I'm home.

Sean MacBride was responsible for growing Amnesty beyond its small London office to the U.S. and other countries. At twelve, he had been tutored by Irish Nobel Prize winners in literature—Sean O'Casey, George Bernard Shaw, and W.B. Yeats, as well as Ezra Pound. The British executed his father during the Irish War of Independence when Sean was thirteen. After that, he joined the Irish Republican Army (IRA), and eventually became head of the IRA. After he left the IRA, he became a successful barrister who freed numerous Irish political prisoners from British prisons. As foreign minister of Ireland, Sean brought Yeats's body back from Europe to be buried in his home turf. Sean was a recipient of both the Nobel Peace Prize and the Lenin Peace Prize.

I had no idea how to find Sean MacBride, so I decided to just check the phonebook. His number was listed next to all of the other MacBrides in Dublin. He picked up on the third ring, and invited me over.

Sean was 81 years old in 1985, but he answered the door of his big old brick house himself. He was well informed on world politics and on Amnesty. We had coffee in a large room with lots and lots of paintings on the wall. He was pleased that I was Irish, and I asked him about the IRA and Irish history. We spoke of his mother, Maud Gonne—a giant of Irish Theater, a great human rights worker, and the fantasy woman of Yeat's poetry. His father was executed in the Irish Rebellion of 1918.

Sean and I discussed the need for a youth movement in the U.S. "Art," he said, "any type of art, that gets these people up, music and painting, these are the ways that we convince people of the importance of doing something other than sitting on their front steps and smoking cigarettes." U2 was a great way to do this. Then, being Sean, he got me to agree to help the Irish section of Amnesty if the concerts raised enough money. A year later, he was pleased when the Irish section received a check for three hundred thousand dollars.

Next, I took a cab to a small, hip office at Windmill Lane. At the top of a narrow flight of stairs I knocked on a large wooden door on which someone had scratched his initials. U2's manager, Paul McGuinness, let me in. Bono came over and shook my hand. At twenty-five, Bono seemed quiet, much quieter than he later became.

I did not have a lot of time because of the connecting flight. I asked Bono, "Are you really Irish?" This rattled him for a minute. I said quickly, "Amnesty is struggling. We're failing to get people who matter involved enough to pay attention to the things that matter. We need help. I need your help to build a movement. We need the young with us."

Bono looked at Paul. Paul looked back. Bono said, "Sure."

I asked Paul to write it up right then, because Bill Graham said it had to be in writing. We said goodbye, and then I tried to hug Paul, but he did not know how to hug. We all laughed, and then we all hugged. I was back in the cab with the signed agreement within eight minutes.

When I got to the Dublin airport, I went directly to the payphone and, emptying my pockets, called San Francisco. Bill answered, already irritated. I had woken him up or interrupted his breakfast or his midmorning meeting or something. When I told him about the contract with U2, he started laughing, and then I was laughing too. The people around me at the Dublin airport that night were staring.

"You crazy bastard. You did it."

CHAPTER 11

The Conspiracy of Hope: 1985–1986

THE CONSPIRACY OF HOPE TOUR TOOK PLACE DURING the summer of 1986 in celebration of the 25th anniversary of the founding of the modern human rights effort by Peter Benenson.

At Amnesty's meeting in Finland, I told anyone who would listen that Amnesty was evolving—that music would be our magical messenger. Music crosses borders. Music will get human rights a stage and explain Amnesty's work and goals. We are on a search for young people for the human rights movement.

Amnesty's Chair, Professor Charles Henry of Berkeley, supported the effort. We wanted a platform of some length so we could explain the mandate of Amnesty as well as recruit a new generation of activists. Amnesty would no longer be a well-kept secret in the U.S. We were twenty-five years old, and it was time to grow up.

With the smarts and friendships of Bill Graham, Paul McGuinness (manager of U2), Miles Copeland, Herb Alpert, Jerry Moss, Gil Friesen, Bryan Adams and Bruce Allen (his manager), Gary Gersch, John Sykes, Tom Freston, and MTV's president Bob Pittman, we began to make it happen. Bono recruited Peter Gabriel and Lou Reed. Gil Friesen and I flew to Vancouver to see Bryan Adams. He agreed over supper. John Sykes and Mike Ovitz of CAA allowed me to hold meetings in their offices when needed.

Norm Pattiz of Westwood One was on board to do the radio work of the shows. My staff at Amnesty USA was smart. My deputy, Curt Goering, held it together while I roamed around doing work out of the office. Mary Daly was our talented press secretary, and James Radner managed administrative operations with ease.

Mary and I met Sting for lunch at his apartment in SoHo. He agreed to join the tour and even agreed to reunite the Police for a concert if we kept it a secret. Bill Graham recruited and added Joan Baez, the Neville Brothers, and Jackson Browne to join us on the six-city tour.

The tour adopted six prisoners. Six was bold, but it did not seem an overreach: six was hopeful, but six was possible. Next we had to select the prisoners to highlight. This was the most difficult part, because it was hard to pick only six. We sat around, late into the night, shuffling through reports of dirty prison cells, no food, no clean water, diseases, and charges for things like distributing poetry. The six prisoners were the reason Bill Graham picked the name "Conspiracy of Hope" for the tour. We did our best to select a representative group of political prisoners. Certainly the ones we chose provided compelling cases:

- Hugo de Leon Palacios, who was in a tiny cell in Guatemala, jailed because he had worked at a school known for grassroots organizing for anti-government politicians.

- Thozamile Gqwetha who sat in a crowded cell in South Africa for membership in the South African Allied Workers Union.

- Lee Kwang-ung, who was placed in solitary confinement in South Korea for distributing poetry attributed to a North Korean artist.

- Riad al-Turk, who lived in a very dirty cell in Syria, because he had joined the Syrian communist party, which was reviled by the Assad regime.

- Tatyana Semyonova Osipova, who was jailed in the Soviet Union, because she had been writing down stories of police brutalization and beatings and rapes by soldiers. Tatyana was later freed and attended the Human Rights Now! tour in 1988.

- Nguyen Chi Thein, who was in prison in Vietnam accused of distributing literature deemed "political" in nature.

We posted each of their pictures behind us at all the press conferences. They were to be highlighted and referred to as often as possible. These six would help explain political imprisonment and also how people could exploit their own freedom to help someone else. The prisoners gave the tour meaning, strength, and clarity of purpose. At all the venues, Amnesty had volunteers to hand out cards and letters to send to the governments holding these Prisoners of Conscience. Tens of thousands of such missives were eventually sent by these new members.

My "office" in LA was the office of A&M Records, home to the Police and Bryan Adams. Jerry Moss and Herb Alpert generously opened their offices for the venture. Bob Pittman, John Sykes, Tom Freston, and Jock McLean of MTV agreed to give us the whole eleven hours for their first big MTV live TV show and all the advertising revenues from the show. Meetings with Viacom produced a syndication show from 7:00 p.m. to 11:00 p.m., giving us a national audience.

A board member from Los Angeles, Sandy Elster, met with me to see how he could help. He told me he knew the Pritzker family that owned the Hyatt Hotels. Their grandfather had died in the Holocaust, and Sandy thought that he could get the Hyatt to give us free rooms for the six-city tour. They generously agreed and saved us a lot of money. Bill Graham loved this touch.

In addition to publicizing the plight of the six prisoners, we wanted the tour to raise the profile of Amnesty. First, we needed to figure out where we stood in the estimation of the public. Who knew about Amnesty, and exactly how irrelevant were we to the ordinary person on the street?

Bill Fertik, an excellent filmmaker, decided to conduct an experiment. We stood next to a coffee shop beside a crowded subway stop in New York City. It was a hot, brutal summer in New York, but Bill was very determined that we "set a baseline," as he called it. We stopped people at random as they left the coffee shop. We asked them what Amnesty International was, or what it did, and then recorded their answers.

Perhaps Amnesty was an organization that advocated for lower taxes, one man suggested. No, no, argued the woman we stopped next. Surely, Amnesty was an organization sponsored by Vietnam-war draft dodgers. We ought to be arrested, or at the very least go back to Canada. The fourth was disappointed that our most recent record had not yet been released, and frustrated that the longhaired drummer had left the band—how had we let that happen?

After fifty interviews, we gave up. We went to have a coffee, and Bill came up with some solutions. He created the message: "Use your freedom for someone else's lack of freedom." He devised a series of brilliant public service announcements that ran on television for years.

We shot for two days. All the actors volunteered their talent. Robin Williams told his hilarious jokes in perfect time for both 30 and 60 second spots. John Huston came in a wheelchair guided by his daughter, Anjelica. John's lungs were giving out, and he had a breathing tube. I was so pleased that he came to do a spot for Amnesty and human rights. It took a while to get the shoot right. Others who were waiting

Bill Fertik, me, John Huston. Bill photographed the PSAs for Conspiracy of Hope that ran for 2–3 years. John Huston is one of my Irish heroes.
Photo by Mitzi Trumbo.

to be filmed began to complain of the time we were taking until they heard it was John Huston. Robin Williams told them they had to be patient when "real" talent was working.

Privately, as an Irishman, like MacBride, Yeats, and my mother, John Huston was one of my heroes. His dad and John and his children were symbols of Irish

Meryl Streep, a long time supporter of Amnesty at the kickoff dinner for the movie, Sophie's Choice, hosted by Rose and Bill Styron. NYC, 1982. Photographer unknown.

talent and ability, and I loved them for that. When John finally finished his 30 and 60 second spots, I asked him if he would allow me to take a picture with him. He shrugged and said "sure." Bill Fertik, our brilliant director said, "I want in that photo." The three of us mugged, and as the photographer got ready, John Huston said, "I am glad to have my picture taken with an ex-priest." Anjelica rolled her father out. The Oscar-winner just smiled the whole time. I asked Bill, "How does he know I am an ex-priest?" Bill said, "Jack, he doesn't know. He is a great casting director."

Meryl Streep, Sam Waterston, Richard Pryor, Marissa Berenson, Jamie Lee Curtis, Richard Dreyfuss, Mike Farrell, Elvis Costello, Carly Simon, Paul Simon, Marlo Thomas, Stockard Channing, Margaux Hemingway, Rosanna Arquette, Susan Lucci, Keith Richards, Tyne Daly, John Taylor of Duran Duran, and Adam Ant all graciously made supporting spots for Amnesty. This ad campaign ran so long and successfully that Robin's manager finally asked that we take the PSAs off the air because, he said, "Robin Williams does not look like that anymore."

A kick-off dinner and press release party was held at Texarkana restaurant in New York on April 1, 1986. Mary Daly, Amnesty's PR specialist, set this event in motion. Bill Graham, Paul McGuinness, Tom Brokaw, Peter Jennings, Glenn Close, Sam Waterston, Jane Alexander, Bayard Rustin, Rose Styron, Inge Morath, and E.L. Doctorow were all there for us. Yelena Bonner, wife of Andrei Sakharov, spoke at the dinner, calling for a new beginning for human rights. The party inspired a five part series on the *Today Show* on national television that ran right before the concerts, as well as spots on *Nightline* and *ABC News.*

Michael Ahern joined the tour as manager, and Ken Regan became the official photographer. Both excelled at their jobs.

We set as goals that we raise $3 million for Amnesty and add 35,000 new members, paying $25 each, doubling Amnesty USA's membership. We sold 180,000 tickets at $36 apiece. In addition, we got 5600 mentions in the press.

Our first concert was in Bill Graham's hometown of San Francisco, at the iconic venue, the Cow Palace. The doors opened at 7 pm, and Joan Baez was the opening act. She walked on with no guitar and began her set with her cover of Bob Dylan's "The Times They Are a Changing." Because it was Joan, it was strong and moving, but there was nobody there to hear it. It was 7:30 when she finished, and there were about 500 people in the 12,000 seat stadium. It was much, much too quiet.

I found Bill and dragged him out to where I had been sneaking peeks behind the curtain, pointed to the empty stadium, and told him the headlines that were surely going to run tomorrow in the San Francisco Chronicle. *Political Prisoners Remain Jailed—Americans Do Not Care. Nobody Cares about Amnesty International.* Bill laughed.

"Calm down, you big loser. This is how rock concerts go. Everybody's gotta get up, smoke their weed, get over those hangovers, and get their asses down here. Wait for it—it'll happen," Bill told me. "Wait till Gabriel hits the stage." As usual, Bill was correct. By the time Peter Gabriel banged out "Sledgehammer," the stadium was packed. When he closed with "Biko," his tribute to Black Consciousness and the anti-apartheid struggle, I was crying like an idiot, joined by most of the audience. After Peter finished, I got Sonny Venkatrathnam, a former prisoner of conscience from South Africa, and we went backstage to see Peter and thank him. We were all weeping. Then Peter asked, "Was I any good?"

The answer was: "Peter, we got a tour."

As Bryan Adams held his guitar over his head following two encores and a standing ovation, Bill nudged me with his elbow. "Your turn, buddy. Remember to kiss the mic, okay?" he said with a big grin.

"What the hell are you talking about?"

"Now; and if you're not better than U2, you'll never see that stage again," said Bill. I had to get on stage and remind the audience why we were there. This was not just a concert, even though everyone was high and happy. There were six prisoners hoping that this concert would change their lives. We hoped the concert would help more people, but there were certainly six.

The crowd of 15,000, packed into the stadium, fell silent as I passed Bryan on my way onstage. He patted me sympathetically as I walked past. The crowd watched, perhaps afraid that I might try to sing or play the guitar. I closed my eyes, and then quite literally kissed the microphone.

"Do you support our campaign against torture? Do you support our campaign to end the death penalty? Do you support Amnesty International?"

The audience screamed its support. Bill was standing on the side of the stage, laughing. He hugged me and told me I'd done a great job, but he could not stop laughing. "Jack," he said. "Kiss the mic is an expression to remind you to stand close to the mic. I didn't mean actually kiss the damn microphone. Rip Van Winkle over here." It was pretty funny.

U2 was the closing band that night. The level of talent on the tour was truly amazing to see, especially close to the stage. Bryan Adams was a stunner. Sting was not with the Police then (that reunion came later). His band of Branford Marsalis, Kenny Kirkland, and Darrell Jones was arguably unrivaled in talent and ability.

Sting's voice was as brilliant on TV as it was on stage. When asked by a TV interviewer to describe Amnesty, Sting said, "It is great to have a dictator as a pen pal." It was the perfect nod to our letter writing campaign. At the press conference, one journalist tried to embarrass the artists by asking how much money they each made. Graham almost went down the guy's throat. Before Bill could do that, I introduced the six prisoners of conscience that we had adopted. That quieted the press. Their pictures hung behind us in the pressroom. That was the real purpose behind the tour. *Good Morning America* interviewed both Sting and Bono during the first week. Peter Gabriel set the tone with "Sledgehammer," followed by the hit song "Biko." "Biko" was the heart of the tour.

Guest host presenters helped on all six stages: Sean Penn, Madonna, Elliott Gould, Steve Reeve, Mia Farrow, Muhammad Ali, Dick Gregory, Robert De Niro, Senator Bill Bradley, and Governor Tom Kean of New Jersey. After my first experience with the mic, I gave a 60 second energizer to the crowd each night.

Our task was to introduce and attempt to free six political prisoners of conscience and to explain our four mandates: No Torture, No Executions, No Unfair Trials, and No Imprisonment based on color and creed.

The day after San Francisco, we had our chartered plane take us to Los Angeles for the

Press Conference for Conspiracy of Hope with Bryan Adams, me, Joan Baez, Sting, and Bono.
© Ken Regan/Camera5.

concert at the LA Forum. Celebratory pillow fights all the way. Those pillow fights were a constant on the tour—relaxation, tension release, and pure fun.

TIME magazine met us at the Los Angeles airport for a photo that started our national coverage. We headed to a press conference, organized by Brian Murphy, our promoter in LA. He had gathered a large and interested press crowd. Each artist spoke of a political prisoner and a certain rhythm and excitement set in. You could feel it now.

One journalist asked if all the artists were against the death penalty. He was expecting at least one negative to write about, but got none. All raised their hands to support abolition of the death penalty.

I got lucky when we went to lunch with my staff members Mary Daly and James Radner. We got to eat with Peter Gabriel. We have been friends ever since. Bill Graham started to add more talent to the performances: Bob Dylan, Dave Stewart, Bob Geldof, Bonnie Raitt, Heart, Don Henley, Tom Petty, Maria McKee, Joni Mitchell, Carlos Santana, Curt Smith, and T-Bone Burnett for the closing jam. The Forum was filled. Madonna and Sean Penn were speakers at the event.

Bono did something I will never forget. He climbed on the equipment with a blindfold on to show the vulnerability of a prisoner of conscience after an arrest. Later he grabbed me, and we did an Irish jig around the stage. U2 was bonding with Amnesty. This was the first time I ever saw backstage. It was a zoo of famous record people and friends. Jack Nicholson asked me how he could help. He said, "I hear Amnesty is Huston country." I grinned, "Jack, we only take good talent."

My second one-minute blast on stage got a little easier, and I learned to just ride the wave. Robert Hilburn, music reporter for the *LA Times,* wrote a glowing review.

Amnesty International's nearly six-hour "A Conspiracy of Hope" concert Friday night at the sold-out 18,600-seat Forum was a dramatic demonstration of how we changed a political "benefit." Lighting and sound were state of the art, the pacing was brisk, and many of the artists were more inspiring than they were at their own paid concerts.[16]

The Denver concert was only half sold. As soon as we landed, all the artists actively promoted the concert. They went around to the local radio stations the morning of the show. They had not announced their arrival in advance; they just appeared at the stations. The local DJs nearly fell over in shock when they got to work and found Bono or Sting sitting on the steps, drinking coffee, and offering to go on the show. The radio studios were elated to see them.

Scott Harrison of our Amnesty staff pitched in vital help. We pumped it up. Graham had a previous commitment, and I wondered why that could be. But the artists did not seem to mind; they played ball and roamed about freely in the hotel.

Coretta Scott King, Aaron Neville, Joan Baez, me, Lee Shin Boom (a prisoner of Conscience from S. Korea) and Bono in Atlanta during COH. Atlanta, 1986. © Ken Regan/Camera5.

It was strange to me that tickets hadn't sold well given the amazing talent line up, but I did not really care because we had two successful concerts and ended on a high note in both cities. The reviews were great, and MTV was saying they were awaiting the next show with great anticipation.

Bill called me and said we are two up and one even. He explained how concerts were like meals. I was bemused by his take that, "the potatoes were just okay, but the salad and appetizers were terrific." I had a long lunch and got to know Lou Reed a little. He took me from the Velvet Underground to where we were that day in Denver. It was a great learning experience. The concerts were building into a movement, and we all were feeling good. The t-shirts were all sold again. Denver might have been the best musical night yet. We boarded our concert plane ready to hit Atlanta.

Alex Hodges was the promoter for the Atlanta concert, and he was ready for us. The concert was already sold out at the Omni. The band REM was in the crowd and later credited the show as having been influential to them. The musicians were eager to visit Dr. King's grave and meet Mrs. Coretta Scott King. U2 was especially eager because of their song about Dr. King. Aaron Neville sang "Amazing Grace." Peter Gabriel called on the Governor of Georgia to stop an execution, and it worked for a short while. The biggest news was that The Police came back together for the Atlanta, Chicago, and New York concerts.

After the concert in Atlanta, all the talent took to the smallish stage at the hotel. Some of the best musicians in the world were just hanging around jamming, only to be kicked out at the witching hour. So they all snake danced out into the lobby.

I knew that if you are the producer, you have to manage or you're nothing.

The Police closed the concert in Atlanta. I was not told in advance they would be closing. This shook me as a producer. Not because they were anything less than great, but I felt strongly that it was my decision as the producer. I was not willing to cede my authority to potential power plays between managers more concerned about their individual groups than the tour as a whole. I knew how important it was to maintain strict protocol and lines of authority. I also was determined to honor all the commitments I had made to artists along the way.

Artists who play as the closing band pick up a buzz that stays with them. I felt strongly that this honor belonged to U2, to whom the tour owed its start.

Peter Gabriel and Joan Baez singing the song Peter wrote to honor and remember Biko, who was tortured and killed. Peter is so damn special. Giants Stadium, 1976. © Ken Regan/Camera5.

Going into a meeting with the artists regarding these issues, Bill Graham told me: "I will block but I cannot tackle." I said, "No problem, I can tackle." Bill replied: "You are crazier than me." That statement gave me pause and continues to do so. Miles Copeland and I eventually resolved most of our differences. But the closing band issue stayed around.

Sting and I sat alone together on the plane to Chicago. I explained the importance of the closing band issue to me. This was not an "Irish" thing, it was simply that U2 was the first band in, and I honored their early commitment. Sting's reaction was powerful, sincere, and wonderful: "Jack, do as you see fit. I am here for Amnesty, and you and I will do whatever is the best for this tour." I went back to my seat thinking, "This guy is someone special." We kept our running order in Chicago. It was another night of great rock.

Then Miles sent Sting's British manager, Kim Turner, to see me. We argued for an hour. Finally I said, "You Brits have had your boot on our neck for seven hundred years. This will stop now." I apologized later because my comment was over the top. Kim was a great guy and they all accepted my apology. But I was still sticking to my guns on the running order.

Chicago was a sold out gig produced by Arne Ginsher. Robin Williams did a fifteen minute introduction for the Police. It was tremendously funny, and the crowd roared its appreciation. Talking to an arena of 12,000-15,000 takes courage, especially in the middle of a rock show.

Before we left Chicago, Bill asked me to address all the artists about the NYC gig on MTV. I did my best, but I wept a bit as I thanked them for their tremendous effort.

Aaron Neville, Joan Baez, Bono, me, Sting, Bryan Adams. I can't sing or dance, but it was great fun to be on stage with this group of talented artists. Giants Stadium, 1986. Photo by Ebet Roberts.

By their rallying for human rights and Amnesty International, Amnesty was becoming the charity of choice, and the American people were getting the message of our four main goals: fair trials, no torture, no executions, and no political imprisonment.

Bill Graham, Bob Guccioni, Jr. of *SPIN* magazine, and the artists wanted to highlight the successes that Amnesty had achieved. We asked Nigerian singer Fela Kuti to join in the Conspiracy of Hope. He was a constant critic of the Nigerian government, a freed prisoner of conscience, and his life had been devoted to human rights. He was the symbol of all we were working toward. Fela and his band arrived in time for the big press conference to discuss the upcoming eleven-hour telethon of music and human rights.

The ticket price remained at $36. Best ticket ever for the price. The concert featured Miles Davis, Third World, the Hooters, Joan Armatrading, Yoko Ono, Pete Townshend (whose father got ill; he was replaced by Joni Mitchell), Jackson Browne, Stanley Jordan, Howard Jones, Peter, Paul and Mary, Pat Benatar, Ruben Blades, John Eddie, Little Steven, and Paul Shaffer to play with the Police, U2, Bryan Adams, Peter Gabriel, the Neville Brothers, and Joan Baez. The promoter, John Sher, had done an amazing job.

At the beginning of the flight to New York someone asked Bill why it was so quiet. He answered, "The wives are here." The quiet was temporary; eventually the usual pillow fight broke out. The pillow fight kept most of the plane busy as we landed in Newark, but I saw the plane bounce and said "too high!" Then slam. Two tires had blown, and we got off where we landed in the middle of the runway. Somewhat shaken, we immediately went to the press conference. Fela's statement was that "we would never do this in Africa." He was referring to Nigerian rejection of human rights. But, it got it into my head that I would try to put on an event in Africa one day.

It was a beautiful day, with just enough afternoon rain to cool things off. All the VJs from MTV were ready: Bob Pittman, John Sykes, Jock McLean, and Tom Freston. Viacom would film from 7:00 a.m. to 11:00 pm. The stadium opened at noon, and young people raced across the field to get seats in front.

The New York show was insane from the start. John Sher, our New York promoter, had set things up to run smoothly. Michael Ahern did a superb job running the show. It was an amazing feat keeping all the acts running on time. It was MTV's first big live broadcast. I asked for an addition to the VJ lineup to allow Amnesty chair, Charles Henry, a chance to speak. The idea was rejected until Bill Graham threatened to cut all the TV lines by ax if Charles was not allowed to speak (Bill could tackle when it was needed).

Reporters were packed backstage. Amnesty had volunteers throughout the stadium, and we sold 30,000 t-shirts that day. The public service announcements by Bill Fertik were running on MTV before, during, and after the concert.

Muhammed Ali and I at the final Conspiracy of Hope concert. I first met Ali when he joined Dick Gregory's World Hunger Run, 1986. Photographer unknown.

Dick Gregory, Muhammad Ali, Robert De Niro, Governor Kean, and Senator Bill Bradley were present to speak about Amnesty. Robert De Niro came over to me. "I have no idea what I'm supposed to say," he said flatly. I told him he could say what he wanted; as long as he mentioned the political prisoners or Amnesty, it was really up to him. He looked at me blankly. I handed him a copy of one of our public service announcements, and he walked onstage, in front of over 50,000 people, pale, shaky, and sweaty.

He began, "I uh…I didn't really know much about Amnesty until…well I'm new to this, really." People in the crowd laughed as he stammered over his words. He looked back at me and glared. "All right," he said, tossing aside the public service announcement. "After 25 years, we at Amnesty know that a government, even one that commits unspeakable crimes against its people, can be affected by your opinion, what you do and what you say. You can stop torture. You can free prisoners. You can stay executions. Join us, here today. Get up out of your seat and join us. Because, what you need to remember, is that all that evil needs in order to succeed is for good men to do nothing. So don't do nothing. Do something." He received a standing ovation.

It was a great speech, and it was followed by equally memorable speeches by Dick Gregory and Mohammad Ali, who addressed bigotry against the Muslim faith and its followers.

U2 continued to help Amnesty after the concerts. Bono also helped me celebrate my 50th birthday. L.A., 1988.

When Little Steven of the Bruce Springsteen band went on with Bob Geldof, he devoted his song and album to Leonard Peltier, an American Indian leader who had been in jail since 1977. Then Miles Davis, known to often play concerts with his back to the audience so he could see his band, turned to face the audience during his segment.

A great moment of the show was when Sting graciously turned over his bass to U2 as if to say, "we were the top and now it is U2's turn." All the bands were great that day, but U2 went from being a popular band to being acknowledged as one of the very top bands. It was great to see that happen to a band that had given so much to others. Sting's strong, quiet demeanor during this enhanced the respect I already had for him.

All the bands and dozens of former prisoners of conscience that were at the event did the closing jam on stage and sat for a picture later.

The Conspiracy of Hope tour sold 138,000 tickets. A new generation struggling for human rights was awakened. Amnesty, and its call for human rights, became famous. The music of rock and roll delivered the message, and young people responded. We hoped more light would enter the jails and the torture chambers and death row and justice systems.

Made in the USA
San Bernardino, CA
01 December 2019

Peter Gabriel and Sting did twenty three more concerts with Amnesty during my time, including Human Rights Now! in 1988 and a Hug to a Hope in Chile in 1990. Those two artists just got it and lived it.

Bill Graham more than lived up to his agreement with me, his family, his nation, and his world. He enriched the movement for human rights.

The day after the tour, I was in the Amnesty office in New York. We counted our new members. Within a period of six weeks, we had more than doubled our membership from 40,000 to 90,000 and had an additional $3 million in our bank account. Amnesty chapters were opening in high schools and colleges all over the country. Six months after the tour, the U.S. section of Amnesty had tripled in size.

A year later, I was in Los Angeles for a meeting. A young kid around ten or so kept following me around the office. Finally, I said to him, "Hi, I am Jack Healey of Amnesty." He immediately shot back, "I am the President of Amnesty International in my school." I felt that day that I was doing my job. Amnesty chapters had sprung up in thousands of high schools, colleges, and even grade schools. Young people had responded.

Conspiracy of Hope team. Every person with a white t-shirt is a former prisoner of conscience, except for me. Giants Stadium, 1986. © Ken Regan/Camera5.

CHAPTER 12

Amnesty after a Conspiracy of Hope

THE LATE 1980s AND EARLY 1990s WERE LIKE NOTHING I HAD ever experienced. Due to the popularity of the musicians, I was on major network news nearly every week, sometimes more than once a week, also appearing on TV super programs such as *Oprah,* CNN's prime time news, *60 Minutes,* and NBC's *Morning Show.* Scholars were calling it the "era of human rights," and Amnesty was at the center of it all.

Press conference at the nation's capital. The concerts drew increased attention for human rights. Photographer unknown.

I was never in the same city for more than two days in a row, accepting speaking engagements at every college or high school that asked. When I landed at an airport and was picked up by the students or instructors, I was never sure of the school's prestige, but it did not matter to me. A voice is a voice is a voice. Spending a lot of time in the air traveling around, I began to get noticed there as well. Passengers and ticket agents would give up their first class seats for me, saying things like, "Hey, you're that Amnesty guy. No, please, I will not let the plane leave with you in coach."

I never really knew how to handle this brief celebrity status. I mostly just nodded and took what was being offered to me. It was awkward to say the least. Strangers would tell me about articles they read, and how they related to what they thought Amnesty should be doing.

What was far more important was the impact our popularity had on the effectiveness of Amnesty. Our name recognition was through the roof. All of the

airtime, coupled with the reliability of our research, gave us instant creditability. The world was changing in our favor as well. I still remember the shocked looked that our Soviet researcher had on his face when we crowded around the television to watch the Berlin Wall fall, or the tears that came to our Latin America researcher's eyes when Pinochet peacefully resigned power in Chile. And my heart still stops beating for a second when I think about the first time I saw Mandela emerge from jail, thrusting his fist in the air to salute the *Umkhonto we Sizwe.*

Artists for Amnesty
June 6 to June 16, 1989, NYC

In the spring of 1989, one of our volunteers, Jennifer Wachtell, suggested that we have a charity art show for Amnesty. At the time Mrs. Jimmy Ernst asked Amnesty to start a fund for refugees in honor of her artist husband, who had also been a refugee. We had just finished the Human Rights Now! tour, and we were a bit worn down from these high profile moments, but Jennifer guaranteed there would be little effort required from my office. That sure sounded good to me.

Mrs. Ernst called and said, "Let's go see Frank Stella." I told her that would be fine. Then I had to ask who Frank Stella was. I learned he was the Bruce Springsteen of the art world. We went to his studio that sported the décor of a mechanic's place back in Pittsburgh. Frank Stella graciously agreed to help us and donated one of his works.

I got wind that Botero, a well know artist and human rights activist, wanted to give a piece as well. I offered to pick up that piece myself. I got to Botero's apartment, and he answered my knock at the door. He looked at me, closed the door without inviting me in, and went to get the piece. When he opened the door again, I got up my nerve to ask him why he painted those wonderful people in such huge proportions. He said that when he was young, he was scared of big people.

Leo Castelli called and wanted to help. He was a firm believer in the anti-death penalty work of Amnesty. Mary Boothe and Larry Gogosian followed suit. Alice Hunsberger and Jennifer Wachtell assembled an honorary committee headed by Steve Martin, Leo Castelli, Virginia Dwan, Jill Revson, Ariadne Getty, Justin Williams, Cathy Graham, Michael Roux, and Robert and Laura Sillerman. These were the greats of the art world.

Robert De Niro, Sr., joined in with a gift. Blum Helman and Germans Van Eck gave us space for the show. Jay Chiat of the Chiat/Day Advertising Agency helped Jennifer organize a kick-off event attended by most of the artists. Collectively, they

donated over 150 pieces of art. We sold every piece. Once the artists heard that we sold out, they donated another 120 pieces to be sold.

Art and artists are an amazing positive force for change. I got a glimpse of that power from the art show. Freedom and universality ride the artists' shoulders and they keep alive those feelings in their art.

The prisoners are free in Swaziland
March 26-27, 1991; six detainees set free

Shortly after the concert tour and art benefit, I met Daniel Nsereko in Johannesburg to co-direct a planned mission to Swaziland. Nsereko lived in Botswana and was a lawyer who looked the part: tall, thin, elegant, and smart. We were both excited to go on an official mission. We flew into Mbabane and discovered that when the government heard we were arriving, they released the half dozen young students they had arrested for demonstrating at the University of Swaziland. We smiled and were absolutely thrilled. This was the true benefit from all the publicity. Amnesty's renown caused power to tremble. Later, I was called a nemesis of third world thugs by *U.S. News and World Report.*[17] I'm not sure I deserved the title, but that day I was proud to wear it.

We visited the government and thanked them for the release and arranged to have supper with the freed students at our hotel. When they arrived, they were trailed by more secret police than we had at our dinner party for nine. The students told us they had received letters of support from the United States. Given the drabness of the jail, they said the colors on the stamps also encouraged them. By the way, one of the students asked, "Who is Thomas Jefferson?"

The notoriety sparked by the Conspiracy of Hope, Human Rights Now!, and Chilean concert tours contributed to an already strong political influence. Reporters from all over the world were now calling our office regularly, asking for quotes on Nicaragua, reforms in China, and opinions about presidential candidates in the U.S. Instead of having to send our interns down to the offices of newspapers to cajole space for a story, newspapers were calling us. Because of the increased income, the budget of the research department in London was now large enough to enable them to hire more researchers and pay for their travel. More research helped generate more action.

The influx of money, members, and chapters necessitated a bigger staff. We had around eighteen people on staff when I started at Amnesty in 1981. By the time the HRN tour was over, we had about 100 people working for us. And we were still hiring. Many of our board members applied for jobs with us. We worked to

hire a staff that looked like the U.S. and included blacks, whites, gays, and people from as many different backgrounds as possible.

We tackled new issues. We had the money, the capacity, and the energy, so why not expand our goals? We grew our vision along with our organization.

The death penalty was increasingly being utilized as a form of punishment. Although reserved for the worst crimes, such as murder, it was too frequently imposed on those too poor to hire a good lawyer, whether or not they were guilty. The Reagan administration cut funding for federal programs like free school lunches, drug treatment programs, and homeless shelters. As the safety net disintegrated, more people were jailed nationwide. Drug use and addiction prompted stealing, prostitution, and other desperate acts which put more Americans in prison. Although Reagan espoused the trickle-down theory of economics, it appeared that money from the top was not really trickling-down but was instead hitting a snag or stopping altogether somewhere before reaching the middle class.

Whatever the reason, the public perception was that crime in America was skyrocketing. News reports of murders, kidnappings, armed robbery, and other horrible crimes gave the Republicans the impetus to "get tough on crime."

Amnesty set a goal to stop the killing of death-row inmates. Charles Fulwood, who directed Amnesty's division fighting the death penalty, suggested that first we find out what Americans thought about the death penalty. The Republicans were frequently on television, touting polls saying that Americans still supported the death penalty.

Charles was good at both statistics and detecting bullshit. He began by breaking down the statistics. He suggested we take our own poll to acquire more nuanced information. We found that Americans generally supported the death penalty, but with some very clear caveats. The majority did not support the use of the death penalty for someone who was mentally retarded, under the age of twenty-one, or in a case where there was evidence of racial bias.

Amnesty had to jettison its former strategy of waiting to protest until after a governor had signed an execution order. Charles pointed out that we would be more likely to be successful if we talked to prosecutors and defense attorneys while a trial was ongoing. Once an order of execution had been signed, it was legally and politically almost impossible to stop the execution. We had to make people both in and out of the system conscious of the unfair use of the death penalty.

We reused the technique that had been successful with our prior concerts. We chose prisoners who were facing the death penalty and made their stories the focus of our campaign. We publicized their names and ages, their backgrounds, the circumstances of the crime for which they had been convicted, and the "fairness"

of the trial. We also started gathering our own statistics. The more we dug, the worse the situation seemed. Our researchers reported that in cases in which the victim was white, the defendant, especially if he or she was a minority, was more likely to receive the death penalty. Indigent defendants often received a shoddy defense. Public defenders were overworked and often were not even familiar with their client's case. They lacked the resources to check alibis, hire psychiatrists, and otherwise mount a decent defense.

Charles was plugged into the community of civil rights activists around the country, and he helped us garner support. Soon, we were meeting with the NAACP and the SCLC, and we sponsored a SCLC -organized "Death Penalty Awareness Day."

I had met Robert Badinter, the man who killed the death penalty in France, at one of my first annual meetings of Amnesty International in 1983. His speech was long but thoughtful. Robert was the French Minister of Justice under Francois Mitterrand and later served as head of the French Supreme Court. I asked him for help with our anti-death penalty fight.

Mary Daly set up an interview at the *Washington Post* to start the media coverage for Robert's visit. We were ushered into a conference room. Colman McCarthy, editorial writer for the Post, stomped in. He slammed his tape recorder on the table and began questioning the French Minister of Justice with this question: "Have you closed all the prisons in France yet?" Robert said that he had not. Colman was not finished insulting the French Minister. Next he asked, "Have you moved back those trees on the highway because they were responsible for Camus's death?" Again, Robert demurred. Colman stormed out in disgust.

Supreme Court Justice Harry Blackmun and Aram Jafarey at dinner in the south of France, 1976.

Robert Badinter turned to me and said, "Ah?" which I took to translate as "what the hell?" I had no answer available. After a few minutes, Colman reentered with his tape recorder and did a standard interview.

In the summer of 1986, I visited Feryal Gharahi in Aix-en-Provence, France. She was a Georgetown law student and had come to France to study case law at the local university. One of her professors was Supreme Court Justice Harry Blackmun.

My second week there, we were invited to dinner at Justice Blackmun's house. Feryal had told him that his position on the 1967 death penalty case, and the fact that he had voted for the death penalty, "made him just like other dictators who punish misbehavior by killing."

I asked whether she compared him to a dictator in front of everyone in the class. "Well, of course, Jack," she said, "and so he invited me to dinner."

We ate and talked about the death penalty and about black men, who disproportionally end up in the electric chair. We talked about how the system was stacked against poor people. And we talked about how black men usually faced an all-white system of judges, juries, and lawyers. Justice Blackmun and his wife said that our findings were not surprising.

At the end of the night, after we had had the cheese plate and another glass of wine and then a final, final drink, Justice Blackmun stopped me as I was leaving. "Stay strong, will you, Jack?" he asked, pleading, maybe.

"With all due respect, sir, it is not me that I am worried about. Thank you for this lovely dinner, and evening." What a couple, and what an evening. I wished my mom were alive so that I could have told her about that evening with Justice Blackmun.

Two years later, when the Supreme Court refused to hear a case involving the validity of the death penalty, Justice Blackmun issued a dissenting opinion stating that he would "no longer tinker in the machinery of death." Justice Blackmun's law clerk said that Blackmun was struggling to "reflect the wisdom gained, and the frustration endured, as a result of twenty years of enforcing the death penalty on the Court."

Moira Stanley and Ian Gray from my old Walk for Development days agreed to write a book about the death penalty. The idea was to give the kids who joined us in big numbers after the tours an answer as to why they should oppose the death penalty. Moira and Ian compiled a series of interviews to answer those questions. The book brilliantly relays the stories told to them by lawyers, clergy, prison personnel, inmates on death row, and families of murder victims. Not only does the penalty not deter crime, it is meted out with alarming inequity.

Our efforts against the death penalty were not entirely successful, but we saw a gradual shift in public opinion and greater limits placed on its use.

CHAPTER 13

Human Rights Now! Tour: 1987-1988

T HE CALL THAT WOKE ME ONE MORNING TO TELL ME ABOUT the 40th anniversary of the Universal Declaration of Human Rights (UDHR) came from one of my predecessors, David Hawk. David and Mary Daly had had supper the night before and had discussed the need to do something special to acknowledge the Declaration. The Conspiracy of Hope tour had been successful, and from that experience I knew music was a powerful tool to be used.

Human Rights Now! press conferences were held in each city to draw attention to the Universal Declaration of Human Rights. Photo by Ebet Roberts.

Amnesty had attracted a new American generation of human rights activists and a growing, paying membership. The advice I had received from another Amnesty colleague, Feryal Gharahi was to "Go bigger. Governments can be fooled

with perceptions and presumptions. If Amnesty acts big, governments will think Amnesty is big."

How do we get that concept of size and magnitude across to governments? We thought we could achieve that with music. Instead of touring the USA as we did before, we would tour the world.

The UDHR is universal, and the tour had to be as well. In order to travel all over, our concerts had to be numerous enough in hard currency countries to afford to play in countries with little or no hard currency. It was the poorer countries with no hard currency that Bill Graham and I were interested in the most.

By 1987, I had watched six years of the Reagan administration's policies with human rights issues abroad and at home. Its commitment to human rights was as ephemeral as a cloud: squeeze it and it disappears. George H. W. Bush was better. His staff had considerable appreciation for human rights, though it was still limited. Terror is a tactic that some governments use to control people. Many people were tired of governments operating that way. I felt there was a growing river of consciousness for justice forming in the mountains that had to spill out onto the plains sooner or later. I could not stop torture, a policy of rape, disappearances, and the brutality of governments, but I could provide a moment of respite and solace and allow the victims to know that there were people and an organization that cared. Our artists could tell the story of the tortured and abused—using music—and the resulting publicity might help.

My team at Amnesty was ready and willing to go again. My immediate nucleus of Charles Fulwood, Magdeleno (Leno) Rose Avila, Mary Daly, Jessica Neuwirth, and James Radner were up to the task. Curt Goering would easily replace me again in the office. Communications, law, and administration were solid. The tour would take me away from the office for a year, so the strong home base was pivotal to success. I went back to Bill Graham for help, and he agreed to produce the tour.

Claude Isakov and Bill Pace, our advance team, set up the London office in Hampstead Heath. Improvisation was crucial to our operation. When we

Promo photo of Bruce Springsteen, Sting, and me for the Human Rights Now! tour. © Ken Regan/Camera5.

couldn't get a phone installed, we "rented" the phone from next door by punching a hole in the wall and using the neighbor's phone from 9:00 to 5:00.

I did not want this tour to be a repeat of the last tour that had focused primarily on Amnesty. Instead, I wanted to celebrate the full Universal Declaration of Human Rights (UDHR) and urge that its provisions become law in as many countries as possible. It was also my small way of saying thanks to the Roosevelts for saving my family. It was time to enact the UDHR. At that time, less than five percent of the world's population had ever read it or knew of it. When I was asked about the UDHR in the interview for the job of Amnesty, I responded ambiguously that the UDHR contains the powerful and helps the poor. "That's gotta be a good thing," I laughed.

Naturally, I called Peter Gabriel and Sting, my British boys. Both agreed to join us. Peter said, "I want Youssou N'Dour of Senegal along." That was fine with me, and we were off to a great start. Jackson Browne called and said that I had to hear this new voice, Tracy Chapman. Bill said, "We should take her; she's got a guitar and nothing else. That works." Graham set my next task by saying: "We need a steak, Jack. Get me a steak. We've got potatoes, vegetables, salad, gravy, and dessert, but no steak. And there are not many steaks in the world. So get me a steak."

I went to see U2 in Los Angeles at the A&M studios where they were recording. Bono and the boys loved the idea of joining the tour, but felt they could not do it with their already overloaded recording and filming schedule. I argued with Bono that the film they were producing was coming too early in their career, and I thought they should drop it. Not having U2 devastated me.

We needed a strong closing band to be the steak. Bruce Springsteen was, at the time, the most famous musician in the world. His angst-ridden lyrics appealed to all. He wrote songs about inequality and racism, lyrics that lined up well with our message. He could sell out an entire stadium within hours of tickets going on sale.

The problem was none of us knew anybody in the Springsteen camp. After much debate and thought, Bono finally suggested that we call Frank Barsalona, the president of Premier Talent, promoter of the Rolling Stones and the Beatles, who had helped U2 in their rise to fame. When we explained that the tour would be a vehicle to promote the UDHR, Frank signed up. He promised to get me an appointment with Bruce Springsteen.

With Frank in hand, and right before I was to meet Bruce in the bowels of Madison Square Garden, I ran into Herb Alpert and Jerry Moss. They, along with Gil Friesen and Gary Gersh were the anchors of the Conspiracy of Hope tour, and so it was a meeting of old friends. They helped calm me down. I went in. Bruce was sitting alone in the darkened room on a big velvet sofa. He was probably tired,

Human Rights Now! musicians: Peter Gabriel, Joan Baez, Youssou N'Dour, Tracy Chapman, Sting, Bruce Springsteen. Photo by Ebet Roberts.

since he had just performed an epic, two-hour concert. I sat on a chair next to him and started off with small talk, thinking he'd want to chat for a while. Bruce interrupted politely and asked, "Why are you doing a music tour for The Universal Declaration of Human Rights?"

I explained that "the UDHR is an essential legal document. Most people don't even know it exists, but all governments should be responsible to uphold it. The anniversary provides us with an opportunity to give the UDHR visibility. We need to take the message beyond the west and show our solidarity with people in Africa, Asia, and Latin America. We want to play the world so the millions of people under oppressive regimes are no longer suffering in silence."

He asked what I wanted him to do. I told him that I needed him for a six week tour. I knew it was a huge request to make of a rock star.

Bruce said, "I'll do it." I froze. I couldn't comprehend that he had just agreed to drop everything and join us. Bruce must have expected a more enthusiastic response than my silence. "Are you happy or what?" he asked. My answer, since I was still speechless, was to jump on him and give him an enormous bear hug. Now we had our steak.

The UDHR would finally get heard around the World. My thought leaving the room was, you got Bruce in three minutes and U2 in eight minutes…Jack, you do keep your meetings short.

The Nuts and Bolts

Ian Martin, Amnesty's Secretary General, received an honorary doctorate from the University of Essex in 2003. Among the many accolades, the presenter said, "Speaking to people who worked in Amnesty at that time, what is striking is the way they describe Martin's management style. One said that Martin created an environment in which he could just get on with his work. If it wasn't broke, he didn't fix it. When he did fix something, it happened so smoothly that it did not disrupt the work being done. That must be the highest tribute that can be paid to a senior administrator. Another simply said, 'He's a class act.'"[18]

Peter Gabriel played a concert prior to the tour just to raise money to pay for the tour.
Photo by Ebet Roberts.

This was my experience with Ian throughout my time at Amnesty. When we started planning concerts, he stood behind the decision to create a legal firewall between the concert work and the rest of Amnesty's work. So, our first task was to organize a separate nonprofit called The Concerts for Human Rights Foundation. To much of Amnesty's board, it existed only for insurance purposes in case of a tragedy. But the members of the Concerts for Human Rights Foundation upheld the firewall as strictly as we could. This resulted in a few battles between the groups. Ian Martin stood up for the separation between the groups, and he helped immensely.

Along with the need for steak, we had to evaluate the cost and the income/loss potential of the tour. Graham and I wanted to schedule concerts in countries most in need of the power of music for human rights, but these were also the countries that would carry a loss. The profit from wealthier nations needed to support those countries. Our team estimated that we would need between $5-10 million even if we sold out the stadiums where the audience paid for its tickets in hard currency. Nations like Russia and Zimbabwe had soft currency. That meant Amnesty received zero return from tickets. We required

144

a team of 300 employees and two DC-10 jets for six weeks. Amnesty advanced $250,000 to get us started. Those funds ran out fast once we began placing holds on the jets and sixteen stadiums.

When the Amnesty funds ran out, we asked Peter Gabriel to play a televised show in Italy and give us the cash. He did. With Peter's help, we kept going. It never ceased to amaze me how quickly top artists contributed to help spread the message of human rights. Their voices thundered.

Eventually, we decided to alter our usual policy and find a corporate sponsor. This risked compromising Amnesty's credibility; we did not want it to look as if we were beholden to any corporate interests. We approached Paul Fireman, Joseph Labonte, and Angel Martinez, Reebok's top executives in Boston. They quickly agreed to underwrite any losses of the tour for up to $10 million and advance $2 million to get the tour started. In accordance with Amnesty rules, Reebok could not use the concert to advertise their product and the Reebok logo would not appear with the Amnesty logo. As part of the agreement, Reebok did control the t-shirt sales to help recoup some of their investment.

Next we had to convince the top brass at Amnesty to support this slightly unorthodox pairing of a sneaker company with the UDHR. We dragged the Reebok representatives in their tailored suits to the Amnesty boardroom in London, where the board members sat at one end of the table and bellowed questions at Reebok's representatives.

The Reebok people did well, fielding every question thrown at them: the working conditions for producers of their sneakers, shipping of their merchandise, and where and how they obtained materials. The Amnesty board members, finally, seemed to have exhausted their supply of questions. IEC member Peter Duffy asked, "Do you use leather in your shoes?"

Before anyone answered, I simply said, "Yes, Peter, you're eating a chicken sandwich."

We had our financial backing. We were ready to go.

Reebok, after consulting with our team, also decided to set up an annual event to honor young people under thirty for their human rights work.

There were three major issues to resolve before the tour. Bill Graham and I wanted to play Turkey, but the research department of Amnesty claimed that people in Turkey did not appreciate rock music. Their real concern was with fundamentalists. We knew that Turkey sold the second highest number of rock and roll albums in Europe. But Bill and I lost that round. The tour was not to go to the Middle East or Near East. This remains a mystery to me even now.

The second decision was where to finish the tour. Bill and I wanted to close the tour in Argentina, though a finale in the U.S. or Europe would have been more

financially sound. But we wanted to choose a place that had seriously debated human rights, where the battle had been won, courageously and openly.

The final debate was whether to do a concert in India. Bill and I strongly argued that we should not play a concert there. The deal just did not look right to us. The *Times* of India, the largest newspaper in the country, was the sponsor. However, the chair of Amnesty mandated that we play India at any cost, so we acquiesced. She repeated, "At any cost."

The HRN tour was not an easy one. Reporters and music historians called it one of the most complicated tours to date to produce. What the audience sees on stage is the polished product: the happy songs, the moving stories. But that show is the result of months of planning, negotiations, organizing, publicizing, and managing staffs internally and externally. The strain of flying around the world for six weeks with several groups of musicians and the full entourage required to make the performances work meant tensions were bound to surface periodically.

Music is a hard business. It is a tough business. Other benefit concerts like Live Aid encompassed many performers, but only two shows. The Conspiracy of Hope ran for two weeks with a year of planning. The Human Rights Now! tour lasted for six weeks and took another year of planning. The upside was the power of the message multiple voices brought. Another unexpected outcome was the lifetime friendships created between artists during the tours. In 2014, twenty-five years after the HRN concluded, I smiled as I watched Springsteen on stage at the Kennedy Center paying tribute to his friend Sting, who was receiving the Kennedy Center Award; it was a friendship germinated during HRN. I always valued these great performers. Not just for their commitments to the tour, but for their kindness, passion, and steadfastness for the cause over the years. But before the victories came the trials.

Mary Daly, Bill Graham, and me. Bill telling me what to do, again. India, 1988. © Neal Preston.

Artists and their managers are used to getting their own way. Managers customarily make hard and fast decisions. They do not generally enjoy cooperative decision making. And Amnesty was all about meetings and moving slowly, especially given the international status of the tour. The international movement

had no structure to deal with the tour, although they tried to exercise control despite the firewall foundation that was in place. Each Amnesty section where the tour played thought that they were in charge of the tour as well. These tensions made the tour more work than fun for me.

I had anticipated a tough go of it, but some surprises left me dumbfounded.

One battle came while reaching agreement with the Springsteen camp. Bruce agreed to join us for six weeks and give up a $21 million tour. But a clash of personalities surfaced between Bill Graham and Frank Barsalona, who was making arrangements for Bruce to join the tour. Frank claimed that Bill was not referring talent to Frank as they had previously agreed. Frank was determined to get an apology. Bill would not apologize.

Since this conflict had nothing to do with me, I stayed quiet and looked for a chance to flee to the bathroom and escape. But Frank said, "Jack, I do not want Bruce Springsteen on a Bill Graham tour. I want him on an Amnesty tour, and you must be the producer of this show. You are the promoter. It is your tour."

I groaned, regretting I had not made a clean escape. Producing the show would be like going to a drug store and asking for some cancer. I knew immediately that Bill thought I had helped make this up. Not only did I not dream it up, I dreaded the job. My role was human rights, promoting the message and image of human rights and doing press work. I did not want to run a tour. I was Bill's angel on the Conspiracy of Hope tour and now on the Human Rights Tour I would be the devil—the boss. Furthermore, Bill was my friend. He made the COH tour a big success. I did not want to do this one without him.

The night ended in the middle of Madison Avenue with Bill screaming at me, "Where am I?" The inability of Frank and Bill to resolve their differences had a profound impact on the tour. I was caught in the middle of two powerhouses of the music industry. It ruined the relationship between Bill and me. He died tragically in a helicopter crash on October 21, 1991, without our having reconciled. His mates at his firm told me that he was about to

Human Rights Now! Tour artists Youssou N'Dour, Sting, Tracy Chapman, Bruce Springsteen, Clarence Clemons. Philadelphia, 1993. Photo by Ebet Roberts.

do so. While I was the nominal producer of the tour, George Travis, Bruce's tour manager, was the real head of the tour. He and his team worked hard and well. Bill Graham's team under Michael Ahern produced the San Francisco, Costa Rica, and India concerts. There were no mistakes anywhere.

The most dangerous struggle came about when the head of Columbia Records went to Bruce after all the arrangements had been made and told him that Amnesty was an anti-Israeli group. Bruce called me and asked me to come to New York to discuss the accusation. I grabbed Amnesty's annual report and flew up from Washington and sat down for a lovely French meal with Bruce and Patti Scialfa, a member of the E Street Band. While Amnesty did not bow to any government, speaking truth to all in power, we certainly did not go after any nation or people with bias.

At the end of the meal, Bruce asked me about what his record company had said. I thought for a minute and said, "Well, let's go together to Israel and the Occupied Territories and examine every claim by Amnesty regarding Israel and the Israeli Defense Forces."

Bruce asked, "You would do that?"

I said, "Of course." We said goodbye, and I said, "If you want to go, call me. If not, let's do the tour." Bruce Springsteen did the tour. We kept our steak.

The discussion on Israel was the first of many times that Bruce proved he was not just a famous musician. He cared deeply about the issues and proved it by continually requesting a thorough briefing on human rights issues. He listened carefully and used the information to speak out during concerts. He was as good with words as he was with music.

Jon Landau, Nils Lofgren, Peter Gabriel, me and Sting. The Universal Declaration of Human Rights finally got a day in the sun. © Neal Preston.

Bruce Springsteen and the E Street Band used their Stockholm concert on July 4, 1988, to announce their participation in the HRN Tour. I was on ABC's *Good Morning America* early the next morning. Right before my segment, there was an announcement that the U.S. Navy had blown an Iranian commercial flight out of the sky and no one survived. It took my breath away. The interviewer asked me why I was so serious. I thought it was more than obvious why. Innocents dying are the essence of human rights.

Bruce understood this essence and supported the work completely. He sent Amnesty $250,000 even before the kickoff in London's Wembley Stadium. He also brought Jessica Neuwirth, our HRN attorney, and me to Berlin for a concert behind the Iron Curtain. Later, when the tour was closing out, he took us all to Ireland for a party, a real party. It was lots of fun for an ex-priest like me.

Instead of adopting former prisoners of conscience as we had during the Conspiracy of Hope tours, we included human rights activists and survivors in the tour. They joined us on the plane and served as informative resources for the musicians, the crew, and the press: Arn Chorn of Cambodia, Navi Pillay of South Africa (later the UN Secretary for Human Rights), Charlotte Holdman (who did anti-death penalty work in the USA), Veronica De Negri of Chile, and Alicia Portnoy of Argentina all participated as voices for their nations.

Robert Johnson and Prudence Fenton organized what we called our 6th band. This band was the UDHR in animation.[19] Johnson and Fenton had traveled to an animator's event in Europe to ask if any animators would do a spot of the UDHR. The result was a powerful animation of the UDHR translated into each native language spoken on the tour. Often all it takes is asking.

The Human Rights Now! Tour was the result of a crazy idea I had with my staff at Amnesty. Many of the board and our members thought we were insane and that a music tour would trivialize human rights issues. Some sections of Amnesty refused to allow the tour to come to their country. The *New Republic* editors agreed with them. They attacked me regularly for trivializing human rights, and they thought that corporate underwriting was a mistake. They wanted Amnesty to get rid of me.

Obviously, I did not agree. The tour could only broaden the audience for our message, and further, we wanted to include all, and that meant entertainers, audiences, and corporations. Both founders of Amnesty, Benenson and MacBride, gave us their blessings. And we sold out every concert. A year after the tour, Amnesty tripled its worldwide membership.

Each concert was started by singing, "Get Up, Stand Up," by Bob Marley to honor Bob and set the stage as an activistic movement.

London

Promoter: Harvey Goldsmith, Avon House
Audience: 82,000

The Human Rights Now! tour opened on Sept 2, 1988, in London at Wembley Stadium. A tradition was started at this opening concert in honor of Bob Marley. The artists entered the stage together to open the show with Bob Marley's "Get Up, Stand Up."

As the rest of the artists slipped off stage, Senegalese pop star Youssou N'Dour brought the stadium to its feet with his pounding performance of his song "Nelson Mandela," who was still in prison at the time.

Though it was still daylight, we had Peter Gabriel play next. Later, Peter Gabriel's mother gave me a word or two about putting her son on stage during the day. I was used to standing up to managers fighting for top billing for their artists, but I was no match for Peter's mother. I didn't make that mistake again.

After Peter Gabriel's set, Bill Graham came to me and said, "Your turn." It was my turn to use my voice to lift that stadium of 82,000 ticket holders to the purpose of the tour. I always liked to give the crowds something concrete to do to help the movement. The response was heartwarming and gave our tour definition if anyone had doubted it.

For HRN we distributed copies of the UDHR and had the audience sign petitions. Tracy Chapman followed next. She was a new artist but wildly popular already, and the crowd joined in. "While they're standing in the welfare lines/Crying at the doorsteps of these armies of salvation/Waiting time in the unemployment lines/Finally the tables are starting to turn."

Sting dedicated his song "If You Love Someone, Let Them Go" to the children in jails in South Africa. Then Bruce Springsteen stepped out to the first few notes of "Born in the USA," and the crowd was ecstatic, filling the stadium with thousands of voices.

Our press secretary, Mary Daly, was crucial to the success of both the Conspiracy of Hope and Human Rights Now! tours. After the opening show in London, the tour was widely covered in the States and across Europe, leading the way to huge crowds in every city. Just as with Conspiracy of Hope, Robert Hilburn provided excellent coverage of the concerts for the *LA Times*.

Paris, France
Promoter: Gerard Drouot Productions
Artist: Michel Jonasz; Audience: 17,000 (twice)

Two shows were performed in Paris at an indoor stadium. Sting and Bruce sang a duet of "River." Tracy Chapman gave the best performance of her career to date. French singer Michel Jonasz was popular with the crowd. Everyone agreed the Paris show was better than London. The team was starting to gel musically. One gap of credibility came when Amnesty's Chair Franca Sciuto read a letter from the Prime Minister of France. The reading violated the tour's strict policy of impartiality. Providing a government with the ability to contribute to our message weakened our freedom to speak the truth about potential abuses in all countries

without regard to political forces. I did not want the Prime Minister addressing our tour. We still had fourteen countries to go. I did not want a governmental message each night, especially in the United States from Ronald Reagan.

Budapest, Hungary
Promoter: Laszlo Hegedus, Multimedia Organization
Artists: Janos Brody, Hobo Blues Band; Audience: 56,000

In Budapest, we were behind the Iron Curtain, but it did not feel like iron. The authorities said we could not distribute the Universal Declaration of Human Rights (UDHR), so Bill Graham and I got the lights thrown, and we tossed copies the UDHR by the thousands into the area for anyone to grab. The concert opened the door to Amnesty to do more work in Hungary and local artist Földes László, lead singer of Hobo Blue Band, received special permission to play despite having been banned in 9 out of 19 counties. Janos Brody, another previously banned artist, also performed. He had a record dedicated to the Universal Declaration of Human Rights in the late 1960s, so his participation was particularly fitting.

Turin, Italy
Promoter: Fran Tomasi
Artist: Claudio Baglioni; Audience: 58,000

By the time the tour hit Turin, the artists and crew were ready for their first day off. This worked out well because the concert there was the last of the season, and the whole city was in party mode. While the others were off relaxing, the rest of the organizers and I were putting out fires. We were still trying to get a show in the Soviet Union, we were increasingly concerned about the demands being made in India, and one of the Japanese concerts had been cancelled. There was no time to rest.

Barcelona, Spain
Promoter: Juan Arzubialde, Promotions DPM
Artist: El Ultimo de la Fila; Audience: 121,000

Barcelona was exceptional for the quality of the music and the size of the audience. 120,000 is a huge stadium, but our artists rallied to greet ticket holders with immense enthusiasm. The Spain section of Amnesty had pleaded for a place in the tour schedule. In a nation recently released from Franco's control, the show was regarded as a celebration and "feast" for human rights. The Barcelona show lasted until four in the morning, and our whole team felt the European leg of

the tour had been a rousing success. The message was getting out, petitions were collected, and the artists were sincerely passionate about the issues. It was at this concert that I first got to know Pino Sagliocco, who in 1990 took me to the top of the stadium in Chile. The song "Biko" by Peter Gabriel, sung by 120,000 people that night, was earth-shattering.

San Jose, Costa Rica
Promoter: Barry Roberts, Bill Graham Presents
Artist: Guadalupe Urbina; Audience: 25,000

Bruce asked me to tell him about some of the issues facing Latin America. His lightning mind quickly got up to speed. He shared passionately with the crowds during his performances.

San Jose, Costa Rico, was played on the back side of a hurricane. We lost $50,000 worth of equipment, but the audience never lost focus. They traveled to the concert from all over Latin America. It was a small region that had lost over 300,000 people to wars and human rights abuses.

On the flight from San Jose to Toronto, Paul Fine of the then-very popular TV show *60 Minutes,* came to the front of the plane and asked if he could speak to Bruce. I told him that while we are in flight it is inappropriate to disturb the artists. It was their only time to relax. I said I was not a policeman, and I would not physically stop him. He decided to go up anyway and spend time with Bruce. When he returned he told me, "You need not worry, Jack. We had a great visit."

That was the last leg for the *60 Minutes* folks. They were off the plane from then on. We had a policy and we obeyed our own rules.

Toronto, Ontario, Canada
Promoter: Arthur Fogel, CPI Concepts
Artist: k.d. Lang; Audience: 16,000

In Toronto I met John Humphrey. He was the United Nations employee responsible for typing up the UDHR and had worked under Eleanor Roosevelt. John was the only critic who could have hurt me if he had been unhappy with the tour. I was worried about his reaction to music, rock, big planes, Reebok, etc. I was afraid he would tell me to get back to the activism that mattered. "This tour," he said, "is the best thing that has ever happened to the UDHR." I left Toronto on a cloud.

Montreal, Quebec, Canada

Promoter: Arthur Fogel, CPI Concepts
Artist: Michel Rivard; Audience: 78,000

A sold out crowd of 78,000 French Canadians joined the movement in Montreal. Singer-songwriter Michel Rivard joined the concert. In 1988 he won two Felix awards, for Concert of the Year and Male Singer of the Year. My staff and I went to visit the Indian tribes right outside of Montreal to get their blessing and gave them a batch of tickets. As a result of this concert, Amnesty chapters started in practically every school in Quebec. The students really organized.

Philadelphia, PA USA

Promoter: Larry Magid, Electric Factory
Artist: Joan Baez; Audience: 102,000

Philadelphia is Bruce's town. All the artists, now joined by Joan Baez, played to a crowd of 102,000. The press conference was massive. Reebok asked to be at the dais, but as grateful as I was for their support, I said no. It was in the contract that sponsors would not be up front. There was talk of withdrawing their support, but I recognized them from the podium and they were fine. We also removed a big Reebok shoe that had been put in the stadium. Philly coverage of the tour was beyond expectation. The crowds and the media came out to support Bruce. It was a hometown party.

Los Angeles, CA USA

Promoter: Brian Murphy, Avalon Attractions
Artist: Joan Baez; Audience: 94,000

Los Angeles's concert ran into some turmoil, because it was on Yom Kippur. Many months before, I had asked Harvey Goldsmith, Bill Graham, and James Radner, who were all familiar with Jewish traditions, whether playing on this date was advisable. "No problem," they had said.

It turned out to be a problem, and we were criticized for holding the concert on a Jewish Holy Day. I called Rabbi Freeling, an old friend, and got his advice. He told us to play as late as possible on that day. We delayed as much as we could, but we lost some of our audience because of Yom Kippur.

Oakland/San Francisco. CA USA

Promoter: Bill Graham, Bill Graham Presents
Artist: Joan Baez; Audience: 50,000

On the flight from Los Angeles to San Francisco, I was informed of a picket line around the hotel we had reserved. I announced the problem to the group. Upon arrival, we set all the musicians on the curb and asked them to wait. I met with the owner of the hotel for an hour trying to work things out. He spent the entire time accusing the union of causing trouble.

So the artists continued to sit on the curb while I found us another place to stay. Most of the people on our bus, Sting and Bono, for example, were not used to sitting around on curbs. It is an understatement to say that I felt pressure to find appropriate rooms. We remained loyal to the union, saying "no thanks" to crossing the picket line. Healeys did not cross picket lines. We stayed in the Hilton.

My insistence that we support the union and not break a picket line did not resonate well with the chair of Amnesty, Franca Sciuto. She felt that my action was outside of the role of Amnesty. I told her she was right. It was in the Universal Declaration of Human Rights (UDHR). We were in the U.S., and I was the Executive Director, and I told the headquarters that this was my decision. In addition, this was on a UDHR tour run by Concerts for Human Rights Foundation, not an Amnesty campaign.

Next I got a telephone call from a representative of the United Farm Workers Union. The man announced that the union would be picketing the concert that evening. I told him that we had changed hotels and were not crossing picket lines. But he wasn't interested in hotels, he was calling about grapes. Apparently, we had non-union grapes in our food arrangements so we were breaking the Cesar Chavez grape boycott. Now, there was another line I would not cross. Cesar Chavez's grape boycott was a human rights issue. I promised the man on the phone that there would be no "scab grapes" at the show.

The morning of the show, I called my regional director Leno Avila. Leno[20] had grown up as a farm worker, had worked with Cesar Chavez, and now lived in Los Angeles. I asked him to find a couple of local kids who could get to the food platters before they made it to the concert. I needed them to steal the grapes—all of them. At the show that night, there were large, gaping holes in the food displays, between the cheese and the celery, but nobody asked any questions, and the picketers did not show up.

Mother Jones interviewed the group and provided great coverage of the HRN tour. But it was a reader's letter to the editor that touched me most.

"The riveting article on Jack Healey, ("Jailhouse Rock," Dec. 1988) is a testimony to a great American whose crusade against human rights abuses has echoed around the world. In this reader's opinion, the following words by Healey are the touchstone in David Beer's searing article. 'On Americans' ignorance of the carnage and repression in El Salvador, Healey laments: 'Sixty thousand people have been killed there and we're still arguing about the damn Vietnam War.'" B.J. Snelgrove, Barrie, Ontario

Tokyo, Japan

Promoter: Seijiro Udo, UDO Artists, Inc.
Artist: Ryudo Gumi; Audience: 42,000

Tokyo, Japan, was almost cancelled, because Japan's leader was on his deathbed. He rallied, and the show went on. The show was a great success, and it was an interesting cultural lesson to watch a revved up rock and roll audience file out quietly as their rows were called over the PA system after the show. *Time* magazine put the tour on the cover.

Peter Gabriel and me at the press conference in Japan.
© Neal Preston.

We had a goal of performing in Moscow, in the center of the Soviet Union, and to do a show that would draw crowds from all over Eastern Europe. We had faith the concert would prove that contact between 20-year-olds in the U.S. and the USSR was possible. The more people we talked to in Moscow, the more aggressively they seemed to keep losing the application, the forms, or the permit.

On the flight from Japan to India, we got word that the Kremlin turned down our request to play in Moscow. Disappointed, Peter Gabriel suggested that we fly the plane over the USSR and have them force down our plane so we could play there. The Kremlin would surely force the plane to land; when we made this unexpected, forced landing, we could just get off the plane and start playing. No need to concern ourselves with such trivial matters as international incidents or jail.

The pilots froze and ran into the cockpit not to be seen again. These people were crazy. But to me, Peter had the real spirit of the tour, and I thought he was channeling Eleanor.

New Delhi, India

Promoters: Arun Muttreja, Amit Chandra, Times of India, Bill Graham Presents
Artist: Shankar & the Epidemics; Audience: 60,000

New Delhi, India, was the best and the worst stop of the tour. It is not easy to get two DC-10s to fly in and out of India in a three day period. The newspaper, *Times* of India, sponsored the concert. They paid all expenses and contributed $50,000 to the tour. In turn, it was agreed that any money made on the event was to go to non-related political nonprofits. Bill and I had warned the leadership of Amnesty not to play India due to a conflict of interest, because the newspaper planned to use it as their birthday bash instead of a human rights event.

When we arrived, the *Times* of India told us that Amnesty could not be at the dais that night. This meant that the chair of Amnesty could not speak at the press conference. The chair called a meeting of the artists and claimed she never gave us instructions to play in India at any cost, and we felt she had. Bill Graham and I were not liars. By this point in the tour nerves were frayed, and this confrontation was deeply wounding to Bill and me. It was too much. It was especially unfair to Bill, who was a volunteer, a great supporter who worked tirelessly day and night, and who was the moral leader of the tour. That bruise took a long time to heal. The vitriolic exchange eroded our support amongst the artists. They were upset and asked me what they should do. "I'm going to the press conference," I said. The artists, Bill, and I fulfilled the contract we had made, even though it ruffled the feathers of the Amnesty chair. We all addressed the human rights issues of Asia and India in particular. Bruce did a great interview saying, "This is not a birthday bash."

Athens, Greece

Promoter: Nikos Sachpasidis,
Half Note Productions
Artist: George Dalaras; Audience: 70,000

The Athens concert sold out in seven days thanks to the outstanding promoter, Nikos Sachpasidis. His father had his feet broken in the military takeover in Greece and later died from those injuries, so this tour was especially important to him.

Future Presidents: Kim Dae Jung of S. Korea, Kim Young Sam of S. Korea, and Ellen Johnson Sirleaf, President of Liberia with Margot Kidder, Paul Simon, and Lou Reed.
Bottom photo by Gary Gershoff.

It was Sting's birthday, so we broke dishes all night. It was a lovely party for a very deserving man. It was especially timely because Sting had advocated strongly to include Greece in the tour. It was a fitting time to celebrate, and we had another million dollars in hard currency.

Harare, Zimbabwe
Promoters: Neil Dunn, Dunn Gould Associates, Andrew Zwe, Avon House
Artists: Ilanga and Oliver Mutukudzi; Audience: 60,000

Africa was a new experience for many of the artists and our working crew. We all flew up to see the great Zambezi River at Lake Victoria in the north, and the sights were amazing.

Ten thousand South African apartheid-era soldiers came to the concert. Our team had also given a large number of tickets to anti-apartheid student movements. Our promoter's new father-in-law handed out those tickets as a favor to his son-in-law. The father-in-law turned out to be General Wall, the man who had led the fight to keep the apartheid system in Rhodesia. I was asked during the press conference about this strange transfer of tickets. All I could say was that Mugabe had given amnesty to all fighters after Rhodesia became Zimbabwe and ended apartheid, so the amnesty must have included General Wall. Phyllis Naidoo, the ANC representative in Zimbabwe, came to the concert and spoke to Springsteen and Sting about how important the concert was to her and the ANC.

During his performance, Bruce knew as he was performing that there were thousands of South African soldiers in the audience. Bruce spoke directly to these young men. "I guess there are a lot of young guys out there tonight who are of conscription age for the South African army. You are being required to support a government that's at war with its own people. I do not envy your position," he said, kindly. "But we're here tonight to celebrate the 40th anniversary of the UDHR. My prayers are with the young men here that you can use your hearts and voices in the struggle for the dignity and freedom of all the African people, because whether it is systematic apartheid in South Africa or economic apartheid in my own country, where we segregate our underclass in ghettoes of all the major cities, there can be no peace without justice and where there is apartheid—systematic or economic—there is no justice. And where there is no justice, there is only WAR!" And then he played Edwin Starr's song of the same name, and the stadium, which had been silent during the speech, sang with him.

Ted Koppel interviewed Thabo Mbeki, the future President of South Africa after Mandela, of the African National Conference on *Nightline* and asked Mbeki if these concerts embarrassed him. His answer was that they were in solidarity with the anti-apartheid movement, and he welcomed them.

Abidjan, Ivory Coast
Promoter: Jules Frutos, S.O.S.
Artists: Johnny Clegg and Savuka; Audience: 50,000

West Africa is Youssou N'Dour country, and he shined with a special glow that night. Earlier in the day, while he was out shopping with other artists, they could hardly move because of the large crowds gathering to see Youssou.

We added Johnny Clegg and Savuka from South Africa to this concert. Their manager made the mistake of asking whether Clegg and Savuka could close the show that night since we were in Africa. I agreed to speak with Bruce, who had no problem with the idea. He was happy to get to bed early. The manager, however, learned a lesson about closing acts. Most people, apparently thinking that the show was over, left the stadium when Bruce left the stage.

Sao Paulo, Brazil
Promoter: Luiz Niemeyer, Mills and Niemeyer Promotions
Artist: Milton Nascimento; Audience: 28,000

The Brazilian concert gave Sting the opportunity to highlight his deep interest in the Brazilian Indians. Brazilian singer/songwriter Milton Nascimento warmed up the crowd with an intensity that was overwhelming.

Peter Gabriel's set, usually the emotional anchor of our tour, was marred when a fan tried to rush the stage during his performance of the song "Biko." The crowd's attention turned to the fan that had to be tackled in that pursuit. This disruption was a big loss for Brazil.

Mendoza, Argentina
Promoters: Carlos Gomez and Daniel Grinbank, Pop and Rock
Artists: Markama, Inti-Illimani, Los Prisioneros; Audience: 60,000

For many of us the highlight of the Human Rights Now! tour was Mendoza, Argentina. Pinochet had refused us permission to play in Santiago, so this was our answer to him.

Shortly after the Conspiracy of Hope tour, Sting asked Mary Daly and I what he could do to further help Amnesty and the human rights movement. We told to do what he does best—write a song. Then we handed him our research on Chile.

Sting wrote "They Dance Alone," which tells the story of the Mothers of the Plaza de Mayo, who for 16 straight years held weekly demonstrations in both Chile and Argentina to keep alive the memory of their husbands and sons who had been disappeared under Argentina's dictatorship. As of this writing, they have been marching for thirty eight years.

The song became an international anthem against Pinochet, the dictator of Chile, just as the song "Biko" by Peter Gabriel came to be the international song against apartheid.

When we landed in Mendoza, dozens of women lined the exit from the airport. The women shouted Sting's name over and over again, to thank him for the song he had written and performed. The women held signs with pictures of their loved ones who had disappeared at the hands of the regime. They wanted us to see the faces of the men they had lost, bodies never returned, cause of death unknown, crimes unclear: more than 3,000 political activists, teachers, and ordinary people.

Chileans poured across the border to see the concert, to disavow the abuses of Pinochet, and to celebrate the election the previous week in Chile in which Pinochet was soundly defeated. More than 60,000 came to that concert from Chile and Argentina. Sting invited the families of the disappeared of both Argentina and Chile to join him on stage as he sang their anthem. Many credited the song for the election victory. The security team, crews, managers, and Amnesty staff lined the stadium, overcome with the beauty of the scene, grateful to witness this healing moment when music met human rights.

Buenos Aires, Argentina

Promoters: Carlos Gomez and Daniel Grinbank
Artists: Leon Gieco and Charly Garcia; Audience: 68,000

The next night in Buenos Aires our performance continued to highlight the brutal excesses of the Argentinian and Chilean regimes.

The Mothers of the Plaza de Mayo began to protest by meeting in town squares every Friday at 5 pm, carrying pictures of their sons and daughters. They would stand for an hour holding those pictures. Slowly, the rest of the world became aware of the mothers in the town squares in Argentina.

Although throughout the tour we had been talking about torture and apartheid and starving children and unjust wars and brutality, we had been somewhat removed from the pain others suffered. In Mendoza and Buenos Aires, seeing the women with those sad pictures made the tragedy of their situation immediate. These two women's groups carried the long fight for human rights in Chile and Argentina.

Sting took the time to meet with every one of the women who wanted to meet him. During the concert, he brought them all up onstage with him. They danced to the song that he had written for them, dedicated to their lost loves.

Impact of Human Rights Now! Tour

Fortunately the challenges we faced during the tour did not have a negative impact on its outcome. The final cost of the tour was $26 million. Reebok had sponsored us for up to $10 million, but since the tour itself raised a total of $23 million we were able to decline the balance of Reebok's offer. It was their seed money that gave us the financial base we needed to get started. The concerts were filmed by Larry Jordan and sold by Phil Kent through the offices of the Creative Artists Agency, netting $2.5 million for Amnesty. There were three airings on HBO, which, along with the live concerts, tripled Amnesty's membership. Amnesty was lifted to a new level as a worldwide charity.

The glory of the tour went to the artists, but also to the roadies who worked on that tour. These unsung heroes, directed by George Travis, Michal Ahern, and the promoters in each of the venues kept the tour on track and the musicians ready. Every artist was on time. We ran a Spartan operation (cheap).

An article in the LA Times by John Voland (LA Times (9/23/88) showed my mood at the time:

> *Though he cited the successes of the tour in promoting human rights causes, Healey was plainly concerned about the toll that the global rock tour—now at the halfway point in its six week schedule—was taking on the staff and crew. "The guys who set up and strike the lighting and sound gear for each show have started calling me 'Mr. 24,' " Healey said with a smile, referring to Article 24 of the Universal Declaration of Human Rights, which calls for "reasonable limitations of work hours."*

Charles Fulwood, the media person who followed Mary Daly, said that after the concert, when Amnesty was exploding, "If you sat next to someone on an airplane and told him that you worked for Amnesty, he would treat you like a damn saint."

Most important to me was that the 40-year-old Universal Declaration of Human Rights finally got a moment in the sun. The real impact of the world tour was that it unleashed the spirit of human rights. New human rights groups sprang up all over the world.

The Final Concert: Istanbul, Turkey

Promoters: Twelve young people of Turkey
Audience: Sold out

Amnesty had not allowed our human rights concerts to perform in the Middle East. There had been no explanation, but Bill Graham and I were deeply disappointed by this inner sanctum decision. For two years after the end of the human rights tour, my secretary Claude Isakov kept getting calls from Istanbul asking when I was coming to Istanbul for the last concert of the HRN Tour.

Finally, I went to Turkey on vacation. I called the number that had been left with Claude and said I would be coming to Istanbul. Since I had been loudly critical of human rights abuses in Turkey, I had some worries about possible arrest, but I figured it would be worth the risk to see the great city of Istanbul.

When we landed, I told my friends that if the agents grabbed me they should go to the other side of the airport and get help. When I got to the customs agent, instead of interrogating me, she smiled and said, "Come with me." She led me into a room filled with journalists and other people. I asked, "What am I doing here?" A woman answered, "We are the last concert on your world tour."

"Where are we playing this concert?" She told me we had a venue opposite the Hilton Hotel. I asked, "Who are we?" The answer was, "Victims of torture, victims of political imprisonment. But we are all citizens of Turkey; there is no difference among us."

That was good enough for me.

I went to the microphones and said exactly that. I raged against human rights abuses here and there and finished an impromptu press conference. I'm not sure how many understood me but I bluffed my way through it. Nine people, all smoking, drove us to a spot in Istanbul where a big poster of the Human Rights Now! tour was splashed across a wall.

I recalled how at the very beginning Bill Graham and I wanted to have at least one concert in the Muslim world. We had suggested Istanbul and a few other places. I remembered the assertion that Turkey was too fundamentalist, despite being the second biggest consumer of rock music in Europe. This was surreal.

I went to the venue on the day of the concert around five, thinking I would take a look, say a prayer and get a feel for the place. As I approached, there were many people outside. I moaned, thinking the gates should be working, letting people in early. I entered the venue to find it already packed. I couldn't believe it. I looked up and saw only big white sheets hanging from each corner of the venue. I had to get out of there, because their hugs were too much and too strong for my little frame. The crowd was ready for rock and roll.

I headed back to the hotel with glee. "We sold out again," I laughed. Of 22 shows only Denver in 1988 was a short sell.

I returned at concert time. I was told that the sheets in the corners were set up to show the videos of the Human Rights Now! tour. This is the connection, the relationship, the bonding. It is an expression of the decency of the Turkey organizing crew. On their own, they somehow felt the need for our Human Rights Now! tour to be more inclusive and corrected the mistake. I could not believe it.

The first band got into gear and let it go. The response was magical. People were weeping and hugging, and the people of Istanbul began a process to rotate the crowd in and out of the venue so everyone could participate. Money was pitched into buckets all around the venue. I spoke through a translator to the crowd. My energy almost carried me through the microphone, I was so moved. After the live bands played, the Human Rights Now! tour bands were played from video. I joined the enthralled Turks, watching the songs of Springsteen, Sting, Peter Gabriel, Youssou N'Dour, and Tracy Chapman, cherishing this final moment of the tour. The artists' spirits filled the venue and were cheered as if they were there. "Biko" by Peter Gabriel stole the night. We celebrated in a disco that night till the sun came up.

On the way to the airport, they bought me a beautiful prayer rug. They asked me, "What do we do with the money?" My answer was that they should give it to the victims of torture. "Just do it as a committee so it is always honest."

That concert is still my favorite of all time, and I had nothing to do with it. It was their dream and their reality. It was December 21, 1990. Two years had passed between the official last concert and the true final concert of the Human Rights Now! tour.

Though neither the U.S. government nor the United Nations ever recognized the accomplishment of this musical tour, the concert in Istanbul spoke to the energy of a universal hope for human rights for all.

I can only hope that, as Matt McGee wrote, "Don't be surprised if a few years from now you find the Universal Declaration of Human Rights printed in your passport. That's Jack Healey's latest project, and what Healey wants—at least when it comes to human rights efforts—he often gets. Or, more accurately, he makes happen."

CHAPTER 14

Amnesty after Human Rights Now!

WHEN THE CONCERTS ENDED, AMNESTY WAS A DIFFERENT place for me. I was constantly asked to appear on television and radio to talk about human rights. There was a renewed interest in human rights. I was asked to talk about U.S. foreign policy, Amnesty's goals for the future, and the conflicts of the day. *Oprah, 60 Minutes,* and the morning shows wanted interviews. I was so busy that I was never in the same city for more than two days at a time, and one university began to run into another, as did conference rooms, and studios.

All this publicity was great for Amnesty. Its name recognition skyrocketed, along with donations and its political clout. Many of my goals had been achieved. However, I was less happy personally with the attention my role at Amnesty generated. I was not comfortable being the center of attention. I was much more comfortable organizing events and letting people like Sting take center stage. The only part I enjoyed in all the frenzy was meeting people and motivating crowds to do more. Random people on planes and trains and in diners would tell me what Amnesty should be doing. Some of them were ill-informed, off base, or totally insane, but there were also people who genuinely cared, who shared great ideas.

The first human rights tours heightened Amnesty's profile in the United States. The second tour had the same effect around the world. Human rights groups were making gains. All of Latin America watched the Conspiracy of Hope live on MTV. The genie was out of the bottle, and the message of Peter Benenson was spreading. This would continue until 9/11.

On my way to the Vienna Human Rights Conference in June 1993, I joined a small youth group called Earth Train. Together we visited Bosnian refugee camps in Croatia. Most refugee camps move in slow motion, and these were no different. One afternoon, I was sitting next to Edin, a Bosnian refugee, watching a soccer game. I nudged him to get into the game. He declined numerous times. I told him I had never played soccer. That astonished him. Finally, I asked him why he would not play, and he answered, "Because the kids and parents I played with in my

village raped and murdered my family." My lame but spoken answer was, "Edin, I hope the day will come when you can run freely on that field."

The Vienna Human Rights Conference was set to redefine the role and nature of human rights work within the United Nations. The American government was present in full force, led by John Shattuck, former vice chair of Amnesty USA. John was a good man, but he did not react strongly enough or quickly enough to the atrocities taking place. Clinton's whole team proved to be weak and ineffective. The massacre of 8,000 Bosnian boys and men and estimated 40,000 rapes of Bosnian women and girls speak to that weakness. Shattock later admitted that the international community and the USA suffered a "failure of imagination" in regards to the war.

The first thing the Chinese government did at the event was to bar the Dali Lama. So Li Lu, one of the leaders in Tiananmen Square, and I led a march and set up to block the doorways in civil disobedience. I went to the Kurds and Kasmirians and requested that they defend me if we got into trouble. They readily agreed. We caught the attention of the press and ended up on the front page of the *New York Times*.

The next day, the conference denied entry to the women of Vukovar, Croatia, whose husbands had been executed by the Serbian militia. Most of the 164 people massacred (163 men and one woman) were hospital patients. Again, we stopped traffic as long as we could. I was thinking what a travesty of a human rights conference it was.

The restructuring of the Human Rights Commission in Geneva had the same result one would expect from such a conference: not much. The United Nations Human Rights Commission was taken over by human rights violators by employing the language but not the intent of most of the human rights advocates who attended the conference. "Your shame must become your glory." These were my words to those who had been abused. "Let your life and the light of the world shine on the injustices of those who would do harm to his fellow man. Where there is truth, the people of the world will rally around that light and your shame will become your glory."

Gay rights were addressed by Amnesty. Historically, Amnesty would "adopt" as a prisoner of conscience anyone who was arrested for *advocating* gay rights but not those who were actively gay. Many at Amnesty, especially in the U.S. and German sections, wanted to enlarge our tepid support for gay rights to support advocacy and activity. Other Amnesty sections viewed this effort as too western or premature for their countries. The gay rights issue came close to getting to the floor for a vote in Brazil at the bi-annual meeting of Amnesty worldwide. However, the elites of the organization quietly tabled the measure until the next

bi-annual meeting to be held in Japan. I thought it was a sly move and knew to watch carefully during the meeting in Japan.

Sure enough, in Japan, when a staffer representing the governing body asked me if we could table the measure again, I was ready. "No, and hell no! It must go to the floor. We will not put this off for another two years. If it does not reach the floor, the U.S. section of Amnesty will resign. If it loses in a vote, so be it, but the members have the right and obligation to vote on it today."

The issue of gay rights deserved open debate. When the initiative reached the floor, it passed unanimously with a big cheer. It was 1990, and we were years ahead of many groups on advocating an important and significant change.

George Herbert Walker Bush (Bush 41) was sworn in as president in 1989. In the first year of his presidency, he supported the military government of El Salvador against a Marxist group called the Farabundo Marti National Liberation Front (FMLN). Like a weak cover of a bad song, the administration supported the government against the Marxist group just as the Reagan administration had done in Nicaragua. And just as in Nicaragua, the government-allied militias attacked clinics, schools, and farms, attacking the FMLN's base of support. The El Salvador government also targeted Catholic priests who preached liberation theology. These courageous priests publicly demanded an end to economic apartheid and supported land redistribution.

The attacks did not deter the U.S. from funding the government of El Salvador. Even the gruesome death of Archbishop Oscar Romero (3/24/80), who was shot while saying Mass, did not slow the flow of money. As the situation for ordinary citizens in El Salvador deteriorated, refugees packed up and began walking thousands of miles north to cross the border. They became undocumented workers and refugees with uncertain futures.

The story had been underreported, both because of pressure from the administration not to look too closely, and because it was difficult to find anyone in the U.S. from El Salvador who was willing to talk to the press for fear of retribution either from U.S. immigration or the government at home. El Salvador became another killing field.

At dawn on November 16, 1989, fifty Salvadoran soldiers surrounded the Pastoral Center at the University of Central America in San Salvador and demanded that the priests come outside and lay on their faces in the courtyard.

Fathers Ignacio Ellacuría, Ignacio Martín-Baró, Segundo Montes, Juan Ramón Moreno, and Amando López were shot as they prayed on the ground. Father Joaquín López, along with the priests' housekeeper, Elba Ramos, and her 16-year-old daughter Celina were shot inside the house.

The soldiers spray-painted slogans on the walls and gate in an effort to incriminate the guerillas. Days earlier, the FMLN had launched a major offensive against the military in San Salvador. Father Ellacuría had tried to negotiate a peace deal involving the ouster of top military officers.

Ted Koppel, of the television show *Nightline,* one of the most influential news outlets in America at the time, called me. He was planning to have the ambassador from El Salvador on his show, and he had some questions he hoped I could answer. I confirmed the report and told Koppel that the Amnesty research department in London had a witness who could verify the connection between the government and the killing spree.

Over the weekend, the *New York Times* broke the story, in which the Salvadoran government denied responsibility and blamed the rebels. Witnesses stated that the Jesuit compound had been surrounded by soldiers in the previous days. Dick Cheney was Bush's Secretary of Defense. He had been instrumental in the decision to support the Salvadoran government, and a when the story broke, Cheney appeared on the Sunday talk shows, saying that there was no way to know who did the killings. ABC asked that I be ready at 6 am Monday to give Amnesty's side of the story. I told them that what Cheney said on the weekend talk shows was not true. The United States and Mr. Cheney knew exactly who was responsible for those murders. America must stop aiding this regime.

And then we published report after report, with irrefutable evidence that government soldiers had committed the murders. The *New York Times* and the *Washington Post* stayed with the story. Slowly, the public began to question and then reject the administration's explanation. And for once, the story and the truth survived. Finally the horrors of Central America were becoming known. Cheney's blatant lies were exposed. During the Reagan and Bush administrations, Central America lost 300,000 lives in conflicts supported by the United States.

Bono continued to stay involved with Amnesty after the 1986 Conspiracy of Hope tour. He flew to El Salvador with some of our Amnesty researchers. He spoke with people who had experienced the civil war firsthand and with members of organizations helping victims. Bono came back and wrote the song "Bullet the Blue Sky" for the *Joshua Tree* album that came out in 1987.

Students at college campuses began to voice concern and to protest the situation in El Salvador. Some young people organized "die-ins" in front of the White House, where they would quite literally play dead outside 1600 Pennsylvania Avenue, demanding an end to U.S. support for the regime.

On December 2, 1980, Sister Dorothy Kazel, laywoman Jean Donovan, and two Maryknoll Sisters, Maura Clarke and Ita Ford, were abducted, raped, and

shot, then buried together in a shallow grave. They had been helping the poor of El Salvador.

Five men, believed to have been ordered by military generals to kill the women, were tried, convicted, and sentenced to thirty years. Two of the five murderers were released early for good behavior. The two generals who are believed to have given the orders retired in 1989 in Florida. The Reagan administration awarded one of these generals the U.S. Legion of Merit, a high honor.

Human rights abuses in El Salvador were given some light by writers Larry and Paul Barber during two episodes of *21 Jump Street* in 1989 and 1990. They highlighted the issue of deportation from the U.S. and disappearance in Central America. U2 and Peter Gabriel donated their music. It was a brave and rare moment for national TV.

In 1990, Saddam Hussein ordered the Iraqi military into neighboring Kuwait, supposedly in response to a dispute over oil production quotas. Amnesty published a report about the invasion of Kuwait. The document, detailing torture and killing of Kuwaiti civilians by Iraqi soldiers, was not particularly unusual. Amnesty published perhaps thirty similar reports about different countries the same year.

President H. W. Bush chose to use this particular Amnesty report for his own purposes. He wrote an opinion piece that was published in 450 college newspapers around the country. Following Elliott Abrams's lead, he cherry-picked facts from the Amnesty report and used it to support the war that his administration was planning to start against Iraq.

The incident that stood out in our report and the one that was used by the President, the Secretary of Defense, and the pundits to obsess about, was the one about the babies. Buried in the long report was a charge that during the invasion of Kuwait, Iraqi soldiers had pulled the plugs on over three hundred incubators in the premature infant ward of a hospital, and that all of the infants had died. The President described this particular action as "Hitlerian."

I wrote a response that was published in the same college newspapers, stating that the administration was twisting human rights information for political purposes.

In the middle of this controversy, the Amnesty report itself came under fire. Middle East experts stated that there was no evidence to support the claim about the babies. They noted that no hospital in Kuwait had 300 incubators.

The House of Representatives asked me to come up to the hill and testify about the findings in the report. I called Ian Martin, Secretary General of Amnesty's International Secretariat, for advice. He spoke to the researchers who had written the story. I asked a researcher from Human Rights Watch, who had done their own research and was among the main critics of our report, to join us on a conference call with the Amnesty researchers who wrote the report.

An hour into the call, the Amnesty researchers were debating loudly, and we were getting nowhere. The call ended with Human Rights Watch unconvinced by Amnesty's research, and our team defending its information. I could only assume the London research team had acted in good faith, and I stood by them. The report was already in the hands of Congress and the White House.

The hearing room was larger than I had expected. All members of the Foreign Affairs Committee were present. After introducing me and the other speakers, the chairman of the committee asked me to read my statement. In front of the congressional committee and the press, I presented the Amnesty International report and said the researchers at Amnesty were very good at their work. I backed the report, never dreaming that they would use one report to justify an unjustifiable war.

Weeks later, I was sitting at my desk drinking coffee. I idly turned on the television and was shocked to see that the United States was in the process of declaring war on Iraq. The vote in Congress was narrow; the Senate passed the declaration 52-47 and the house 250-183. Seven senators who voted for the war cited the story about the infants and the incubators in their remarks.

Months later, after coalition forces had launched their assault to "liberate Kuwait" and had succeeded in driving out Iraqi forces, reinstating the Emir in Kuwait and causing the deaths of hundreds of thousands of Iraqis, we found out that in all of Kuwait there were fewer than 130 incubators. But 500,000 children died of hunger because of the trade embargo the UN imposed on Iraq in the aftermath of the war. Only 130 incubators, and 400,000 Palestinians were expelled from Kuwait as punishment for supporting Hussein. Amnesty's report could not possibly have been true. The damage had been done.

Amnesty had published and then confirmed incorrect information. Amnesty let people down, and damaged its own credibility. Worst of all, our work had been exploited for a terrible cause. I don't know how the researchers in the International Secretariat got the story so wrong. It took a year for Amnesty to issue a public apology, further burning those of us working for Amnesty.

CHAPTER 15

The National Stadium of Death: 1990

TWO YEARS AFTER THE HUMAN RIGHTS NOW! TOUR HAD been denied permission to perform in Chile, we had our chance. The director of the Chilean office of Amnesty, Ramón Farías, asked Amnesty USA and me to help Amnesty Chile stage a two-day concert in Santiago.

Chileans had endured great suffering over the sixteen years of Pinochet rule, and many had worked bravely and tirelessly to win back their democracy. Pinochet's government had suppressed dissidents with violence and death. But in 1990, Pinochet was forced to step down after an electoral defeat that he could not manipulate. The Human Rights Now! tour had celebrated that election in Mendoza, Argentina, two years before, and we were eager to close the circle by bringing music back to the people who had forced Pinochet and his brutal, blood-tinged regime to cede power. Chile had succeeded in doing what so many social movements and leaders claimed was impossible: take out the bad guys without bloodshed. Santiago was truly a city on a hill. It was a huge victory for Chile, Latin America, and the human rights movement around the world.

Sting was my first call. Not only had he helped with the other Amnesty tours, it was his song, "They Dance Alone," that had been so meaningful to the mothers and widows of Chile. I said, "Sting, we have to go and re-baptize that stadium. song was meant to be sung in Santiago, Chile, at the right time and right moment. This is the time and place."

Wynton Marsalis. © Neal Preston

He agreed instantly.

Peter Gabriel, Jackson Browne, and Irish rock star Sinead O'Connor also said yes. Ruben Blades, a Panamanian musician, lawyer, and actor who had joined Sting on the "They Dance Alone" recording, was pleased to be invited and joined the celebration. The young American pop stars, New Kids on the Block, were extremely popular in Chile, so we invited them to play, even though some people feared that they were too lightweight for this kind of show. I thought their youth was on their side, and they proved themselves in the press conference, by giving strong, articulate interviews.

I wanted Wynton Marsalis, the great American jazz trumpet player, to play this show. When I contacted Marsalis's manager Ed Arrendell to ask to play, Arrendell asked, "Why do you want a serious jazz performer, one of the best the world, to play in the middle of a rock n' roll show?"

Good question, I thought, and I had a good reason. "Back in 1973, Secretary of State Henry Kissinger and the Nixon Administration helped Pinochet topple the Allende government, replacing an elected leader with a military man who suppressed democracy in Chile. They know the worst of what Americans can do," I explained.

"What I'd like the Chileans to see at this concert is the best of what America can do for others. Jazz is a truly American genre, created by Americans, primarily in the black community. Wynton is the best jazz player to represent the American people and our decency as a people. Chile saw the indecent America, now they will see the decent America." Ed was convinced, as was Wynton, who joined the concert roster.

The Chile section of Amnesty recruited Inti-Illimani, a Chilean group banned during Pinochet's rule. They were a part of the Nueva Cancion (New Song) movement celebrating indigenous cultures in Latin America and supported the political struggle for indigenous rights and social justice. Inti-Illimani was on tour in Italy during the 1973 coup d'état and they weren't allowed to return to Chile. They had remained in Italy until 1988 and performed in Mendoza,

Press conference for A Hug to a Hope concert in Santiago rocked the stadium in Santiago, Chile, 1990. Photo by Ebet Roberts.

Argentina with the Human Rights Now! tour. Also performing were Luz Casal, Congreso, Los Ronaldos, and Fernando Saunders.

The artists were solid in their commitment to human rights. They learned how to use their celebrity to further the growth of the movement and spread the message. The day after the concerts, Jackson Browne went to a prison where two journalists were held as political prisoners. He managed to help put enough pressure on local authorities that the journalists were released from jail while he was there, and he left with them.

> As Sting remarked in an interview, "I think you'd have to be blind, deaf and dumb not to know that this was more than just an entertainment. I'm not sure what percentage of the people who came to see us will go away with a seed planted inside them. I don't know how long that seed will take. But I believe very strongly that in 10 or 15 years, when these young people who came to our concerts inherit the political and social infrastructures of their respective countries, the seed that's been planted about human rights will come to fruition." [21]

The two-day concert was called: "Desde Chile, un abrazo a la esperanza" (From Chile, A Hug to a Hope). The was buzzing with energy, excitement, and hope. We wanted this to be one of the biggest human rights events South America. We wanted the world to celebrate Chile's bloodless human rights victory.

The venue was the National Stadium of Chile Santiago, the site that epitomized the treacherous years of General Pinochet's military dictatorship. It was used as a massive holding pen in the weeks following the September 11, 1973, military takeover of President Salvador Allende's government.

Thousands of Chileans were imprisoned, interrogated, tortured, and killed in this place. Survivors reported that everyone was sorted according to colored discs. Prisoners who had red discs were certainly going to be executed, while those who had either yellow or black discs stood a small chance of surviving. Prisoners were herded like sheep, sleeping more than 100 men to a cell. The prisoners were packed so tightly that the only way they could sleep was by lying in rows and alternating feet and heads.

Occasionally one of the prisoners would be taken away for interrogation. If they came back at all, they returned to the cell bloody and barely able to speak. The interrogators would beat the prisoners across the head with a wooden bat.

Bruce Springsteen's and U2's production teams added their technical power and ability under the capable hands of film and music producer Allen Kelman and Bob Koch, who organized the technicians to run the two-day concert and handled the administration. Though none spoke Spanish, they worked closely with the local promoter and his team.

Pino Sagliocco, the promoter for the Barcelona concert, secured twenty hours of live television broadcast for all of Latin America, including Mexico and Spain. Arturo Vargas of Uruguay handled the Latin American distribution.

I'd been waiting for this moment for a long time. In 1976, an exiled Chilean diplomat, Orlando Letelier, a former cabinet member in Chilean President Salvador Allende's government, was working at the Institute for Policy Studies, a liberal tank in D.C. On September 21, 1976, he and his American secretary, Ronni Moffit, and her husband, Michael, were driving to work. As they drove past the Chilean embassy, a bomb blew up their car, killing Letelier and Ronni Moffitt. Michael Moffitt survived with injuries. A later investigation implicated Pinochet's government in ordering the killings. Chile's secret police had reached into the U.S. and murdered perceived enemies of their state.

People in Washington were outraged and a large public procession was organized for the day of the funeral. I volunteered to help and was stationed at the actual site of the explosion on Sheridan Circle. As I stood there, I looked up and saw the Chilean embassy and realized that the people in the embassy had probably watched the car explode. I determined to get these people back one day. No one should get away with reaching into the United States to kill like that.

I headed backstage at the stadium to make sure everything was running on time. The backstage was actually below the bleachers and the stage, so it wasn't as secure as the concert venues Amnesty had used in the past. A steady stream of people began to wander into the backstage area, moving from room to room as if they were lost. I could tell they were neither performers nor crewmembers and they worried me. I needed to find the backstage crew to find out what was going on and help me get them out.

"What are all these people doing back here?" I yelled down the hall at three members of the security crew as I made my way toward them. "Get them out of here."

The last thing I wanted was crowds bothering the performers. Many of the musicians had just spent nineteen hours on a plane getting there, the least I could do was guard their privacy and make sure they weren't mobbed by adoring fans.

A few minutes later our attorney, Surita Sandosham, came looking for me. "Jack, you're right—they're not backstage people. But they're not looking for the rock stars either. They're trying to find the rooms where their family members were tortured or killed. They want to see where their loved ones died."

Her words jolted me back to why we were in Chile in the first place—to give this stadium back to the people. I understood that we had to open the underbelly of the stadium where people wanted to be, because that was where their loved ones had been. They wanted to lay flowers and candles as tributes to their loved ones.

"Let in as many people as you can," I said. I decided we could work around any problems this caused. We tightened security to protect the artists and let the people in to find their places of loss and pain. Sixteen years is a long time to wait.

The next problem arose outside the gates. Even though the military no longer ran the government, the carabineros, the national police force run by the military, still managed security at the stadium and armed guards surrounded the fenced stadium, monitoring the gates, halls, and aisles.

"Jack, we need you over here," one of the crew shouted. I followed him to one of the gates where we witnessed thousands of people slamming into each other trying to get in. The carabineros were beating people back, and I saw young men and women injured, some bleeding, and others lying on the ground.

Tear gas suddenly blasted through the gate, and I found myself gasping for air. I shielded my eyes and ran to a place where I could breathe. "What the hell is going on here?" I yelled, though no one was listening. was pure chaos.

This was real trouble, and there would be more to come if it wasn't handled quickly. I ran backstage looking for someone who could help me to those in charge of the operation. Ariel Dorfman, Chilean poet, playwright and human rights activist, was in the middle of a conversation when I interrupted.

"Ariel, I need you to translate for me. Please, come with me," I yelled as I grabbed by the arm. We rushed back to the gate where people were trying to get in to find out why concertgoers were being beaten. The guard told us that thousands of people were trying to get in with counterfeit tickets, and they didn't know

The National Stadium was packed. It was a day of cleansing. © *Neal Preston.*

which tickets were authentic. We walked over to the gate and asked a young man who was trying to get in what was happening.

"They say my ticket is no good," he explained. "We paid for our tickets but the guards won't let us in. Isn't there something you can do? Please help us."

We discovered that someone had sold 15,000 counterfeit tickets to each show. The concert was sold out both days so we didn't have extra seats, but we also couldn't just turn people away. Someone in Chile made a million dollars off these counterfeit tickets and gave me a terrible problem to solve.

Ariel and I asked a guard to take us to their leader to deal with this problem. He said there was nothing he could do and passed us off to the sergeant. I banged on the nearest door. The officer, in his highbrow military-style police hat, opened the door and let us in.

"Tell him to stop his guards from beating the crowds and using tear gas; otherwise I'm going to have to shut this concert down!" I said to Ariel, barely able to contain my rage. "I am not going to be pushed around by these guys."

"Jack, I can't tell him that," Ariel said to me under his breath, turning to avoid facing the officer. "These people are beasts. You know the history of our country."

"Ariel, please tell right now, otherwise I'll find someone else to translate for me or I'll really have to shut this concert down."

Ariel understood that he had to convey my message. We watched the blood slowly rise in the major general's face. It was likely that this was the first time in sixteen years he had had to listen to a citizen, and a gringo at that. The office was stocked with military artillery-grenades, rifles, bazookas, and tear gas canisters. Confronting this guy was a risk, but otherwise we'd have a riot on our hands.

"We have to let as many people with tickets in as possible, because we don't know which ones are counterfeit," I said. He didn't say anything.

After several pleas, threats, and arguments, he agreed to let in as many people as he could. But about 14,000 went home without seeing the concert.

Ariel and I left the office relieved we had worked something out. Fifteen thousand scabbed tickets made someone in Chile a millionaire, but more important, the show would go on.

This particular concert had been a long time in coming. was time to give the stadium back to the people of Chile—to the 35,000 victims of human rights abuses, with 28,000 tortured, 2,279 executed, and 1,248 "disappeared."[22] Music cleansed the stadium.

People who have never lived under state-controlled media have a hard time understanding that a nation held under a military dictatorship doesn't always have the full story about its government and the severity and extent of its abuses. Not

all Chileans knew about the Caravan of Death (Claws of the Puma) that carried an Army squad a Puma helicopter around the countryside and executed opposition leaders and others. After sixteen years of censorship, this concert created an uncensored media event naming the human rights abuses and violence of the past. It also celebrated a new vision for their society as described by artists and activists and watched on television throughout Latin America and the world.

Veronica De Negri, whose son Rodrigo Rojas was set on fire and killed by the Chilean police, had traveled with us during Human Rights Now!, speaking about her experiences as a survivor of torture. We asked her to join us Santiago to introduce the bands as they came on the stage. Veronica, along with Carmen Gloria Quintana, Rodrigo's friend who survived having been set on fire with Rodrigo, and Peter Gabriel, kicked off the live broadcast throughout Latin America.

We had wondered how Wynton Marsalis be received by screaming crowds expecting rock and roll. Our worries were wasted. Wynton and his band took the stage in their cool suits. He started to play his trumpet, and after the first few notes the whole stadium began chanting with the music. I asked people around me for an explanation, but nobody knew what song he was playing. It turned out Wynton was playing a song by Duke Ellington called, "Play the Blues and Go," which sounds very similar to a song Chileans sing at soccer games. Wynton had arrived several days prior to the concert and invited local jazz musicians to jam with him at his hotel. It was during these many jam sessions that he learned their song.

Wynton and his band brought down the house. © Neal Preston.

The Chilean song had become especially popular when they hosted and placed third in the World Cup in 1962. They still sing the song at soccer matches. The crowd went absolutely berserk and they were all singing their victory song, filling the stadium with powerful voices: "We won!"

Marsalis and his band brought the house down. The concert rocked on for hours, and the crowd's youthful energy carried us into the night. The activists were able to tell their stories to the crowd. ear the end, every artist came out on stage to join in singing Bob Marley's rousing classic, "Get Up, Stand Up."

It was time for the closer. Sting took the stage, and the band began playing the first notes of "They Dance Alone," while the Mothers of the Disappeared slowly danced onto the stage with the pictures of their disappeared loved ones on their breasts. There was not a dry eye in the stadium as the thousands of young Chileans remembered and wept for the suffering that the disappeared and their loved ones endured. All the performers came on stage, dancing to "They Dance Alone," together.

As we danced on the stage in the stadium where so many were tortured and killed by Pinochet, I said to myself, "Take that for killing Ronni and Orlando in Sheridan Square."

I woke up early on the second day and drove to the stadium alone. I wanted to get a good look at this place that had been "re-baptized" by the people of Chile and the musicians with their horns, guitars, drums, and voices, who sang of a new

Sting played "They Danced Alone" as the wives and mothers of the disappeared took to the stage. © Neal Preston.

era of human rights, freedom, and justice. I had once again witnessed music as a magical newspaper and a healing force for humanity. The National Stadium is one of the few in the world used after human rights abuses had been perpetrated in it. Usually they tear down these centers of death.

I pulled up just outside the stadium, and as I went to off the radio, John Lennon's song "Imagine" came on. I listened to the song and began to weep.

"Imagine all the people/Living life in peace…You may say I'm a dreamer/But I 'm not the only one. I hope someday you will join us/And the world will live as one."

I was overcome by the reality that I, a scrappy, half blind, dyslexic kid from Pittsburgh had been given the chance to work for human rights with people from all over the world. In the stadium that morning, I felt the significance of the place and the enormity of what had happened. I said a prayer of thanks, grateful I had been able to play a part. My mother and Feryal had urged me to think of the victims first. This time I got it right, because I had listened to their voices.

CHAPTER 16

The Work Continues at Amnesty

Free To Laugh, Wiltern Theatre, L.A., California—March 8, 1992

Jessica Neuwirth and I noticed that a large majority of prisoners of conscience were men. These were the men adopted by Amnesty members, who wrote letters on their behalf. This effort by the grassroots supporters worked over a thousand times a year. As we looked at the data, we could see that there was a bias, but the research department in London told us that any such bias was unintentional.

To help address the gap, I decided to produce a concert to highlight women in human rights. We chose Women's Day, March 8, to stage a show in Los Angeles. Bob Meyerowitz, who had worked on the Human Rights Now! tour, would assist me in getting this done.

We put on a three hour show on Lifetime network, entitled *Free to Laugh,* that was performed live at the Wiltern Theater in Los Angeles. The show was a mix of music and humor, hosted by Tom Arnold and Roseanne Barr Arnold. Halfway through the show, it became clear over an open mike that the couple wanted to do their whole shtick without interruption and then leave. I went on stage to correct this misjudgment on their part. I told the audience, "We're sorry, Tom and Roseanne have to leave now." They left in a huff, but other acts were finally able to get on stage. I received some nasty notes about this later, but it was well worth it. Tom called me a sick liberal.

The comic talent included Richard Lewis, Howie Mandel, and Nora Dunn, and the performers were Vanessa Williams, Woody Harrelson, Jackson Browne, David Crosby, Kathy Sagal, Lily Tomlin, Robin Williams, and Sinbad. The long list of contributing writers was led by Maxine and Sally Lapiduss and Don Foster. Presenters were Anjelica Huston, Marlee Matlin, Daryl Hannah, Susan Sarandon, Andrea Martin, Richard Gere, and Marlo Thomas.

The human rights part of the show featured the stories of women survivors. These women are survivors and activists working to free others: Nomgcobo Beatrice

Sangweni, South Africa; Ninotchka Rosca, Philippines; Veronica De Negri, Chile; and Susanne Riveles, USA. The show was a powerful mix of human rights, music, and humor and was nominated a month later for an ACE award.

Speaking Truth to Power

When William Jefferson Clinton was chosen as the candidate of the Democratic Party, CNN asked me to make some comments. I walked into the room, the producer strapped a mic to my shirt, and the commentator asked me one simple question. "What would you like to see Bill Clinton do for human rights?" I answered that I wanted President Clinton to listen.

I wanted him to listen to the voices of the losers. Those who had been silenced by the international discussions—the American Indians, the Kashmiris, the East Timorese, and the Palestinians, and N'dabelli in Zimbabwe. I said he should bring them together in a big forum and ask them what they wanted their futures to look like, and how the United States could work together with them to achieve that future.

My frankness shocked the folks lingering around the television studio, the producers, the cameraman, sound engineers, and the like. When I walked out of the room they gave me a standing ovation. However, that speech was to earn me much condemnation within the organization. Some felt that I had moved too far from Amnesty's mission. I believe I was speaking for people suffering from a huge number of human rights abuses. A new era in politics might signal new interest.

It was not the first or last time I spoke truth to power and encouraged others to do the same. I have been relentlessly bi-partisan in my criticism of U.S. policies on human rights from Nixon on through to President Obama.

The future of Amnesty as I saw it

Hans Wahl had delivered a paper in 1992 about the future of Amnesty and human rights work in general. The paper was in response to a request from my friend Ian Martin when he completed his excellent term as Secretary General of Amnesty. The presentation was to the governing body of Amnesty (the International Executive Committee). The assembly was held in London and was also a way to introduce the new Secretary General, Pierre Sane, a friend to be. By then the Berlin Wall had fallen, and the Soviet Union had collapsed.

My assessment of the most effective future for Amnesty included a change in the role of Amnesty in the human rights movement. Cameras had become

a swifter messenger than pen and paper. We had to move from Gutenberg to computers. CNN footage exposed areas of abuse before Amnesty could. In the past, Amnesty reports had provided the story to the media. The paradigm had changed, and now the 24-hour news networks told the story first, which allowed for change in Amnesty's role.

Amnesty could focus on in-depth research to expand the narrative. I recommended more regional offices closer to the actual work. Benenson had always wanted Amnesty to move to a place like India. Young people in small non-governmental entities are able to get closer to the issues of the poor and abused and respond more quickly.

Computers allowed far more expansive communication between the field and the home office. Amnesty workers in regional offices could get a better perspective on issues, and were more likely to be trusted by the victims. We could make the human rights movement more accessible and more useful to people. Hans Wahl helped me with that paper, and it went over well, but my ideas were not implemented for quite a while.

Key suggestions for Amnesty

- New Human Rights issues should be pursued: ethnic strife, homophobia, racism, killing, and torture necessitate expansion from the sole focus on prisoners of conscience.

- The dragon slayer has become the dragon—we need to get our fighting posture back.

- Amnesty International needs be on the ground doing human rights work, not behind a desk filing it.

- We need to shift the focus from the sad victim image to one of strength, leadership, and inspiration.

- Amnesty International's watchful eye must strive to cover the entire globe, even if it can't get 100%. The fact that we can be nearly everywhere multiplies our power.

- Amnesty International should be known as the hard-hitting voice of human rights.

- We must always remember how our work helps prisoners or victims of human rights violations and give them credit and support their work through the skills and information Amnesty can provide (training, internationalizing the issue).

- Integrate development of local human rights groups into our strategy. Adopt local human rights organizations as campaign strategy. See to it that our campaigns have a lasting impact on the ground.

- Don't be afraid to build on successes of other human rights organizations that come up with good, innovative ideas (e.g., Peter Gabriel's Video project).

- Empower and unleash Amnesty membership expertise and influence.

- Amnesty needs to enhance the image that it is a tough fighter for human rights on the ground. Our membership wants to take action. One of the unique things about Amnesty is that we have work for members to do. If we give them real human rights work to do, we will bring activists into the movement who know how to make a difference. If we give them marginal work to do, we will get people who are marginally active and influential.

- Co-groups (experts), who are our most astute and sophisticated resource, say they are used as automatons to move papers rather than as participants in an interactive process that uses their expertise and contacts to the limit. This must change so that Amnesty can develop the best human rights strategies possible.

- Computer communications/inter-active capacity: there have got to be more effective methods to involve more people in consultation and decision-making.

- Decentralize the responsibility for actions/initiatives. Make the most of section/regional opportunities to break with policies and practices of the rich over the poor—our traditional human rights work. Give sections responsibility to plan and organize.

Amnesty had historically focused on individual rights specific to the Soviet Union and the third world, for example, the gulags or torture in Africa. We no longer operated in a bipolar world, ruled by an ideological conflict between two superpowers. Amnesty needed to change by advocating for extensive human rights—not just freedom of speech and the freedom to vote. Economic rights belonged in the forefront. People desperately needed food, medicine, and housing. Our narrow focus was turning Amnesty into an instrument of Western hegemony, rather than a neutral human rights organization.

I thought that in addition to economic rights, we should focus on criminal justice, the fight against the death penalty, and the necessity for fair trials. These

were issues in almost every country. We also had to fight the use of torture, but I thought we should try to do so in a more even manner, acknowledging police brutality in the U.S. as well as in jails in Sudan.

Amnesty and the human rights effort needed to improve its emergency responsiveness: when a political prisoner was arrested, an Amnesty team had to be ready to provide support, send a lawyer, or find a local one. If a report of a death penalty case in Texas came up, we wanted to have local contacts ready to provide legal aid as well as to protest the sentence.

It was vital that Amnesty continue to engage young people through art and music and television. I told the crowd that I would not be at the helm of the U.S. section of Amnesty much longer, but this was the future. This prediction was my public recognition that both Amnesty and I were ready for new directions. Ian Martin had retired. I knew I was not far behind him.

In truth, I'd been a part of Amnesty's growth from a small organization that moved quickly to a slow-moving ship I couldn't turn fast enough. We'd been successful to the point of exceeding the size I was comfortable with. I like to grab an idea, jump on a plane, head into a back stage dressing room, and get the job done. I was the eight-minute Bono meeting, not the yearlong board meeting type leader. Neither way is necessarily better. Both speed and caution have value. The LA Times called me irascible. I can't argue with that. But I knew my time was almost up. My style no longer suited the organization I helped to build.

The *LA Times'* "irascible" description was apt, despite a dozen years in seminary and my mother's finest attempts to make me as gentle as she. Or perhaps my wise mother groomed me to be this way, knowing I would need the tough with the gentle. Why else would she send me to handle a legal issue at the age of fourteen to get help for my brother? Why else would she tell me I'd be a man only when I could stand for those who couldn't stand up for themselves? With this personality and a drive to make a big difference quickly, it is not surprising that I offended my share of folks along the way. By the end of the concert tours, Amnesty USA's annual contributions were $21 million, and membership and staff had tripled in size. I was not done with human rights work, but I was about done with coping with a massive board.

Dealing with a board is the most challenging part of working for a nonprofit for me. In the course of twelve years, 140 board members had passed through our offices, and eleven different people had been chair of the board. The majority of the board members and chairs were supportive, open-minded, and eager to applaud new ideas. But I was stepping on leadership's toes with mosquito-like annoyance. I was losing patience with the political games, and I had been in the crosshairs of the

latest board chair a few times.

We had very different styles, and it was clear that we were not going to coexist smoothly. Things had been a little rough between us since we had gone together on an outreach trip to Europe, the West Bank, and Israel. As we were

Fellow Amnesty directors saying goodbye. Boston, 1993.

leaving together after having visited the West Bank, I was stopped at the airport in Tel Aviv. Israelis looked at my passport and began questioning me. "Give us a list of who you've visited," they said. "Tell us where you've been and what you have been doing." Airport authorities typically ask questions when one visits the West Bank. But, I felt it completely reasonable to tell them it was none of their business. Of course, I did not make my plane. The future board chair went on without me, leaving me at the Tel Aviv airport. Perhaps he felt it completely reasonable to let me handle the result of my response myself, but it did not sit well with me to not have that support.

My level of frustration with Amnesty's size and board was not sustainable, and I was ready to move on. No doubt they were ready for a little peace and quiet as well. I suggested a two-year contract instead of the standard four-year term to provide sufficient time for a smooth transition. I was offered a one-year contract instead. I rejected their offer. I signed a six month non-compete clause and an agreement not to speak about the exit terms for two years. This agreement was made ostensibly to avoid questions amongst the membership and media, but it had the opposite effect. Rumors of all sorts spread as people speculated at such a sudden change in leadership. Thankfully, three directors (Philippines, Australia, and Ireland) with the support of the full International Executive Committee (Amnesty's worldwide governing body) put an end to all such rumors by breaking the silence and saying some incredibly kind words to the membership about my role at Amnesty at the bi-annual international meeting in Boston:

> *"...In the time since you became Executive Director, the U.S. section has grown from about 35,000 members to over 400,000, and the section's income has increased from $2 million to $21 million annually. That increased income has resulted in millions of additional pounds being available through the*

international assessment. It has meant our movement has been able to undertake new areas of activity, increase the number of countries we research, and strengthen its campaigning capacity. Today the U.S. section contributes about 1/3 of the international budget, and the translation of that extra money into action is the realization of your dream of a more effective worldwide campaigning movement.

In his remarks at the start of this Council, Curt remarked on what it was like to be part of the U.S. Section in this international movement, describing it as being somewhat like an elephant trying to do ballet. Yet on the HRN! stage in Buenos Aires you showed us you were prepared to turn somersaults for this movement. However, too rarely have we let you know how much we have appreciated your commitment to human rights and AI work worldwide.

In your time as Executive Director, you have challenged this movement to face new developments and to widen our horizons. The rock tours were the most obvious of these to us internationally. Through them, millions of people became aware of human rights and AI's work. Recently, Pierre Sane mentioned that it was the HRN! tour which lead to him joining AI. We never imagined the rock tour would recruit our next SG. Maybe the IS personnel office will have to modify its recruitment process to incorporate music. Yet there are a great many other movement initiatives with which you have been associated which may not be widely appreciated.

From your recognition that with more supporters we will be able to campaign harder and better, and an appreciation that the future of the human rights movement lies with youth, you led your section into that sector of the community. I am sure others like me have met with young people here in Boston in the last week and cannot but be inspired by their support for AI's work.

The move to more direct and more diverse actions are innovations that have inspired many of the discussions which have culminated in our consideration of SYSTEC over the past few days. On behalf of your colleagues of the movement-wide staff I want to publicly share some things with you.

Last night someone described the developing network of senior staff throughout this movement as "a bracelet of precious stones," and we feel we've lost one of the gems.

Over the past 7 years there has been greater contact between the senior staff of the movement, and you have been a driving force behind that development. Your efforts have fostered a spirit of collegiality amongst a group of key people in this movement, particular the Section and IS Directors, people who have often felt alone and vulnerable through their unique position in their respective parts of the movement. You pleaded for a fair deal for all AI staff.

You have sought to have this movement address the difficulties of board- staff relations. In addressing this ICM about the challenges facing this movement, Ross Daniels identified board-staff relations, and this ICM has finally acknowledged that this is an issue which must be addressed. We cannot afford to continue to lose

valuable staff and board members as has happened over recent years, and at long last something will be done to stop this bleeding.

As a friend and colleague you have shared with us your energy, creativity, and enthusiasm for new ways to make this a better world.

While many of us derived our understanding of this movement from the decisions of bodies such as the AGM and the practice current at the time, you also went back to "the source." You were able to convey to us the inspiration of Peter Benenson and Sean MacBride, people with whom you have spent much time, and who were instrumental in establishing our movement.

Jack, in conversations we've had, you have often remarked that whatever our position in AI we are only what our movement wants us to be. Your colleagues want you to be part of the much needed struggle for human rights.

There are still too many injustices in the world for us to not heed your words in the final plenary in Yokohama, so let me repeat them to you, Jack: "LET'S GO."
— *Harris van Beek, Director Australian section.*

Final Address to the IEC

Following this and a few other tributes, the International Executive Committee gave me the privilege of addressing the meeting. Three other directors introduced me to the audience (Australia, Ireland, and Philippines). It was quite an honor for me. I prepared for the talk by reading the speeches of Chief Joseph of the Nez Perce Indian nation in Oregon, who had fought the U.S. military from Oregon to Yellowstone and up to Montana and then into Canada with 300 men, women, and children. (Chief Joseph was trying to join Sitting Bull in Canada, who had defeated General Custer at Little Big Horn River.) I quoted Chief Joseph quite extensively to remind the audience that we were on Indian land.

Final farewell to Amnesty in response to my speech. Boston Amnesty international conference in 1993. Photographer unknown.

Leaving Amnesty was not easy. Like an amicable divorce, there was peace and pain simultaneously. Though I was ready to head in new directions, I was going to miss these folks. Amnesty had been very good to me. The board had allowed me to try every crazy idea I had and supported our efforts to advance the human rights movement.

I tried to inspire the movement in its future important work. Something good must have happened during our years, because I got a standing ovation for an embarrassing amount of time. I thanked the International Executive Committee for giving me such a nice goodbye. It was truly a healing moment.

CHAPTER 17

Human Rights Action Center: 1994–Present

THERE IS A TERRIBLE EMOTIONAL COST ASSOCIATED WITH major life changes, and I was facing another one with my departure from Amnesty. At every break of my life, I had to remake myself: leaving the priesthood, working with teenagers to end hunger, working with the Peace Corps in apartheid South Africa. This change was the toughest. I fought anger, self-doubt, and hurt.

I was fifty-five and had almost no savings. When I started at Amnesty it was unimaginable to make big bucks at a nonprofit that speaks for the oppressed. So, while my replacement started at well over a hundred thousand, I had taken a $20,000 salary cut from my Peace Corps job to start at Amnesty at $34,000, and my salary advanced slowly over the years. Though I got a small severance that was soon to dry out, I had this feeling that I had just stepped off a roller coaster, and the room never quite stopped spinning. The transition from working 70-hour weeks to having to build my own life was disorienting, to say the least.

I started yoga and made it one of my best friends. Pulling and pulling at my back muscles, I could feel my fingers reaching closer and closer. Finally, after about three weeks, I could feel the tips of my longest finger brushing up against my big toe. This gave me an odd sense of accomplishment. The next day I booked a plane ticket to California.

In San Francisco a friend was producing a fundraising concert like none that I had ever seen before, and he asked me to join him backstage for the show. Political hip-hop duo, The Disposable Heroes of Hiphoprisy, which consisted of an artist named Michael Franti and another named Rono Tse, opened the show with ravaging beats that had the audience bopping their heads. They were followed by The Breeders, which was fronted by Kim Deal, formerly of the Pixies. A quintessential '90s act, they captured the audience with their hit "Cannonball." Then the all-female grunge band, L7, followed with thrashing guitar riffs and upbeat and screaming lyrics.

Three working class white boys from Washington State had put the show together. Named Kurt, Krist, and Dave, their incredible breakthrough album Nevermind had knocked Michael Jackson off the top of the charts and ushered in a whole new era of rock. Overnight, Kurt Cobain went from sleeping under a bridge to one of the most recognizable faces in entertainment.

Nirvana was a stage presence like no other. Instead of the neatly toned bodies that I was used to seeing lead singers sport, Kurt Cobain appeared about 5'8" and 150 pounds. Not to mention, he played every note like he was barely hanging-on to the rhythm, power cords with heavy distortion and the reverb turned all the way up, and with a raspy voice, making the music hard to ignore. And as to the production, the light show of flashing shapes that felt like the Velvet Underground gone punk made it impossible for me to keep my eyes on anything but the stage.

I could feel the energy filling my body again. This was a great concert for a great cause. The child of Croatian immigrants, Krist Novoselic had become concerned about the war in the former Yugoslavia and had recently returned from a trip around Bosnia-Herzegovina, where he saw the impact of the war first-hand. The show raised money for the Tresnjevka Women's Group, which was working with the victims of the rape in Bosnia. During that war a policy of mass rape was orchestrated by the Serbian military in Bosnia. They were backed by the Serbian government under Milosevic against most of the population in Bosnia, as well as the Croats.

Feryal Gharahi at the Adriatic Sea on a mission to rebuild a factory for multi-ethnic citizens.

The conflict was one of competing ethno-national identities and outright anti-Muslim attempts at ethnic domination. Ethnic Serbian armies expelled the mostly Muslim Bosnians and Catholic Croatians from towns that they were trying to establish as fully Serbian. Though living in Bosnia, these Serbs were backed by Slobodan Milosevic in the neighboring country of Serbia. For Nirvana, this conflict was both personal and political.

For a brief moment, I was able to chat with the artists about the goals of the concert, and they had humbleness about them, combined with anti-corporate politics that were new to me. They were concerned about the

way that their concert would portray its victims. Krist noted that the media made Croatia look like it was one giant starving child, and he did not want any part in that. He also understood that there were people attending the concert who would not necessarily be interested in the actual crisis going on in Croatia, but that there would be literature in the back for those who wanted it. Kurt seconded Krist's concern that they not pretend they were doing much more than they were.

"This is not some corporate rock, 'we make you feel like a hero for having donated a couple bucks to a cause' kind of thing," he said.

Though I thought they were underestimating their own power, I was extremely impressed by their sincerity. It gave me a lot of hope. It also helped me snap out of my own quiescent state.

I was beginning to imagine what it would be like to build a new organization for human rights. I have talked all my life about "What One Person Can Do." I wanted to return to that truth. I wanted to create a one-person organization that could be as effective as a medium-sized human rights group with a lot less money. New technology made this possible. I didn't want meetings. I wanted simplicity and its power. I also wanted to take advantage of the 24-hour news cycle, the internet, and social media, all which were brand new.

On that same trip, I went to visit Joe Strummer, a rock star whose presence I had been seeking for years. By the time I arrived at the pool hall, working class hero Joe Strummer, lean, with his hair in an Elvis puff, had already finished one bottle of wine. In the 1980s The Clash had been dubbed "the only band that matters" because of their willingness to take on tough political issues in that otherwise stagnant time. While I fumbled around, missing shots, and sinking the eight ball, Joe was in the pocket with every shot. As we played, we chatted.

"I know this place is a far cry from London."

"Well, it's a far cry from Pittsburgh as well."

"The world is changing. The Labor Party in England is not what it once was and neither are the Democrats in America. Ever since Thatcher and Reagan broke the unions, both parties have increasingly had to look towards the banks for funding. The poor are increasingly left out of the conversation, even on the left. It's all about privatizing this, closing that public park, making way for the mall. We live in increasingly myopic times."

"Yeah, Joe. It's depressing, but there's hope, too. Mandela is out. White minority rule has ended in all of southern Africa."

"Sure, sure, but my concern is about the poor. In South Africa, what type of victory will it be if the white elite is just replaced with a black elite? In England, working class kids like me could never make it today the way I was able to."

"You know the Universal Declaration of Human Rights guarantees everyone the right to health care and education. It also guarantees people freedom from the want of hunger."

"Is that a fact? So, is that what you plan to be working on, promoting that document?"

"Yeah, Joe, among other things."

"Well, then let's do something that will get the word out about the Universal Declaration of Human Rights. How about a *Punks For Human Rights* album? I can wrestle up all the young punks who love the Clash and get them to donate songs. All the money we make from the album can be donated to your new organization."

And that was a contract. We would get to work on the album soon. My excitement was growing and growing. Jason Rothberg, a smart and dedicated producer, made it happen.

I was at an opening for a new law firm opening offices in Los Angeles. I wasn't sure why I was there, but after a few minutes a tall, smart looking guy walked up to me.

"Are you Jack Healey?"

"Yup."

"I want to be your lawyer."

"Okay," I said. He introduced himself as Matt Burrows, and he has been my attorney ever since. Matt has become one of my closest friends and a trusted advisor on strategy and legal issues for Human Rights Action Center.

It was settled then. I had a lawyer, a financial backer, and a musician who returned phone calls. Now all I had to do was get to work.

Matt Burrows and Robin Hurley, architects of the album "For the Lady," at the Aung San Suu Kyi dinner. Matt Burrows offered his legal services to the work and has become one of my most trusted advisors. © ABImages.

I named the new organization Human Rights Action Center (HRAC) and it has defined my work since 1993. I determined to keep HRAC small enough to respond quickly. I wanted to be an advocate for places I had been and people that I knew. I did not want to be isolated from the actual work on the ground as I had often been at Amnesty.

Bosnia, 1994

Bosnia became our first focus. In December 1994, I had a conversation with my Amnesty coworker Feryal Gharahi about the unfolding genocide in Bosnia, particularly the targeting of women by Bosnian Serbs. I had seen reports of rape camps operated by the Serbs, and I suggested that she travel to Bosnia on a fact-finding mission. A few months prior to our talk, Feryal had been approached by a former colleague at Amnesty, Jessica Neuwirth, to start an organization for global women's rights. They had formed Equality Now, an organization that continues to address the violation of rights of girls and women around the world.

Feryal Gharahi with Bosnian refugees, 1993.

Feryal Gharahi with Bosnian Prime Minister Haris Silajdzic at the dedication of the factory.

Feryal's trip, arranged with help from The United Nations, allowed her to collect information. She spent two weeks in Croatia and Bosnia interviewing hundreds of people, mostly Bosnian refugees who had fled their homes. She returned with a harrowing account of what was happening in Bosnia: an asymmetrical war of aggression and ethnic cleansing waged by the well-armed Serbs against a Muslim civilian population that was under an arms embargo imposed on it by the West.

She was asked to testify to Congress with two Bosnian women who were rape victims. The congressmen at the hearing were sympathetic but reluctant to

A visit with Bosnian refugees during the war, 1993.

intervene. I suggested that Feryal go to the media to publicize the plight of women in Bosnia, hoping it would generate a public outcry for a policy change.

In 1994 the United Nations formed a Commission of Experts and charged it with investigating war crimes and crimes against humanity in the former Yugoslavia. The Commission hired twelve international lawyers, one of whom was Feryal. The team of lawyers was dispatched to Bosnia and Croatia for a month to probe the charges. Their findings formed the basis for establishing the War Crimes Tribunal in The Hague that has successfully prosecuted Slobodan Milosevic (the former president of Serbia), Radovan Karadich (the president of Bosnian Serbs), and many others for crimes against humanity and war crimes.

Feryal was deeply affected by the events in Bosnia and wanted to do something tangible that would have a positive impact on the daily lives of the people there. So Feryal went back to see what we could do. She came across a destroyed garment factory that had been a major source of employment in the town of Fojnica outside the capital of Sarajevo. She met with the former director of the factory, who was a Bosnian Serb married to a Bosnian Muslim. They discussed what was needed to rebuild the factory and provide much-needed jobs.

The major problem was financing. After months of searching, Feryal found a group of American bankers in Sarajevo who were looking at different development projects. Feryal met with the head of the banking group, David Proctor. David is a tall, elegant man blessed with unusual intelligence and kindness. He agreed to finance the rebuilding of the factory. Feryal hastily arranged a meeting between Nenad, the former director of the factory, and several of his colleagues and David Proctor to discuss the details of the financing.

Agreements were reached to reconstruct the factory. Nenad agreed that the work force would be multiethnic. Serbs, Croats, and Muslims would all be hired, and war widows would be given first priority.

In 1997 Feryal received a call from Nenad inviting her to the formal opening of the rebuilt factory. It was fully operational and producing sports gear. Since this was an economic success for that region, Prime Minister Haris Silajdžić

attended the ceremony and cut the ribbon. Feryal was also asked to serve as an election supervisor for Bosnia.

Belfast, Northern Ireland—November 9, 1993

Ireland has always been magical for me. Sean MacBride and U2 had become my friends while I was at Amnesty. I once attended a Van Morrison concert with Bono in Dublin. I was hearing Van's powerful voice in one ear while Bono's voice was in my other as he sang along. Two great Irish voices at once. It was a lovely moment in my life.

I saw U2 perform in Dublin at an indoor arena as well. My people are originally from Mayo County in western Ireland. Whenever I could, I would go through Shannon Airport in the south of Ireland and drive around the west of Ireland for days.

But Northern Ireland had been a troubled region for 700 years. Tensions were high between the Catholic Irish that wanted to be rid of British rule and Irish Protestants who relied on the British for protection. Rita Mullan, a neighbor of mine in Washington, D.C., helped me understand the difficulties of working in Ireland. Her mom had been killed by British troops, but Rita had remained committed to nonviolence. She knew who the players were in the battle zone.

I was asked to observe a trial in Belfast, Northern Ireland. The case involved the execution of Fergal Caraher and the wounding of his brother, Michael Caraher, by British soldiers. I flew to Manchester, England, and then took a short flight to Belfast. The customs people in Manchester questioned me endlessly until I finally told the custom officer, "I am done now with this."

Later, on the plane, I understood their concern, because Ian Paisley, the firebrand of the Protestants, was on the flight as well. The hostesses treated him like a rock star. My taxi ride took me by the site of an IRA hit on a meat store where a number of people had died. I then asked the Belfast taxi driver to take me by some spots hit by the Protestants. He passed on that.

The trial was for two British soldiers from the unit 45 Commando, Callahan and Elkington, who had fired over twenty armor-piercing shells into Fergal's car, killing him and wounding his brother. The spent shells were later collected and hidden, so there was no evidence of who did the shooting. The Caraher family believed that the soldiers had passed the boys through a checkpoint and later that night open fired on them as they left a nearby pub. I asked the father what he thought and what I might do to help. His answer was: "We will not get justice in this court."

IRA prisoners were typically brought to court in chains and with head coverings. The British soldiers on trial came in wearing uniforms and were able to walk around and speak to people.

There was another American in court. I never got his name, because he wanted to keep his distance in order to be totally independent. But unknown to him, his "independent guide" for the next two days was actually close to the IRA. The British soldiers were acquitted of killing Fergal and wounding Michael.

The Carahers looked like my family. Very Irish, red faced, some big and some small. I was moved by the family. I asked Mr. Caraher if I could visit his farm. I asked questions about their lives. One part that struck me hard was that British soldiers would descend quite often on the Caraher farm and knock on the door. If the door wasn't opened quickly enough, they would break into the home, harass the children, and accuse them of being IRA members.

This kind of activity was constant, Mr. Caraher told me. I suggested we try to stop that activity or at least give them a little respite from the aggravation. I wanted to figure out how to stop this invasive practice.

When I returned to the U.S., I really wanted to do something for that family. I thought that we could print large signs for both the front and back doors that would say something like "if you enter this home, you will be filmed, recorded, and a fax will be sent to ten American families telling them you are in our homes unlawfully."

Each of ten American families contributed $100, with which we bought a fax, a camera, and a small tape recorder—the equipment needed to carry out this attempt at non-violent protection. Word spread, and many families liked the idea. Before we tried to implement the "Families for Families" campaign, successful peace negotiations began. Finally, after 700 years, the troubles came to a rest. Although the "Families for Families" campaign was never implemented, I think it was worth the exercise of finding a method for outsiders to help when a society is under severe pressure.

Much later, the wounded Michael Caraher was arrested and convicted of possessing arms and belonging to the IRA. He was later released as part of the peace agreement.

St Patrick's Day, March 20, 2000

Years later I wrote an op-ed that ran in the *Washington Post* and reran in the *Herald Tribune* calling on the Irish Diaspora (mainly in Irish bars) to stop funding the IRA. The peace process needed a boost. We American Irish had to stop giving them money so that the IRA would be more motivated to seek peace in Northern

Ireland. Many in the Irish community did not like this call for stopping the cash flow, and they let me know how they felt. So I felt grand when an invitation came to attend the White House Saint Patrick's Day celebration at the urging of the British government.

All was smooth as I joined the line to meet President and Mrs. Clinton. I went to shake the President's hand, and he turned quickly and did not allow a picture to be taken. Eventually, as happens after White House events, I received a picture in the mail, but mine was with Hillary Clinton. I guess he remembered that during his presidential campaign I told his fundraisers, Miles Rubin and Smith Bagley, that I would not reach out to Bruce Springsteen for the Clinton camp because Clinton supported the death penalty. Shortly after they had asked for help, Clinton pointedly left the campaign trail to return to Arkansas to permit the execution of Ricky Ray Rector, one of the four executions performed during Clinton's tenure as governor. As President, Clinton pardoned only one death row inmate.[23]

While I strongly opposed Clinton's death penalty stance, his work with Prime Ministers Bertie Ahern of Ireland and Tony Blair of Britain got the peace process to work in Northern Ireland, and this became a large part of Clinton's legacy.

Joe Strummer's Nobel to me, 1997

I find it hard to write about Joe Strummer. His music was unique, challenging, and powerful. In person, he was simply a grand friend with whom one would cry from laughter. I first met Joe at Moira Sher's home, where I had stayed for over thirty years when work took me to LA. His former father-in-law, Tom Salter, would come by and we would spend long, strange nights filled with fun and banter. Shooting pool at Tom Salter's Hollywood Athletic Club was an experience in cheating, laughing, bumping, yelling, and friendship. Joe was so decent and caring. He missed feeling important in music, but he wasn't driven by fame. Meals with Joe were a true experience in existential life. They were a mixture of laughter and wine and talking to everyone in the restaurant.

Joe Strummer, lead singer of Clash. My first celebrity endorsement and support at Human Rights Action Center, 1994.

When Joe rehearsed, he liked to be surrounded by the flags of many nations. For me, studio work is more yawningly called "over and over." But when Joe worked on the song "Generations," Jason Rothberg, a young and very talented producer, and I listened for hours. At the end of the final cut in a long recording session, I heard his voice singing ever so softly and ever so kindly the words "Jack Healey." Joe had ended "Generations" by adding my name. I have always treasured this moment as my *Nobel.*

We produced a video to go along with the song. Filming included a pregnant woman lying on the back of a station wagon shooting video while Joe and I drove a Presley-type Cadillac along Mulholland Drive in the hills above LA. I told Joe that if we included the words of the Universal Declaration of Human Rights on the video, MTV would never run it. "Okay," he said, "let's include the same words in Chinese and MTV will never know it, but one fifth of the world will understand." I loved this plan and we did it.

Joe used the song "Generations" on the album *Generations: A Punk Look at Human Rights,* produced by Jason Rothberg and Miles Copeland, Sting's manager at the time. Green Day, Bad Brains, Pennywise, BUGS, Jelly Beans, DFL, Electric Doghouse, Good Riddance, Lagwagon, Pansy Division, Swamp Dogg, Red Ants, and the Vandals all donated their music. An artist created what can only be described as punk portrait of Eleanor Roosevelt, with lines from the UDHR printed underneath. The album came out in 1997 to great reviews. I was thrilled.

Joe was truly a friend. One day he returned home from a peaceful walk, laid down, and died. After his funeral, the local firemen drove his body around London to the pubs where he had played his music. He deserved an easy passing. It was just not that easy for the rest of us. I still miss him and his raw and vital spirit and his cheating at cards and pool.

The Anthem, 1997

Two young filmmakers, Shainee Gabel and Kristin Hahn, asked if they could interview me for a documentary and book they were producing, asking if the American Dream was still alive at the end of the 20th century. Their book and film, *The Anthem,* included interviews with some of my old buddies, including Studs Terkel, the great American historian and theoretician, and Hunter S. Thompson, the gonzo journalist with whom I spent surreal time during visits to his Colorado ranch. The filmmakers and I walked two blocks from my house and set up my folding chair on the steps of the Supreme Court. It seemed the most appropriate backdrop to discuss the state of the American Dream. Ironically we were chased away and had to find another spot at which to complete the shoot.

South Korea—May 21, 2003

Korea is not a country that Americans think about much. But Amnesty could not ignore the situation in South Korea in the 1980s. The country was under military rule.

Lee Shin Boom, a former prisoner of conscience, made it out of South Korea to the U.S. on April 12, 1984. Shin Boom was young, smart, and working to help South Korea to reach higher ground on human rights. He had spent time in jail fighting for human rights in South Korea; he had proven his mettle. Lee gave my staff and many of our Amnesty meetings a little understanding of South Korean human rights abuses. He was one of the prisoners of conscience we highlighted the day of the MTV show on national TV.

I guess for this reason we were visited later on by Kim Dae Jung and Kim Young Sam, both of whom went on to became Presidents of South Korea. Dae Jung was a natural human rights leader, having been tortured and jailed and stolen out of Japan; Kim Young Sam was more of a business kind of guy. Kim Dae Jung was nearly elected as head of the South Korean parliament in 1971. He lost because of restrictions placed on his candidacy by the ruling party. He was ultimately placed under house arrest for publishing an anti-government manifesto. Amnesty had adopted him as a prisoner of conscience in the '70s. When Kim was released in 1980, he came to New York and asked for our help in returning democracy to South Korea. Kim spoke at Amnesty conferences and any other events he could about South Korea.

Protests against the military government were suppressed and dispelled with tear gas and water cannons. In 1987, the South Korean government tortured a student to death, and the country rose up against the coup's leaders. Kim Dae Jung returned to Korea to help reestablish democracy. I spoke at his going away events in New York City and Los Angeles. He was elected President in 1997 and served from 1998-2003; he won the Nobel Peace Prize for his efforts to make peace with

Feryal Gharahi with Woo Yong Gak, a prisoner of conscience who spent 41 years in jail in S. Korea, 1994.

North Korea. He thanked us publicly for our help in supporting the people of South Korea.

Years later, Human Rights Action Center (HRAC) sent Feryal Gharahi to South Korea to interview Woo Yong Gak, the longest serving prisoner of conscience in the world as he was being released. Initially they were not going to let her in because she did not have proper credentials as a journalist. Lee Shin Boom, by then a press officer for President Kim Young Sam, heard the noise and straightened it out by telling them to let Feryal in. "Jack Healey did more for South Korea than any other American," he said. We were both grateful for the kind remark, and she was able to meet Woo Yong Gak, released after forty-one years.

CHAPTER 18

Groundwork: October 14–22, 2001

B OB PATTERSON, A LOCAL EMPLOYEE OF THE FOOD Agriculture Organization (FAO), asked me if I would do some work to raise money for small agriculture projects presented directly by farmers around the world. I told him that I had directed Freedom from Hunger Foundation from 1968-1973, which was an arm of the FAO. It took me awhile to be convinced, but I agreed to do a concert.

Here's what the *LA Times* had to say about the event:

> *SEATTLE—He's dumped the T-shirt and put on a good sport coat for this, a tie, for God's sake, good shoes. But his gray hair is still splaying out of his ponytail. He's still urgent, still mad. It's like they say: You can take the man out of the street, but you can't take the street out of the man. Jack Healey isn't about to let the world forget its shortcomings.*
>
> *"Do we know what the hell we're doing? What we're about?" he asks, and when no one raises a hand, he goes on. "I'd like to think that in the last century, governments didn't do very well, and we the citizens, the average, the poor, the wounded, the confused, we are [now] going to make it work the way it never did before ... a citizen boom that would reach out to the whole world. My God! Wouldn't that be a moment? An earthquake. An earthquake of decency, a century of such uncommon decency that we can all look each other in the eye with equality, and justice—and something to eat."*
>
> *Healey is back...the man who spearheaded the unprecedented Amnesty International pop-rock tours in the 1980s has put together a concert series again, this one on behalf of the U.N. FAO's Groundwork 2001 anti-hunger campaign... (All)for a cause (world hunger) that has absolutely nothing to do with global terrorism. Or at least, FAO liaison officer Bob Patterson says, not until you think about it.*

Usually producing concerts entails a search for money and talent. In this case, we had money. The bubble had broken open in the tech world, and Adobe was

interested in supporting the concert to fight world hunger. After a rather short meeting with Adobe's staff, we were guaranteed the money to do what we wanted. Adobe generously gave us offices, phones, and financial support, and they were great supporters on many levels.

Our first hire was Melanie Ciccone, to be our talent recruiter. She brought her sister Madonna in as the chair of the event we called *Groundwork,* and Madonna made a generous contribution. We chose Seattle as the concert site. I suggested a five-day music festival, because I thought an idea like the "right to food as a basic human right," would take a while for the public to get.

Groundwork concert. Director General of FAO, Jacques Diouf, thanks me and my team for five days of music in Seattle to fight world hunger. Photo by Fred Clarke.

Seattle reminded me of Pittsburgh when it was a thriving steel town, before the bust occurred and rust settled into the factories. Seattle was in the midst of a big boom, and it gave me an eerie feeling. I wondered how long the bubble would last. Seattle's lack of mixed communities reminded me of days past as well.

Three local Seattleites helped me with the daily chores. Susan Silver managed most of the talent to come out of that area. The Westside Café owner prepared meals of all sorts for the long nights, and the Spoonman became the face of the concerts with the help of Bob Peterson. We shot a public service announcement of him and ran them when and where we could. The Spoonman turned out to be a walking, talking guru of human rights. We gave him the stage of TV, music, and concert presentation. He did it justice.

Since Melanie handled the recruiting so well, my only contribution was to get Joe Strummer to play. Joe was home when I called. He yelled out to his wife, Lucinda, "Jack is on the phone. Come listen to him and find out where and when he needs me."

Melanie and I met with the Starbucks people to discuss producing an album also called *Groundwork.* Seattle-based Starbucks was excited to help in the cause of fighting world hunger. They offered two options: $500,000 for an album up front or a percent of the sales on the back end. We took the half million dollars and

Melanie produced *Groundwork,* which sold in their stores for a number of months.

Dave Matthews and Nancy and Ann Wilson of Heart came to the press kick-off for the concerts. They were solemn and serious and spoke of their children. Dave and I got to speak privately about our love of southern Africa. A large class of Seattle students was at the press event, and their teacher came up afterwards and asked Dave to come down and speak with the children. In a few minutes Dave came back and said, "They want to speak to the old guy." Months later, Dave called and donated to my work.

The talent list was extremely strong due to Melanie's hard work. The first night's performance was at the 3800-seat Paramount Theater and featured Dave Matthews, the Blind Boys of Alabama, Emmylou Harris, and Daniel Lanois. The next four nights were at Paul Allen's beautiful EMP Museum and included Chris Whitley, The Wallflowers, Joe Strummer and the Mescaleros, DJ Cheb i Sabbah, DJ Nasir, Afro Celt Sound System, Shawn Smith, The Gents, Ann and Nancy Wilson, Heart, Chocolate Genius, Joe Henry and Michael Franti, and Spearhead. We closed at the 18,000 seat Key Arena with Femi Kuti and the Positive Force, Mana of Mexico, Alanis Morissette, Pearl Jam, and REM. The emotional highpoint was Pearl Jam playing with Rahat Fateh Ali Khan, a Pakistani vocalist.

After the dreadful 9/11 attacks, Adobe left it up to

Susan Silver, manager of the Seattle talent, with Spoonman. Spoonman was famous for playing spoons every day in the Seattle market. He was the featured artist for Groundwork. My Hero. Photo by Fred Clarke.

us whether to continue with the project. Most events like this were canceled after 9/11. But we had already sold out all our tickets, and we went on with the show. We were glad we did. Seattle's artists worked hard and well, and we would have done even better if the concerts had not followed 9/11. But even given that, we sent over a million dollars to the small projects of the farmers from developing countries.

The Secretary General of FAO, Jacques Diouf, thanked the artists and the organizers over a nice long supper. Large organizations have a hard time explaining where the money is spent. We Americans are blessed with a curse and a solution. We have money for this sort of thing, but we also have a cynicism that the money

might be wasted. The real issue in funding a project is that there must be risks taken for it to succeed. If you admit this, few people will want to give to that project. But risk is the necessary coin of change. So our effort to supply funds to small farmers bringing in their own projects seemed reasonable and sensible. We may even have been correct.

The week of music in Seattle was a rare opportunity to speak to the issue of hunger as a basic human right. This issue is rarely addressed, even among human rights organizations. To me, this is obvious. If you are dying from hunger and thirst, what good are human rights? Money is always short for the relief of world hunger. Seattle gave me the chance to address the issue directly as a human right, as written in the Universal Declaration of Human Rights. The Seattle show also gave me another chance to allow all thirty articles of the UDHR to come to life and get exposure for a minute or two.

Our final effort was to produce two one-and-a-half hour videos of the shows for FAO. These productions were given freely to all the developing countries in FAO. Billions of people got to enjoy the shows. Sandra Hay did the post production work in her garage.

CHAPTER 19

Aung San Suu Kyi Campaign

I MET MICHAEL ARIS IN 1990 AT AN AMNESTY CONFERENCE IN Boston. Michael was a British citizen, married to a Burmese woman named Daw Aung San Suu Kyi (ASSK). Michael had been separated from his wife since she'd left Oxford for Burma in 1988 to care for her ailing mother. Once back in Burma, ASSK found herself swept up in the democratic movement there. She joined the protests and became the head of a fledgling movement advocating democracy in Burma.

The military junta placed her under house arrest, and Michael left his post at St. John's College and began to petition for his wife. He asked me for help, and I said "of course." It was to become one of the longest lasting campaigns of my time in human rights work.

All human rights campaigns must achieve particular goals if they are to be successful. I included these goals for our work for Burma.

Great friends: Dick Gregory, Wynton Marsalis, Jenny McCarthy, Jim Carrey, Bruno Battaglia, Jacob Donnelly, David Bruce, and Feryal and Firouzeh Gharahi joined me for my 70th birthday at Jimmy Miller's home. Photo by Daniella de Varney.

First, we needed to educate the public on both the leader and the antagonist. This was paramount. In cases where this isn't accomplished (e.g. Darfur), confusion remains until the issue drifts into silence. Second, given the difficulty of pronouncing Suu Kyi's name, I knew we had to start there. Third, we had to funnel her worldwide support into one place. Fourth, we needed to let the world know what she looked like. Of course I looked to the arts and artists to help achieve these goals.

Jim Carrey solved the name pronunciation in a short and powerful video that went viral. Shepard Fairey solved the image problem with his art. Jeremy Woodrum and I introduced her to Americans as "the Mandela of Asia." This established immediate credibility for her cause. Stan Salett helped me get a movie going showing all the support around the world for ASSK.

Amnesty had opposed the human rights abuses of the military junta in Burma. The junta was extremely repressive and imprisoned political activists, conscripted children into the military, and seized land from poor farmers. Aung San Suu Kyi was the daughter of the famed liberation hero, Aung San, so it was not surprising that she led the National League for Democracy (NLD) that pledged to unite the country's ethnic factions, restore democracy, and bring about change. She was first placed under house arrest in 1989 and ultimately spent 15 of the next 21 years under house arrest (July 1989 – November 2010). "In a clear showing of the people's will, Aung San Suu Kyi's party, the National League for Democracy (NLD) won 81% of the parliamentary seats and the government-backed party won only 2% of the seats," said a report by the Asean Inter-Parliamentary Myanmar Caucus.

With Feryal Gharahi in Burma. 1999.

In 1991, ASSK received the Nobel Prize for Peace, but was unable to attend the ceremonies. Until she was released in 2010, Human Rights Action Center and its supporters devoted most of their efforts to this campaign.

A few years after I met Michael Aris, a Burmese student by the name of Zar Ni spoke to the crowd at the University of Oklahoma. My friends Michael Johns and David Slemmons, who organized a free musical event for human rights each year at the University, were in the audience. They were moved and told Zar Ni to call me. He had started the Free Burma Campaign. We got together on August 12, 1998. Some students from American University had been arrested in Rangoon for supporting ASSK. This action gave the movement momentum. Recent college graduates Jeremy Woodrum and Dan Beeton and I joined the Free Burma Campaign and then eventually started the U.S. Campaign for Burma under the auspices of the Human Rights Action Center. We worked together for the next dozen years.

In February 1999, I went to the refugee camps and hospital of the Burmese along the Thai border. As in most refugee camps, conditions were miserable. I met some of the leaders of the 88 Generation who had helped in the victorious election of ASSK and then had to flee the country. Many of their co-leaders were in jail. In Bangkok, HRAC colleague Feryal Gharahi and I applied for visas to Burma and received them after a long interview on the purpose of my visit. We pretended to be tourists and antiques dealers.

At the Rangoon airport, I was lucky to meet Mr. Synge, a taxi driver who became our driver and escort. Mr. Synge spoke English and knew his way around. We ate noodles at stands along the sides of muddy roads. We toured Burma and the surrounding countryside. I saw so many pagodas I was ready to convert. I followed the news; ASSK had been officially "released" from house arrest but was still mostly confined to her home. I visited the U.S. Emissary in the hopes of some good information on how to reach ASSK. "No, that will not work," they said.

I shared my problem with Mr. Synge. He said, "She gives out rice once a week to her people at the headquarters of the National League for Democracy. But no one knows the schedule." I decided to watch the place and see when people showed up. I walked back and forth looking at antique stores for hours. Finally, one day there were many people going into the building and just

Visiting Aung San Suu Kyi in Rangoon, Burma at the National League for Democracy headquarters. February, 1999. Photo by Feryal Gharahi.

as many soldiers across the street watching them. A white Toyota arrived and quick as a flash the lady in white jumped out and went into the building.

Feryal convinced me that she could slip inside the building unnoticed, dressed as she was in traditional Burmese garb. She seated herself on a small wooden bench and waited. Daw Suu soon appeared in front of Feryal. Feryal quietly explained who she was and asked if I could come in. Daw Suu graciously welcomed us both.

I was struck by the energy and calm Daw Suu radiated. She is a stunningly beautiful woman, tall, thin, and incredibly focused. We spoke for ten or twenty minutes. I told her I would commit myself to her cause, and that I would not give up until democracy came to Burma. I got her autograph and a photo for a friend. ASSK asked me to take the message back to her American supporters, especially the Burmese in America: "Stay united and stay focused on the goal. We have a long way to go."

But the authorities in Burma had eyes everywhere, and that night I was told to leave the country. I flew out after the customs agents performed a very long inspection of my bags, which were incredulously short on antiques. Thankfully we had hidden our autographed photos very well.

I went home and started the work I had promised to do. I began by learning a little about Burma, its colonization by England, and the long years of military rule. There was little international focus on Burma despite a long history of human rights abuses. Actually this was a rare time when American leaders were ahead of the American people. Clinton and both Bushes supported ASSK and the Burmese people. Jeremy Woodrum, Dan Beeton, and I established the U.S. Campaign for Burma as a lobbying group dedicated to freedom for Suu Kyi.

A month later HRAC funded a film crew to go to Burma and interview ASSK. Ebet Roberts and Nancy Anderson conducted an in depth interview on camera with her that made the rounds for years. I wanted to give the tape to a CNN producer. He told me that CNN only covers news: I was making news. My answer to that was that she could not call a press conference when she was under house arrest. But he stuck to his aphorism.

Not long after this, Zar Ni convened a quiet meeting of the exiled government and some active Burmese leaders at Harpers Ferry, West Virginia. Over the next three days, Hans Wahl, a former colleague from Amnesty, and I did our best to shape and record the meeting. It was time to nationalize the name and face of Aung San Suu Kyi. The few Americans who had heard of her could only refer to her as "that Lady over in Asia." I thought that the least we could do was teach people her name.

With the help of Jimmy Miller and Eric Gold, who together represented him, I met with actor Jim Carrey at his home in Malibu. It was great to meet the very funny comedian, whose movies I love. I expected that elastic body of great humor to be present, but it was not. He was business-like, a warm host with a soft touch. His house was long and narrow with a great ocean view. We sat for a while on the windy deck and watched the waves. The campaign to free ASSK was in a rough spot. We were having trouble getting enough (or, for that matter, any) attention for the cause, and we needed publicity. We wanted to make video spots featuring different celebrities, describing the situation in Burma and the plight of Aung San Suu Kyi.

Within five minutes of my arrival, Jim agreed to get involved. He knew what was going on in Burma and was anxious to help. He devised two plans for video spots: one was to sit in an expensive restaurant, calmly eat the majority of his meal and then stand up, look at the camera, and just scream for all he was worth. Then he'd sit down and say Burma. The other one, and the one we eventually decided to

use, was designed to address the total lack of awareness about ASSK, and Burma in general, among Americans. We would do a spot of Jim Carrey teaching people to pronounce her name, thinking that the campaign would go nowhere unless people could say her name, Aung San Suu Kyi. I left feeling terrific. It was a short and sweet meeting with a quick move to action. Just my style. Human rights in action.

This time, CNN decided that Carrey's spot was newsworthy, and its coverage helped our spot go viral. The healing power of humor delivered the traction to get our campaign going.

We followed up with a 30-day campaign entitled *Burma: It Can't Wait,* with celebrities talking about a different aspect of Burma each day. I flew to LA three times looking for backers and was about to leave town in defeat when I stopped for a quick lunch with my good friend Dan Adler of Fanista.

Dan organized his team of Prudence Fenton and John Solomon to bring the campaign together. Prudence served as Creative Executive Producer for the thirty-seven short videos. The spots were produced by Kristin Hahn, Francesca Silvestri, Kevin Chinoy, Robyn Wholey, and Jorge Berlanga. June Guterman came in for fifteen of the spots. Michael Abbott and partner pitched in with their talent.[23] Joseph Fiennes, of *Shakespeare in Love,* called from London to tell me about the three-minute spot he had done. Rob Schwartz of the TBWA in LA developed a whole campaign with our guidance. Will Ferrell and Judd Apatow kicked off this effort. After this, the project was easy.

Amy Poncher coordinated it all for the HRAC. The campaign received coverage in the *New York Times, Newsweek,* and the *LA Times.* We ran a new ad each day starting on May 1, 2008. *The Burma: It Can't Wait* campaign received millions of hits on YouTube. It is still frequently viewed on the HRAC site and YouTube.

A terrible cyclone hit Burma on May 3, 2008. We continued with the spots and extended them to include pleas for Cyclone Nargis relief. Anjelica Huston joined Jeremy Woodrum and I at a news conference at the United Nations regarding the cyclone. Later that month, I found myself eating whole grain, sugar-free cookies on Jim Carrey's jet as we flew to New York so he could address the United Nations. There was no comedy when Jim said, "It's a brutal and sadistic regime that has for decades tried to squash the will of its people through mass relocation, rape, and murder." It was a brilliant talk.

Anjelica Huston, who served as Chair for the campaign, helped us organize a large dinner and fundraiser at the Hyatt in Los Angeles, where we spoke to the film community about ASSK. Damien Rice sang at the dinner because he had traveled to the refugee camps and wanted to help. Maggie Q did the same and brought her friends to the dinner. Sony executives Doug Belgrad and Jonathan Kadin

Anjelica Huston with (L–R) Wendy Willis, Jacob Donnelly, Eric Torres, Tony Roman.

came, as did the Mosaic staff. Mosaic covered a van with the image of Aung San Suu Kyi.

We produced an hour-long film, originally imagined by my friend Stan Salett, using the many endorsements ASSK had received and tapes showing the wide support for a free Burma. We called it *Douye,* meaning *struggle,* which was the word the Burmese shouted while demonstrating at the Burmese Embassy. The film included spots from Bill Clinton, Anthony Kiedis, John McCain, Anjelica Huston, REM, and Bono.

Sandy Berger of the National Security Council arranged a couple of meetings for the Burmese activists to brief the White House staff. Later the George W. Bush people would do the same. Laura Bush was deeply interested in ASSK. Jeremy and I showed the *30 Days for Burma* campaign to Laura's staff.

Matt Burrows, HRAC's lawyer, arranged a meeting for me with Rhino's Robin Hurley. Robin responded to our request for help, and we developed the album called *For the Lady,* a two CD set of eighteen of the best musicians in rock.

Shep Fairey's artistic poster of Aung San Suu Kyi made her face known to the world. © Shepard Fairey

Lock Bingham from San Francisco moved to Memphis to help coordinate this effort for HRAC and the U.S. Campaign for Burma. Featured artists included U2, Sting, Peter Gabriel, REM, Paul McCartney, Eric Clapton, Pearl Jam, Coldplay, Ben Harper, Talib Kweli with John Legend, Bonnie Raitt, Avril Lavigne, Ani Di Franco, Damien Rice, Bright Eyes, The Nightwatchman, Lili Haydn, and the great Natalie Merchant, who was the first to sign on.

Brian Sirgutz and Levi Felix arranged for me to meet Shepard Fairey, whose poster had been instrumental to the Obama campaign. I wanted to give Shepard a gift to thank him for bringing so many young people into the last

election with his art. I gave him an original art piece by Sister Corita that had been a gift to me from her for my work on the Walks for Development. Shep was stunned. He had been an ardent fan of Sister Corita for years. I asked him to make a

At Harmony 1999 concert in Bankok for Aung San Suu Kyi. Photographer unknown.

poster of Aung San Suu Kyi. Shepard kindly created the iconic artistic portrait of ASSK. His poster has become the image of her that is recognized worldwide. We printed and distributed thousands of posters over the next few years.

My intern, Grace Powell, arranged for a Burmese child soldier now living in New Zealand to speak at a congressional hearing (Burma had tens of thousands of child soldiers). We wanted Congress to hear a direct story and see a real child soldier. Our hope was they would act on this critical issue. There are over a half million child soldiers in the world (Kaplan, 2005).

A friend of mine, Jorge Berlanga, called one day and said, "Jack, these soldiers in Burma love soccer. I will get Maradona for your campaign." Maradona helped bring a ton of publicity to the campaign. In order for folks to move to grasp her importance, we connected ASSK to Nelson Mandela by calling her the "Mandela of Asia." The press copied our language and this gave us a further boost.

Another friend of mine in Las Vegas gave a month-long spot to our campaign on an outdoor billboard. Sylvester Stallone did a movie about oppression in Burma and kindly added Jeremy and I to the director's cut so we could discuss the non-movie version.

Friends like John Taglioli, Maria Anaya, and Steve Strauss helped me pull off a concert named "9999"

Me with Aung San Suu Kyi at HRAC dinner in her honor, 2012. © ABImages

Amanda and Shep Fairey meet Aung San Suu Kyi, years after he created the iconic poster of her.
© ABImages.

on September 9, 1999, in Bangkok. Raven-Symone was the headliner. The Black Eyed Peas, while on tour in Bangkok, did a dedication to ASSK as well and received major headlines. 9999 is a significant number for many in Asia. It means bad news.

Ten years after I first met her, the Lady who had inspired so many was released from house arrest. The government allowed Aung San Suu Kyi to take her seat in Parliament. The battle was not over; her party was still not in power, and the regime was still in charge, but it was a start. In 2012, when she was in the U.S. to accept a Congressional Medal of Honor, ASSK's office called ours (technically, my basement). She wanted to have dinner, to meet and thank the Human Rights Action Center and others who had worked so hard on her campaign.

On a warm evening in early September, at the stately Bel Air home of my good friends Jimmy and Cheryl Miller, we hosted a dinner for 150 people. There was beautiful light from candles and paper lanterns and, most especially, from Aung San Suu Kyi herself. She sat casually among us, radiating her particular charm and magnetism. Lili Haydn and Tom Morello provided music. Many of the celebrities and Burmese who had been part of the *Burma: It Can't Wait* campaign

Jimmy Miller, fellow Pittsburgh native, has been a supporter of human rights work for decades.

and other activities over the years attended the dinner. Shepard Fairey spoke, and we all got precious time with the lady.

At the end of the evening she stood up on a small, wooden podium and spoke. "The battle," she said in her lilting quiet voice, "is not yet over. We cannot give up the fight against injustice."

CHAPTER 20

Symbols of Hope

I HAVE ALWAYS FOUND COMFORT AND POWER IN HAVING MY own symbols of hope. Some are obvious, and others are not. I heard Dr. King speak at the Lincoln Memorial, but I never really met him. I did get to know Dick Gregory, Father James Groppi, Fannie Lou Hamer, and Muhammad Ali.

Internationally, I looked to Mandela of course, but also to his lawyer Denis Kuny. A playwright, Barney Simon, inspired me, as did Chris Hani, Khalaki Sello, and Kuny during my time in southern Africa. They moved me into thought and action.

Dick Gregory won the Dawson Award in fall of 1976 for his Run Against Hunger, and Ms. Hamer also received an award. We were all together at a Hilton Hotel for a Black Caucus dinner when Fannie leaned over and whispered to me, "Jack, I'm dying. Don't fret. I'm okay. I'm with Christ." I knew she was indeed.

I was invited to give a speech at the University of Denver. Another speaker or two from a contested area of the world usually accompanied me and also spoke. I was first up in a room of about three hundred people sponsored by an Amnesty chapter. Earlier in the day, I'd taken the chance to pay a visit to two of my favorite Amnesty members, Marketa Freund and her mother Henrietta. These kind women lived in a tiny house in Boulder filled with boxes and files. They were unknown to the outside world, but they were the real deal in human rights. The Nazis had marked their arms during the Holocaust, but their hearts were marked with love for their fellow humans, particularly anyone under governmental oppression in Latin America.

They tirelessly made phone calls, wrote letters, sent faxes, and contributed money for the good of prisoners of conscience in Latin America. They served meals to human rights workers—luckily, including me—and fussed that I was working too hard. Their purity of work always inspired me and lifted my spirits. Their humor, insight, and advice on what I should be doing next was always valuable. They never failed the movement or any of us in it. You don't have to leave the front room to make a difference. That was the message I gave that evening at the University of Denver.

The second speaker was a Peruvian Indian from the south where there had been war going on for years. He told us how he and his village would look at the river to see how many bodies were floating by. The number of bodies floating by would be their indication of whether they should travel that day. These brave villagers continued their work for human rights deep in the jungle despite the river of death facing them daily. And then he said in his broken English, "There are two ladies who live in Boulder, Colorado, who if you can get a hold of them, can get you out of jail. He was referring, of course, to Marketa and Henrietta, who never left their home but could free prisoners in Peru. One gets a lot from people who just are the real deal. I drink from their souls.

Cancer: A Fear That Rocks

I called on these heroes often when I faced the hardest battle of my life in 2006. I noticed a black, domelike spot on my left shoulder and thought it was strange but chose denial and ignored it. Within a month I went to Washington Hospital Center and found out it was not only a cancer, but it was the melanoma kind, a possible killer. While the care and expertise at Washington Hospital Center was terrific and compassionate, the diagnosis rattled me and took away a lot of confidence. With my doctors, I chose surgery, which went better than we were told to expect. But fear and anger swirled in my belly as I graduated to the 2nd floor, land of chemotherapy and interferon. Interferon was recommended to me by the doctor who handles it. He said it would boost my immune system but terrified me further by showing me the odds of cancer's return.

The treatment would require me to inject myself three times a week under the skin. Most patients drop treatment because of side effects like depression and possible suicide. I rejected this option after a lengthy discussion with my doctor. I also checked in with John Hopkins, and they said not to do it.

Instead, I sprung my mind and body into fight mode. I isolated myself and pursued aggressive treatment that ultimately brought victory. I set out to get my confidence back. Fear had such a grip on me. I had even stopped

Henry and Carol Goldberg, here with Feryal Gharahi and me, gave me a good retreat at which to recover.

flying, which I had done for so many years. During that first year of recovery, any ache, bump, or red spot scared me into a terrific worrier. I had to get my spunk back. My family, friends, lawyer, and Feryal Gharahi rallied me.

My friends the Goldbergs gave me a retreat to recover on my own. I decided that my immune system would be strengthened by me. I got heavier into yoga than I had been in years. I added weights and the treadmill. I added eight to ten hours of sleep, and fruit, nuts, and vegetables became an intricate part of my diet, and I lost weight. It worked. I still had to get a lesser cancer off my ear and brow, but they were not melanoma. It took a year for me to regain my confidence and spirit. The cancer bullet came close, but the wind from that shell enriched my life with a new view and a new gratitude. Good friends, good doctors, good eating and exercising are cures, too. I have been cancer-free for nine years now, and today I fly again.

CHAPTER 21

Haiti: February 2, 2010

O N FEBRUARY 2ND, 2010, *POLITICO* RAN AN ARTICLE BY STEVEN Van Zandt regarding the future of Haiti.[24] Steven made the important and necessary argument that Haiti must not return to a state where many of its people routinely suffer starvation, malnutrition, the lack of clean water and electricity, and have little opportunity for quality education or health care. Steven advocated a steady hand for the distant future by organizing a group of wealthy and powerful people to rethink and remake Haiti. In other words, rebuilding Haiti was a long-distance jog, not a quick fix. I could not agree more. Much of my rationale is based on my own experiences in Haiti, aiding various development projects, dating back to 1970.

Amnesty commissioned a boat to search for Haitians fleeing to the United States. President Clinton stopped the boats and sent the refugees back. He was wrong. Per international law, people have the right to run from harm's way, 1993. Photographer unknown.

I was in Haiti in 1998 to review the operations of a center that treated the victims of torture. Our team stayed at the Montana Hotel where many later died

in the 2010 earthquake. In an effort to assess the general state of human rights in Haiti, I insisted we visit the prisons. Everyone wanted to know why, since jails were not on the agenda. My answer was that we could learn about justice or the lack thereof more quickly in the prisons than in any other place. In the prison housing adult male inmates, there were many inmates claiming that their cases had not been reviewed by any discernible judicial standard. Many prisoners had already served their time, but they had no way to obtain release, because the courts would not hear their cases. The courts often did not hear cases for weeks or months.

We visited two prisons for minors. As far as I could tell, both were unconstitutional by the standards of the Haitian Constitution. The facilities were astonishingly inadequate: basic resources, like bedding and medicine, were in very short supply. There was one bed for 162 boys. The medicine cabinet contained two aspirins. The juvenile girls had organized their prison room into areas that resembled their economic system, with the richest girls bunking at the door exiting the facility and the poorest girls bunking at the door entering the facility.

This look into the prison system said it all. I met with many Haitian lawyers who were prepared to right the system and do what was needed to fix it, but the situation was beyond their grasp. Haiti was a country where one could be killed for twenty dollars. More than half the nation was under the age of eighteen. The government did not seem to work for any one.

In contrast, the Center for Victims of Torture was an extremely well run organization headed by Dr. Herve Razafimbahiny and gave much solace to those who came to it. I recommended it to continue at its work. Despite this recommendation, the United States government, for whom the report was written, made the decision to close the center.

Haitians saw Aristide, their democratically elected leader, removed by an American Secretary of State and exiled to the Central African Empire (CAE). Aristide moved from CAE to South Africa, where he lived while seeking permission to return to Haiti. Aristide was allowed home in 2011 after seven years in exile. Our government's interaction with Haiti has been a mixture of good and bad.

When I was at Amnesty, I arranged to rent a boat to go into the Windward Passage to pick up lost Haitian refugees who were out at sea and in distress. I wanted to return with them and get arrested, because Clinton was preventing them from fleeing their oppressive circumstances. Under law, the United States government has an obligation to take in refugees and hear their cases. In my view, President Clinton was wrong to turn Haitian refugees away, and I wanted to confront the administration. The right to run from harm's way is basic and guaranteed by law.

Clinton was in violation of international law by having the navy pick up those folks and return them to Haiti. Unfortunately, during my one day at sea, I did not encounter any refugees to save even after we sent a plane up to search.

Haiti's past is clearly not worth repeating. Those of us who care are worried that, once the media interest wanes, the world will leave, and Haiti will fall back into its old patterns of citizen abuse. Steven Van Zandt was right: a new paradigm needs to be put into place. Haitians deserve nothing less. I hope that Steven's article will be read by everyone who has ever heard his music and seen him entertain. He helped snap the bond apartheid had on South Africa. He is at it again in advocating Haiti's cause, and I pray that the result will be the same: a new Haiti.

CHAPTER 22

Defend Our Native People

A S A CHILD, MY BROTHER MIKE AND I WOULD HEAD TO AN old movie theatre in Crafton, outside of Pittsburgh, to enjoy our Friday night movies. The price was a dime. And it was a double feature, too. Per usual, we cheered for the soldiers chasing the Indians. But on the way home, Mike would make me the Indian and chase me all over the place. This little role playing continued when I was alone in the woods. Our home in Oakwood had some wooded areas to play in. I think it was this child's game that made me curious and interested in Indian history and Indian people.

In 1972, as director of Young World Development, I joined many of my friends, including Barbara Body of the Children's Foundation and Anselm Rothchild, the Buffalo leader from Freedom from Hunger, on a trip to Nebraska to do a seven-day fast on an Indian reservation. We knew by then that our idea of the walkathon was working, not only for our

Leonard Peltier has been in prison for 40 years. It is time for clemency. Photo by Dick Bancroft.

organization but also for other organizations that had a much bigger footprint. The goal of the fast was to get our minds clear and perhaps find a vision for the future of our movement and work. Fasting was not new to me, but it was extra difficult in the heat of the summer. Father James Groppi was along, and he jokingly said, "If they fast, they will think they are under Rome." The Indian leaders of the village led us through the process in a good and positive way. They also spoke of their history, their struggles, and their hopes. That visit opened my eyes like never before to the issues Indians were facing. It was less than 100 years after the

1890 Wounded Knee massacre, and the Native people were neither assimilating into American culture as the government hoped nor thriving on their own land, because they were unable to live in their traditional ways of hunting and fishing.

Most of us were knowledgeable of the American Indian Movement at that time. It sprung up out of the turmoil of the sixties and early seventies, inspired by the Civil Rights Movement and the anti-war movement. Many of the young men from the reservations were returning from Vietnam with both anger and a wish to help their own people. Many of our local chapters had funded this movement, and we had gotten to know some of their leaders, including Dennis Banks, Russell Means, and the Bellecourt brothers.

Our group never did find or build another fundraising tactic, but we found something more important on that Nebraska reservation. It was time to move on to bigger and better things. We all left the reservation feeling renewed and inspired to put ourselves to work again for the common good.

In early 1973 my attention was riveted like the rest of the nation's when the American Indian Movement took control of the village of Wounded Knee on the Pine Ridge reservation in South Dakota. They held it for 71 days in an attempt to bring attention to the poverty and neglect people were experiencing on most of the nation's Indian reservations at that time. It dominated the evening news for weeks. There was an attempt in Milwaukee by Dick Gregory, Father James Groppi, and Marlon Brando to influence the occupation so there was no bloodshed. Both Groppi and Gregory, as close friends, filled me in on news of this event. But there were two American Indian men killed, and one federal marshal badly wounded during the long siege.

Tensions remained very high at Pine Ridge after the Wounded Knee occupation came to an end. In June 1975, another gunfight erupted at Oglala, some fifty miles from Wounded Knee. This time three people were killed: FBI agents Jack Coler and Ron Williams, and Native American Joseph Stuntz. Two Indian men named Bob Robideau and Darrell Butler were tried for the deaths of the two agents in Cedar Rapids, Iowa, and found not guilty on grounds of self-defense. This left only Leonard Peltier to face charges. He had fled to Canada and was facing extradition hearings. He was eventually returned to the United States, but the circumstances of his extradition were widely questioned. A mentally disturbed young Native woman named Myrtle Poor Bear was coerced into signing three separate and conflicting affidavits. This did not become clear until much later when it was too late to help Peltier. He stood trial in Fargo, North Dakota, in 1977. The fairness of the trial was immediately questioned by Amnesty International. Peltier was convicted and sentenced to two consecutive life terms, to be served consecutively.

Ironically, he would have been acquitted if he had not fled to Canada and had been tried with his friends in Iowa.

My return to the Peltier case came about when I was appointed director of Amnesty International in 1981. In most of my talks at hundreds of colleges and universities, I would raise this case as one of the trials that needed to be rerun, along with the Geronimo Pratt conviction, another dubious trial. I would raise the alarm for these two leaders of their communities. Beyond that, as director of Amnesty, the rules kept me out of American cases of imprisonment. That was left to other sections and the international secretary in London.

In late 1993, I got an opportunity to meet a Canadian Indian, half Cree and half Ojibway, by the name of Larry Morrisette. We were at a meeting in California organized by Sue Kiel, a former South African activist. Knowing an issue is different from knowing another person who is immersed in that issue, so I welcomed this new friendship. I got to hear in quiet and easy conversations the history, traditions, and ways of life as Larry saw them. Many questions were answered. This relationship enriched me deeply. In fact, when I decided to leave Amnesty, I went to the Winnipeg to council with him in the hopes of gaining some wisdom and to settle my mind on my future.

Years later, I was asked to be part of a documentary being filmed by a company from Great Britain about the life and times of Leonard Peltier. My response was "gladly." We did the shoot, and I did my best. I was saying goodbye to the camera crew when my cell phone rang. It was Leonard on the phone. He simply asked me to help, and I said sure.

I looked over the almost successful campaign to free Leonard at the end of the Clinton administration. At the last minute, Clinton chose to grant clemency to a rich guy instead of Leonard. He told his supporters that he did not know how to sell the release of Leonard to the American people. This was greeted by shock and dismay in Indian country. Thus, I decided, this time, in the Obama years, we would run a YouTube video every month or two, and by the time we get to the end of the Obama administration, we will have half of Hollywood and half of the musicians, and a great look into the Indian life through their own eyes, their own faces, and their own history. Leonard Peltier has languished in prison for almost forty years and at 70 is in failing health.

This is a campaign I know we can win, and we must in the name of justice. Readers wishing to support this ongoing effort can find more information at: www.humanrightsactioncenter.com or on YouTube under "Leonard Peltier: I Will Clemency Campaign."

CHAPTER 23

Chen Shui-bian Vengeance in Taiwan

THREE YEARS AGO, PROFESSOR JAY TU OF NORTH CAROLINA State University wrote me concerning the plight of the former president of Taiwan, Mr. Chen Shui-Bian. Mr. Chen was jailed immediately after his two terms as President of Taiwan for corruption, real or imagined. Jay felt no one was paying attention to this prisoner's treatment in jail or the false charges against him. At first I did not see much of an issue, as I got the same impression as everyone else—that Mr. Chen was a corrupted politician. But Jay continued to send me articles and updates. Finally, after many phones calls and email exchanges, Jay said to me, "Jack, take this case over. It is a real human rights issue."

There had been a few writers, mostly on the right, reporting on the conditions and environment of the prison for this prisoner. A few Republicans added their voices, but not many. One U.S. congressional delegation went to Taiwan for the inauguration of the second term of President Ma, and they were not allowed to even raise the issue at the insistence of one congresswoman from Miami. The charges were nonviolent charges. His jail sentence was 27 years for alleged corruption charges while in office as President of Taiwan, out of more than eight charges, most found innocent or still in trial. The law in Taiwan caps the maximum sentence to 20 years unless it is for life in prison.

Without money.

Without fame. Just action.

Impact is all that matters.

The background to Mr. Chen is important. He comes from the green side, represented by the Democratic Progressive Party (DPP), the party of those who for the most part were born and raised in Taiwan. The blue side, called Kuomintang (KMT), is controlled by those who followed Chiang Kai-Shek to Taiwan from China after Chiang lost to Mao Tse-tung in 1947-48. The KMT held military rule under martial law from 1949 to 1987 and basically had only two presidents, Chiang Kai-Shek and his son, both served until they died. The KMT still held every presidency after 1987 except from 2000-2008 for that of Mr. Chen, who came from the green side and is a non-mainlander. He was a success story of the

new Taiwan. In jail, for good or bad reasons, Mr. Chen remains a symbol of the Old Taiwan under military rule.

I had visited Taiwan twice, once while it was under military rule, once right after the martial law was lifted. But this story was not on my radar until Jay called.

As I looked into it, I wanted to make sure my Human Rights Action Center (HRAC) was doing the right thing. I sent two friends from the human rights movement over to visit the man. Hans Wahl and Harreld Dinkins were expecting to see a reasonably healthy man who once had been a great corporate lawyer, mayor of Taipei, and a president twice. Instead, they found a weakened old man with all kinds of ailments. HRAC proceeded then to start writing blogs on the *Huffington Post* to right this wrong. But I still could not figure out why so few human rights groups and Congress folks were looking out for this man, with the usual letters, visits, Congressional mentions, etc. He was forgotten. And he was in bad health. Our blogs, along with a dedicated few, kept pressure on the government of Mr. Ma and eventually he was moved to a bed in a hospital room. But the history of rushed doctor visits and drive-through hospital exams, in particular the inhuman prison conditions—23.5 hours trapped in a small cell, under bright lights and surveillance cameras, no bed, no table, no flush toilet, and no hot water, and little time out of the cell (thirty minutes a day)—broke this man's health and mental powers. He was declining into a mess of health problems.

Some solid voices started to come into the picture: Republican and Democrats, like Senators Sherrod Brown of Ohio and Dick Durbin of Illinois. HRAC's articles appeared regularly. The Secretary General of Amnesty International visited, and he added his voice. Prof. Jerome Cohen of New York University School of Law, whom President Ma brought to Taiwan as his mentor, even spoke up and called for medical relief. More people in Taiwan started to join the loyal few supporters of Mr. Chen. The blogs of HRAC were gaining large hits. The election of the new Mayor of Taipei in November, 2014 put pressure on the Ma government to release Mr. Chen. This new Mayor is the chair of an unofficial, voluntary medical team, advocating medical rights for Mr. Chen.

Former President of Taiwan, Mr. Chen Shui-bian, served a number of years in jail, but with the help of his friends and HRAC, we were able send him home. Photo by Bryan Chen.

Mr. Chen gained medical release in January 2015. The people of Taiwan celebrated, and I was surprised to learn that my face and writings were all over Taiwanese television as having played a significant role in getting him home. Without money. Without fame. Just action. Impact is all that matters.

CHAPTER 24

Words have Power and One Document Can Lift the Whole World

SOMETIMES I THINK THAT THE FOOD DUMPS OF THE WORLD, where children gather their daily sustenance, might be the best places to drop as many copies of the Universal Declaration of Human Rights (UDHR) as I can. This neglected document from 1948 remains the best kept secret in the world. The Western and now Eastern Powers have neglected it. Who will wake up these governments to the UDHR and its power, its vision, and its promise? It just might be one of those poor children hunting for a bite to eat. There is a great river of consciousness in the world that wants governments to behave and let people alone in their lives and beliefs. Rather than sticking people in jail to torture and kill, we need to turn the power of government into a force for unity, sustenance, and strength of character.

> Torturers need to be pushed into the sun and taken to court to face trial, our own leaders as well as those abroad. A free people must work for an unfree people.

Power, real power comes from agreements, written, signed, and kept. The Constitution and the Bill of Rights are examples. Now it is the time of the Universal Declaration of Human Rights. It is time to dust off the old document and let its strategy and vision become the law. Progress in interpretation and implementation will be slow just as they were with the Constitution and Bill of Rights and the Civil Rights Bill of 1964.

By the 70th anniversary of the UDHR, we pray that the wealthier countries will be flying drones over the poorer countries in order to help the hungry, the needy, and refugees. The mighty are only truly mighty if they do not dance on the heads of the poor.

*For several years I gave a human rights workshop at Esalen Insti-
tute in Big Sur, CA. These weekend retreats were a chance to spread
the importance of people finding their voice. Brazilian TV personality Maria Paula attended and immediately went to work for the
Brazilian Indians who were being driven from their homes by oil.*

The Human Rights Now! tour of 1988 was not a symbol of hope. It was a
clarion call to rally to the Universal Declaration of Human Rights to be printed in
the passports of every nation. It is the best idea I believe I ever had.

Hank and Carol Goldberg, generous supporters of HRAC and my hosts on
Martha's Vineyard for over 15 years, recently asked me why I continue in my
human rights work. Before I answered, I asked Carol if she had ever heard the song
"Little Victories" by Bob Seger. The song is about the power of little victories in
many walks of life. It tells the story with energy and force—just as I feel when I
think of the victories we have had in the human rights movement. Little victories
bring big victories!

Some human rights leaders are so famous their names alone invoke their causes:
Dr. Martin Luther King, Jr., Nelson Mandela, Aung San Suu Kyi, Gandhi, and
Steve Biko. Lesser known but just as important were the activists who achieved
victories like ousting the military dictators in Latin America; gaining majority
rule in South Africa, Rhodesia/Zimbabwe, Southwest Africa/Namibia, and
Mozambique; the Soviet Union dissolving without a violent revolution; Cambodia,
El Salvador, Chile, Argentina, and Bosnia settling scores with people like Pol Pot;
establishment of an Assistant Secretary for Human Rights at the United Nations;
and the creation of the International Criminal Court (ICC).

I had the privilege of being a part of some of these achievements, although the size of the role I played varied. The true credit goes to the human rights parade that perhaps few notice, but I do, because I meet people from these places and those times. These folks energize and inspire and mobilize the human rights movement. Their blood and their sweat, their torture and their disappearances move us all. Albert Camus spoke of those who receive the lash and those who count it; the latter is mine, but the feeling of victory is shared. We the people of the earth are winning, even though it does not always look that way. Those who survive human rights abuses are witnesses to life and its power to survive and live and just be.

The battle is not left and right, Democrat and Republican. It is the battle between good and evil; decent and indecent; and between power and love. Torturers need to be pushed into the sun and taken to court to face trial—our own leaders, as well as those abroad. A free people must work for an unfree people.

CHAPTER 25

One Person Can Lift
the Whole Damn Thing

HUMAN PROGRESS—HUMAN RIGHTS—IS PLAYED OUT IN THE blood of many, many thousands of people. Blood has to be spilt—ours, too. We have to get knocked over regularly and come back. That's all.

We just have to get back up on the balls of our feet and fight again. Just come back up. Get over your little depression and think about something bigger than yourself and go back to it.

Creating your future is not just a possibility; it is a responsibility; one that we owe ourselves, our family, our community and our world. It is about shedding limitation and accessing our power, embracing our fears, and owning our courage. Nietzsche says dare to dream big and the whole universe will conspire with you to bring it to reality.

You don't need money, status or an Ivy League education, but you do need a vision, boldness and willingness to access one truth—one standard—that is immutable and unchangeable. That truth is the inherent dignity and equality of every human being. This is where I started, and it is what I used as the foundation of my work throughout my life. A single standard was my metric by which all governments would be judged in their display of respect for the rights of their citizens.

These days, when I give a speech, I address the most confused kid in the room. I figure the others will be okay. I talk to the smallest kid, the least educated, the least powerful person in the room. I tell them they can do it, because I did. I am that confused, lost, undereducated kid, too. I've got all those lesser things in my life. If they understand that some little jerk went in front of them and did it, maybe it will give them the courage to reach for something higher. All we need is one champion somewhere.

I saw it with Dr. King. I saw it with Fannie Lou Hamer. I saw it with Mandela. I've seen it everywhere in the world.

One person can lift the whole damn thing. So become that one person and lift the whole damn thing.

As the work continues, I remember my friend Fannie Lou Hamer's last words to me when she told me she was dying:

"And you," she said, "Keep on keeping on...do not stop till you join me."

Credits

Honorary Degrees

- Doctor of Philosophy, Doctor of Humane Letters, May 31, 1987. Southeastern Massachusetts University
- Doctor of Philosophy, Doctor of Humanities, May 22, 1988. Providence College
- Juris Doctor, Doctor of Laws, May 29, 1988. Northeastern University
- Doctor of Philosophy, Doctor of Public Service, May 27, 1989. Bridgewater State University
- Juris Doctor, Doctor of Law, May 9, 1992. Notre Dame College
- Doctor of Public Service, Bridgewater University
- Doctor of Human Letters, Old Dominion University

Honors and Awards

- Special Recognition Award, Humanitarian of the Year. MTV Video Music Awards, 1986
- Pollstar 1988 Readers Poll Award of the Amnesty International Human Rights Now! tour, named the Concert Industry Event of the Year. Pollstar, 1988
- International Rock Award Tour of the Year Elvis Presley Award. The International Rock Awards, 1989
- Bill Graham Award. Fox News. 1991, *Billboard* Magazine
- Martin Luther King Jr. Spirit of the Dream Award. House of Blues Foundation, 1996
- Person of the Week, *ABC World News* with Peter Jennings
- Guest editor, *SPIN* Magazine
- Thomas Merton Award, 1976, for World Hunger

Press

- *Arise* Review - Anger and Outrage (Silencing of Journalists in Egypt)
- *LA Times* - Magical TourLA Times
- *US NEWS & World Report* - Mr. Human Rights
- *Pittsburgh Press* - Crusader For Amnesty
- *Washington Post* - Burma Crisis
- Anthem Jack - ANTHEM
- Rock and Roll Hall of Fame - Peter Gabriel Biography (Mentions the Conspiracy of Hope and Human Rights Now! tours)

Burma: It Can't Wait

DATE	ARTIST	DATE	ARTIST
Day 01	Will Ferrell	Day 19	Ellen Page
Day 02	Woody Harrelson	Day 20	Hank Azaria
Day 03	Jason Biggs	Day 21	Sylvester Stallone
Day 04	Sarah Silverman	Day 22	Felicity Huffman
Day 05	Julie Benz	Day 23	Diego Maradona
Day 06	Eddie Izzard	Day 24	Kim Kardashian
Day 07	Jorja Fox	Day 25	Dream Bath
Day 08	Sarah Silverman	Day 26	Joseph Fiennes
Day 09	Wally Langham	Day 27	James Cameron
Day 10	Davood Roostaci	Day 28	Damian Marley
Day 11	Jackson Browne	Day 29	Jennifer Aniston
Day 12	Graffiti Wall	Day 30	Tila Tequila
Day 13	Judd Apatow	Day 31	Sheryl Crow
Day 14	Thich Nhat Hanh	Day 32	Brett Dennen
Day 15	Rosanna Arquette	Day 33	Marionettes
Day 16	Eva Longoria	Day 34	Giovanni Ribisi
Day 17	Child Soldier	Day 35	Leaders
Day 18	Steven Seagal	Day 36	Norman Lear
		Day 37	Myanmar Celebrity

References

[1] I had been enrolled in school in Mike's, above my age group peers. It was a great surprise to me later that I may not have been as small as I always felt. I was actually just in school and sports with kids older and thus larger than me.

[2] Everywhere I travel I meet Steelers fans because of the mass migration from Pittsburgh that occurred as mills closed.

[3] (Hilston 1983), Regional Jobless Rates

[4] (King 1967), Beyond Vietnam speech

[5] (Black Backlash Programs Set 1968)

[6] (Schultz 1971), Tireless Young Walkers Rack Up Blisters, Cash

[7] (Burns 1972), Thousands Join Hunger March Despite Rain

[8] (Houck 2011), I'm Sick and Tired of Being Sick and Tired, Mrs. Fannie Lou Hamer

[9] (Young 2012), The Man who Raise the Black Power Salute

[10] (Steve Biko, Black Consciousness Movement Leader, is buried 1977)

[11] (The Death of Stephen Biko n.d.)

[12] (Biko 1978), I Write what I Like

[13] (Phyllis Naidoo n.d.)

[14] (Peace Corps Times 1980)

[15] (Lardner 1991)

[16] (Hilburn 1886)

[17] (NewsOK 1999)

[18] (Honorary Graduates 2003)

[19] (Video: The Universal Declaration of Human Rights 2008)

[20] (Magdaleno.org n.d.)

[21] (Henke 1988)

[22] (Report of the Chilean National Commission on Truth and Reconciliation, 1993)

[23] **Full list of Artists:** Will Ferrell, Woody Harrelson, Jason Biggs, Sarah Silverman, Julie Benz, Eddie Izzard, Jorja Fox, Sarah Silverman, Wally Langham, Davood Roostaci, Jackson Browne, Graffiti Wall, Judd Apatow, Thich Nhat Hanh, Rosanna Arquette, Eva Longoria, Child Soldier, Steven Seagal, Ellen Page, Hank Azaria, Sylvester Stallone, Felicity Huffman, Diego Maradona, Kim Kardashian, Dream Bath, Joseph Fiennes, James Cameron, Damian Marley, Jennifer Aniston, Tila Tequila, Sheryl Crow, Brett Dennen, Marionettes, Giovanni Ribisi, Leaders, Norman Lear

[24] (Van Zandt 2010), Don't Rebuild Haiti; Reimagine It.

Bibliography

Biko, Steve. *I Write What I Like: Selected Writings.* Edited by Aelred Stubbs. Chicago, IL: The University of Chicago Press, 1978.

"Black Backlash Programs Set at Frostburg State College." *The Cumberland News.* May 16, 1968. http://www.newspapers.com/newspage/18418892/.

Burns, Kathleen. "Chicago Tribune." *Hikers Cheerful Despite Rain.* May 8, 1972. http://archives.chicagotribune.com/1972/05/08/page/1/article/hikers-cheerful-despite-rain.

Headlam, Bruce. "The New York Times." *The New York Times.* March 13, 2009. http://www.nytimes.com/2009/03/14/theater/14greg.html?_r=0&pagewanted=print.

Henke, James. *Human Rights Now!* Edited by Kim Ronis. Topsfield, MA: Salem House Publishers, 1988.

Hilburn, Robert. "LA Times." *Pop Review : Amnesty's State-of-the-art Benefit.* June 9, 1886. http://articles.latimes.com/print/1986-06-09/entertainment/ca-10371_1_benefit-concerts.

Hilston, James. "Regional Jobless Rates in the Early 1980s." *Pittsburgh Post Gazette.* April 1983. http://old.post-gazette.com/pg/images/201212/20121223unemployment_80s_543.png.

"Honorary Graduates." *University of Essex.* April 3, 2003. http://www.essex.ac.uk/honorary_graduates/or/2003/ian-martin-oration.aspx.

Houck, Davis W. *Speeches of Fannie Lou Hamer, To Tell it Like it Is.* University Press of Mississippi, 2011.

Kaplan, Eben. "Child Soldiers Around the World." *Council on Foreign Relations.* December 2, 2005. http://www.cfr.org/human-rights/child-soldiers-around-world/p9331.

King, Jr., Dr. Martin Luther. "The King Center Archive." *The King Center.* April 4, 1967. http://www.thekingcenter.org/archive/document/beyond-vietnam.

Lardner, George. "Abrams Pleads Guilty in Iran-Contra Affair." October 8, 1991. http://www.washingtonpost.com/archive/politics/1991/10/08/abrams-pleads-guilty-in-iran-contra-affair/a6958d53-0c3f-40ac-81da-ae0d16eaaf5e/.

Magdaleno.org. n.d. http://www.magdaleno.org/#!about/aboutPage.

"NewsOK." *Groovefest Raises Awareness for Human Rights.* April 15, 1999. http://newsok.com/groovefest-raises-awareness-for-human-rights/article/2649602.

Peace Corps Times. July 1980.

"Report of the Chilean National Commission on Truth and Reconciliation." *United States Institute on Peace,* 1993.

Schultz, Terri. "Chicago Tribune." *Tireless Young Walkers Rack Up Blisters, Cash.* May 9, 1971. http://archives.chicagotribune.com/1971/05/09/page/415/article/tireless-young-walkers-rack-up-blisters-cash-in-hunger-hike.

South African History Online. n.d. http://www.sahistory.org.za/people/phyllis-naidoo.

"Steve Biko, Black Consciousness Movement Leader, is buried." *South African History Online*. September 25, 1977. http://www.sahistory.org.za/dated-event/steve-biko-black-consciousness-movement-leader-buried.

"The Death of Stephen Biko." *South Africa: Overcoming Apartheid*. n.d. http://overcomingapartheid.msu.edu/sidebar.php?id=65-258-4.

Van Zandt, Steven. "Politico." *Don't rebuild Haiti: reimagine it*. February 2, 2010. http://dyn.politico.com/printstory.cfm?uuid=8B5A5A49-18FE-70B2-A8D3001B60157E3B.

Video: The Universal Declaration of Human Rights. October 7, 2008.

Young, Gary. "The man who raised the black power salute." *The Guardian*. March 30, 2012. http://www.theguardian.com/world/2012/mar/30/black-power-salute-1968-olympics.

Ziemba, Stanley. "Thousands Plan Hike on Hunger." *Chicago Tribune*. May 8, 1971. http://archives.chicagotribune.com/1971/05/08/page/2/article/thousands-plan-hike-on-hunger.